Praise for

THE JOY

"*Life-saving.* That is the most accurate description of *The Joy Plan*. As I devoured the transformative words of this book, I wished I'd had it during a desolate time in my life…but it is not too late. Whenever fear, worry, anxiety, or negativity grip me, I simply open *The Joy Plan*. Waiting to shed light into my darkness is a strategy, an inspiring anecdote, or well-researched fact with the power to bring me back to hope, peace, and positivity. *The Joy Plan* is much more than one woman's journey from rock bottom; it is a universal lifeline for reviving the world's long-lost joy."

—Rachel Macy Stafford, *New York Times* bestselling author
and founder of *Hands Free Mama*

"If you are in the midst of a joy drought, so to speak, this could be the book for you. Part memoir, part universally applicable joy strategy, *The Joy Plan* tells the author's story of suffering and lays out, step-by-step, the process that helped her experience much more happiness. Kaia Roman writes in an engaging way, so reading this book feels like listening to a friend."

—Sharon Salzberg, author of the *New York Times* bestselling
Lovingkindness: The Revolutionary Art of Happiness

"All of us need to learn how to shift from stress to joy. *The Joy Plan* is a positive, practical guide to help you experience more of the happiness you deserve."

—Dr. Barbara De Angelis, #1 *New York Times*
bestselling author of *Soul Shifts*

"*The Joy Plan* is easy to read, engaging, and full of great scientific advice as well as fun and enlivening stories to get you motivated to find your joy on a daily basis. Don't let the stress of modern life weigh you down! Take responsibility for steering your course toward happiness with this well-written and researched book."

—MeiMei Fox, *New York Times* bestselling coauthor
of *Bend, Not Break*

"*The Joy Plan* was birthed through direct experimentation in the laboratory of Kaia Roman's own life, qualifying her to wisely and tenderly guide readers to discover and cultivate the seed of joy that has been implanted within us all. Follow the steps in this book and watch how joy—the spiritual dimension of happiness—blossoms in your life."

—Michael Bernard Beckwith, author of *Life Visioning*

"If you're looking for more meaning, purpose, and joy in your life, then *The Joy Plan* is for you!"

—Jason Wachob, founder and CEO of mindbodygreen

"I love *The Joy Plan*! We create plans for our work, our finances, our life—but hardly ever for the most important things in our life: gratitude, optimism, and joy. This book will help you achieve exactly that—more joy! And who doesn't need that?"

—Michaela Haas, PhD, author of *Bouncing Forward:
The Art and Science of Cultivating Resilience*

The JOY PLAN

HOW I TOOK 30 DAYS TO STOP WORRYING, QUIT COMPLAINING, AND FIND RIDICULOUS HAPPINESS

KAIA ROMAN

Published by Sourcebooks, Inc.
P.O. Box 4410, Naperville, Illinois 60567-4410
(630) 961-3900
Fax: (630) 961-2168
www.sourcebooks.com

Library of Congress Cataloging-in-Publication data is on file with the publisher.

Printed and bound in the United States of America.
VP 10 9 8 7 6 5 4 3 2

For Kira and Nava, my fiercely joyful role models.

When I grow up, I want to be just like you.

CONTENTS

"We cannot solve our problems with the same thinking we used when we created them."

—ALBERT EINSTEIN

INTRODUCTION

It was cool on that early October day. The afternoon Santa Cruz fog had rolled in and covered our town house in a blanket of gray. But I was sweating. I paced the floor in my small home office, listening with disbelief to the conversation taking place with my business partners over the web conference on my laptop.

Even though I was the only one home that afternoon, I locked the door to my office and drew the curtains closed tight. I needed to somehow block out the world so no one would see my rising shame. The words "shut down the company," "buyout," and "bankrupt" sounded as if they were spoken in a dream as white noise began to fill my ears.

Feeling dizzy, I stumbled to my desk and tried to focus on the computer screen—but all I saw was black. The sound in my ears was growing, and I was falling into it. What started as static had become a scream, and I felt it reverberate through my entire being: NOOOOOOOOOO!!!

Not this. Not now. I had put it all on the line, and I had failed. All that time. All that money. And Dan. *Oh shit, what would I tell Dan?*

"Please trust me, this business is going to be a huge success! Within a couple of years, you'll never have to work again if you don't want to. I just need you to give me time," I had begged my husband when we first discussed my investing large amounts of time and money into a start-up business.

But now the time had run out, and I had crashed and burned. Dan would not be retiring anytime soon. I would not be making millions of dollars. And I had little to show for my eighteen-hour workdays except for the twenty pounds I'd gained from sitting at a computer all day, every day for months on end. The irony of this was not lost on me, since all the work was for a health and wellness company that helped people, among other things, lose weight.

In the days that followed, I numbly signed papers, closed accounts, handed over passwords, and cried in the bathroom. I felt like crawling into bed and not coming out for a year. But that wasn't possible. My two daughters, Kira and Nava, were six and eight years old. I had responsibilities I couldn't escape. So as I went through the motions of my life, I just tried to get through another task, another checklist, so that another day would end.

I've read that when you have depression, you don't care about anything, and when you have anxiety, you care too much about everything. But what is it called when you have both at the same time?

I felt the anxiety most in my chest, but it was more than a rapid heart-beat. It felt like my lungs were in a vice grip, each gasp for air tinged with panic. My mind was racing on red alert, but rather than having productive thoughts, it only said the same thing over and over again: *Oh no. Oh no. Oh no. What do I do? What do I do? What do I do?* And yet in this state of panic, even as fear prickled my mind, all my body wanted to do was sleep.

While anxiety yanked me upward—panting, grasping, scratching, clawing for breath, for safety, for answers, for *anything but this*—depression heaved me downward. "Sleep," depression said. Perhaps if I could sleep, I would wake to find it was all a dream. Perhaps if I could sleep, I would come up with a solution in the morning. But sleep didn't bring relief, only fitful dreams and waking in more panic. I dreaded the prospect of leaving the bed, even though things weren't any better from there. I quickly slipped from being a capable executive leading multinational teams and complex marketing campaigns to an apparition barely capable of taking a shower. Usually ambitious and organized, I was now a shadow of my former self.

From the time I could talk, I had been organizing things—even if they were my stuffed animals—and taking practical steps to achieve my next plan. I was so good at making plans that I even got paid to make them for other people when I grew up, as a marketing and event planner for businesses and organizations. Throughout my life, each time one of my plans was complete, I would already have another one in place. But when this plan, my *grand plan*, took a nosedive, I was caught completely off guard, with no backup plan or direction.

"It's just a business," some rational voice—mine or another's—would say from time to time. But it wasn't just a business. It was *my plan*. My plan to create financial security for my family. My plan to free Dan from the job he hated. My plan to make an impact—and an income—that I could be proud of. I had already played it all out in my mind: the company's success, our eventual expansion, my cut of the profits. I was so sure the plan was foolproof. But now I only felt like a fool. And what felt even worse was that I didn't have a plan for what to do next.

Knowing I was desperate for a way to move forward, my friend Niko told me about a concept she'd heard recently: you could turn your life around if you made your own joy your top priority for thirty days. Granted, this "concept" came from a rather supernatural source—a "channeled" message from a spiritual teacher that Niko turned to from time to time for inspiration. But with no other ideas and a small buyout that was enough to float me for about a month, I decided to give it a try. Which shows you just how desperate I was: spending a month focusing on my own joy actually seemed like a viable plan for changing my life.

I figured I didn't have to believe in the spiritual aspect of this idea for it to work. I knew enough about brain behavior to understand that my thoughts are formed by neural connections, and those thoughts influence my outlook, my actions, my choices, and eventually my life. Perhaps thirty days of intentional joy was long enough to get my life back on track—either from the magic of outside forces or from the power I possessed within. If this strategy didn't work, I promised myself I would get a job and go back to contributing to society after thirty days. But if I was going to try it, I was going to give it my best shot.

Luckily, my husband was supportive of this crazy idea. Not necessarily because he thought it would work, but mostly because after fourteen years with me, he knew that once I get it into my head to do something, it's futile to try and stop me.

So for thirty days, I dedicated my daily actions to the hot pursuit of joy from all angles, from the spiritual to the physiological and everything in between. I called on the body of scientific and personal research I had amassed over the years involving hormones, neurotransmitters, psychology, and mindfulness, and synthesized it into a single, deliberate plan: the Joy Plan.

Because I think like an entrepreneur, I decided to approach my Joy Plan like a business plan. I thought I'd fully analyze the background and circumstances that led to the project, set my joy objectives, implement my joy-creation strategy, assess and tackle any challenges that came up, call on the strengths of my support team, measure my results, and predict joyful outcomes for the future. As a planner, I was thinking in terms of practical action; I was going to "do" the Joy Plan. But although all areas of my business plan–based idea were eventually addressed, what actually unfolded was very different from what I expected. I came to realize that for my real joy to emerge, I had to "be" on the Joy Plan and allow the plan to reveal itself to me. As it turned out, the plan that revealed itself was the best plan I (n)ever made.

What follows is a written record of the biggest epiphany of my life. It details an experiment that was carefully planned and executed, although the process itself and the results I experienced were often surprising. It was a practical journey to ridiculous happiness. And through this planned-yet-spontaneous process, I changed my life in ways that I think anyone can, including you.

I do recognize how rare it was that I had an entire month to dedicate solely to my own joy. And because I actually had this rare opportunity, even though it started off as something I was doing just for myself, I really did it for you too—because I had the time not only to do it but to write down what worked along the way. Now that I've written it down, I believe it can be done under any circumstances, including an already busy life.

The Joy Plan is a practical memoir, a guide that's illustrated through my personal story. And by the time you finish it, I hope you'll be inspired to create your own Joy Plan too.

PART 1

Background

HOW DID I END UP HERE?

The "Background" section of a business plan explains how an endeavor came about. While *The Joy Plan* is not a business plan, it is helpful to understand the backstory. This section isn't just my personal backstory but rather the backstory we all have in common, the one that's been happening inside our brains since we were born. Before starting a Joy Plan, it's important to go through a process of self-reflection and discovery. Think of it as preplan planning; you may need a week or two to prepare. We all experience joy differently and have our own unique barriers to attaining joy. Understanding what makes you tick helps you develop a plan that's tailored specifically for you.

CHAPTER 1

NOW WHAT?

"Sometimes not getting what you want
is a wonderful stroke of luck."

—DALAI LAMA

A couple of weeks had passed since the official collapse of my business, although without work to keep me on track, I was starting to lose track of the days of the week. Each day that passed was just another that I hoped would end. October was normally my favorite month, when the Indian summer sunshine brought balmy bright days and pleasantly cool evenings. But now I found the sun stressful. I kept the blinds in our two-bedroom town house closed tight as often as I could to shut out the offending brightness. I didn't want to be reminded of the world outside my door, to see that life continued and there were people out enjoying it.

I'd poured my heart, soul, sweat, tears—and a considerable amount of money—into the business, an epigenetics-based personal health assessment service. Based out of Santa Cruz, California, I—along with my business partners and a team of fifty people in six different countries—had been working eighteen-hour days for months on end without a break. But now all the electronic noise that had frantically filled my world and kept me chained to my desk—barely having time to pee or grab a snack— had just stopped.

I sat at my desk and stared at my phone. Its usual steady barrage of dings, chimes, and numbers that indicated mounting emails, voice mails, and texts was hauntingly absent. I thought I'd check, just one more time, to see if anything urgent had come in since I'd last looked five minutes earlier, but my phone was quiet. It was astonishing, really, how quickly I could go from hundreds of emails flying back and forth—from deadlines and managing teams and responsibilities and people who were waiting for important things from me—to silence. I was no longer important, needed, or relevant. Now that my business was gone, I felt like I was gone too.

Of course there were still a few people who needed me. My husband, Dan, had patiently supported me while I built the business, invested our savings, and retreated from our family to work nearly around the clock. For years, he'd been wanting to leave his "soul-sucking" software sales job to pursue something he could feel passionate about, and yet I'd continually pleaded with him not to quit. Now we depended on his income more than ever. Although he did his best to shield me from his disappointment, I could barely look at him without drowning in guilt.

To my daughters, Kira and Nava, the collapse of the business seemed like a good thing. All of a sudden, Mommy was out of her office. Listless as I was, for my children, a warm body is good enough to play with. While they excitedly showed me their latest art projects, dance routines, blanket forts, and tricks they'd taught our dog, Lovey, I feigned a smile and tried to be encouraging. But I wasn't really present. During those weeks, I wasn't really present in my own life at all. I was slipping away, sinking into the grip of depression while also jacked up on the panic of anxiety.

Between the crushing pull of depression and the shrill push of anxiety, I was immobilized—frozen in limbo and powerless to make a move.

During the day, with my children off at school and Dan away at work, I found myself—for the first time in a very long time—without a to-do list. Free time was a curse to me then: face-slapping evidence of my failure and uselessness. Moreover, I was annoyed with myself not only for failing but for wallowing in my own despair instead of just moving on. I tried to tell myself that this wasn't such a big deal. I knew I still had an enviable life: I was married to a wonderful man. We had two healthy children and a cute dog. We lived in a beautiful beach town. The failure of an Internet business was a perfect example of "first-world problems." However, this event felt like the last straw in a long string of failures that all pointed to my many shortcomings.

My inner dialogue played on repeat like a broken record that went like this: *I am stupid, worthless, and untalented. I might have some good ideas sometimes, but they only make other people successful and never do me any good. I pretend like I'm this smart, empowered woman, but the truth is I'm completely financially dependent on my husband and will probably never be able to stand on my own two feet.*

This running mental commentary wasn't new, unfortunately; it had been around for years. But by being fervently engrossed in work, I'd managed to suppress it. Through my role in the business, I felt I could finally prove that I was worthy and smart and had something of value to offer the world. I could finally be a real success! And now what? I was thirty-nine with no plans, no prospects, and no ideas about what to do next.

In the past, I had always had a plan. *I was a professional planner, for God's sake.* Throughout my life, I was always working on a project, in the process of creating something, making projections, and taking steps to achieve my next goal. I started my first business when I was nine years old and hadn't stopped since. No wonder I was struggling to deal with life without a plan.

When we were testing the algorithm for the personal health software that was the foundation for my latest business venture, I'd had the opportunity to have my brain activity measured with an EEG (electroencephalogram) device. The software was programmed to make estimations about brain behavior in order to provide personalized wellness tips based on individual physiology. With the EEG, I found out that the area of my brain that I primarily use is the T6, located in the right posterior temporal lobe, which drives visioning into the future and predicting what will happen next.[1] This is literally the part of the brain that forecasts the outcome of events. It turns out I have an innate skill at being a fortune teller, which is basically a glorified strategic planner—with a little bit of magic sprinkled in.

Watching my brain's EEG results light up on the computer screen was fascinating; my T6 was activated every second or two. During the process, I was asked all sorts of unrelated questions—math problems, emotional questions about my children, descriptions of food—and my brain skipped from the appropriate areas (cognitive reasoning, emotional center, pleasure center) back to the T6 to check in *constantly*. The T6 is like my brain's command center, and I'm always touching base with it. So when I can't use the area of my brain that I'm so accustomed to using—when my T6 can't function properly because there's no plan to project and no clear future to predict—the rest of my brain totally freaks out.

This means that the lack of a plan is much more traumatic for me than for someone who primarily uses a different area of their brain (such as, for example, the P3, which is located in the left parietal lobe and concerned with physical movement and spatial tactics). It feels uncomfortable for me in the way that a pulled muscle might feel uncomfortable for someone else. It feels like my T6 actually *hurts*, and the only way to find relief is to make a plan.

So there I was, feeling intense anxiety and doing everything I could think of to come up with a new plan as quickly as possible. But I found fault in every job I considered, and I doubted I could ever be successful as an entrepreneur again. My mind kept spinning back to all the ways I'd failed. I obsessed about the rapid downward spiral the business had taken, with some of my greatest professional life achievements now going unrecognized. I simply couldn't go on in this negative tailspin, even if the vortex of negativity existed primarily in my mind. Something had to change.

I decided to try going to the gym to see if exercise would help snap me out of my misery. I knew that exercise induces endorphins in the brain, which reduces the sensation of pain, and at that point, any reduction in my suffering was welcome. Plus it had been weeks since I'd moved my body in any significant way, and I was worried it might go in the same direction as my spirit: toward atrophy.

I thought that if I exercised first thing in the morning—and if exercise did actually help me feel better—then maybe that improved feeling would carry on throughout my day. So I got up one morning at six o'clock to hit the gym before my family woke up. The moon still illuminated the dark sky, and heavy fog hung over the road. I felt ridiculous, making an effort to fit in a quick workout as if I had a busy workday ahead of me. My usual litany of negative thoughts kicked in with vigor as I berated myself for the mess I was in.

As I was driving along, boiling in my own stew of putrid, acidic thoughts, a skunk ran right in front of me, stopped in the middle of the road, lifted its tail, and sprayed the front of my car before running away. If the skunk had only wanted to cross the street, it could have easily just kept running the whole time, but I believe it very intentionally stopped right in front of my car and did its business, just to spray me back into my senses.

If you've never had your car sprayed by a skunk, I don't recommend it. The stench goes everywhere and stays around for a long time. But the message was received, stinkily clear. I had to stop these "skunky" thoughts of mine, and I was desperate to figure out how. After the early-morning skunk encounter, I gave up on going to the gym. Instead I went to the library and checked out a huge stack of self-help books. Over the next week, I scoured the books voraciously. But no matter how many of them I read, I still couldn't help myself. Many of the books recommended meditation, but when I tried to meditate, the droning on and on of my thoughts was always too loud, and I couldn't quiet my mind, no matter how Zen I tried to be.

About a week after my run-in with Pepé Le Pew, I called my friend Niko. Niko is the friend I call when I can't figure out what to do next, because she always knows. As an inspirational speaker and executive coach—two really handy qualities in a best friend—Niko talks me off the ledge of my fears and anxiety for free, while other people have to pay her big bucks for it. However, in my state of desperation over the past month, I hadn't reached out to Niko—or to any of my friends and family, for that matter—and she was surprised to hear how bad it had gotten. Thankfully I did call Niko, and the pearl of wisdom she gave me that day changed the course of my life.

"I heard this idea the other day that might just be crazy enough to work for you," Niko told me. "But brace yourself, it came from a channeled spiritual teacher."

As a seeker of truth and student of life, Niko is open to wisdom from any god, goddess, deity, spirit, or magical force willing to lend a hand. She's also goal-oriented, practical, and professional—a planner just like me. In fact, in some ways Niko is even more of a planner than I am; her love for spreadsheets is extreme. But perhaps because her background is in what's known as "design thinking"—an innovative method of solving complex problems—Niko has a different way of seeing the world. While I usually choose the established, proven path, Niko is always looking for a different angle, the outside-the-box approach, and has no qualms about finding it in the spiritual realm.

"At this point, I'm willing to try just about anything," I said, "including a lobotomy."

So Niko told me about an idea that if you focused only on feeling good for thirty days, your life would change completely. All you had to do, according to this theory, was make your own joy your top priority for thirty days, and miracles would occur in your life that you could scarcely imagine.

Joy for thirty days will turn my life around? Okay, that's definitely a hard concept to swallow, I thought. *But I sure could use some miracles.*

Niko said the idea was based on the Law of Attraction, which is a belief that our thoughts, feelings, words, and actions produce energies, and those energies attract similar manifestations.[2] Positive energies attract positive things, events, and people, while negative energies attract negative experiences and outcomes. There's a famous quote, often attributed to Buddha, which pretty much sums up the Law of Attraction: "What you think, you become. What you feel, you attract. What you imagine, you create." Niko explained that the only reason we ever want anything is that we think we'll feel good when we have it. So if we can feel good now, the things we want will come to us now.

This wasn't the first time I'd heard about the Law of Attraction. Like many hippies of their generation, my parents were into New Age books like *The Path of Least Resistance: Learning to Become the Creative Force in Your Own Life* by Robert Fritz.[3] I remember my dad telling me when I was ten years old that if I wanted to manifest something, all I had to do was visualize it and then imagine a rubber band stretching between me and the thing I wanted. The "structural tension" of the rubber band between me and whatever I wanted would draw it to me, he said. I grew up believing that if I wanted something and worked toward it, I would have it.

But I had always taken a very goal-oriented approach to manifestation. I wanted the degree, the husband, the career, the travel, the house, the car, the kids, the dog—and I went for them with full force. I made one-year plans and five-year plans and business plans and savings plans. And each time one of my plans was complete, I would already have another plan in place. I never stopped to think about the emotional motivation behind all this planning and creating; I just focused on what I thought the goal or objective was. However, in spiritual self-help books that address the Law of Attraction—like *The Secret, Ask and It Is Given, Life Visioning, Think and Grow Rich,* and many others—the major emphasis is on the *feeling* rather than the *goal.*[4]

According to the theory of the Law of Attraction, when we pay enough attention to something, we'll get it. The Law of Attraction doesn't discriminate between what we want and what we don't want; it just gives us what we focus on. Did that explain why I was experiencing something I very much *did not want* in my life? With so much at stake, I'd been gripped with anxiety about the business for months. Had my fear and worry about the business failing, rather than the excited anticipation of it succeeding, gotten the most air time in my thoughts, words, and actions?

Perhaps my "vibe" had attracted my reality, or perhaps it was just my brain. While there may be a higher power or deep, inner wisdom that answers the call of the desires I wish to manifest, I know my brain also plays an important part in the equation. Every thought creates a connection of nerve cells, or neurons, in the brain. Repeated thoughts form clusters of these nerve cells, called neural networks, which grow stronger and larger each time they're activated. The more these neural networks are used, the stronger they become, eventually clumping together to form neural pathways, which are like highways our brains prefer to use because they're well-worn and familiar. In other words, our repeated thoughts become habits, which eventually shape the way we see and experience the world.[5] Our brains also favor memories with a strong emotional charge. That means when thought is combined with emotion, neural connections grow even faster and stronger.

In addition, we're programmed with a cognitive bias, known as the negativity effect, which steers our attention more readily to negative information than to positive information.[6] In fact, we require three positive experiences to balance the impact of one negative experience, because negative memories are more salient for the brain.[7] Because of these combined mental tendencies, when we notice something negative and focus on it, our brains naturally provide similar information to match our focus. This can quickly become a self-fulfilling prophecy: if we frequently focus on problems, we'll notice more problems in our lives. Stored memories that match our focus are often played on a feedback loop, activating strong neural pathways and triggering repeated thoughts, behaviors, and thus experiences—whether negative or positive.

What if I was caught in a feedback loop of negativity in my brain and just needed to create enough positive experiences to counterbalance the strong impact of the negative experience I'd just been through?

I wondered, is the Law of Attraction based on an outside force (spirit/God/universal energy) that responds to our thoughts and feelings, or is it simply our own reality being created by our minds as our brains form new neural pathways? If we shift our perception of reality by reframing our thoughts toward a positive outlook, thanks to neuroplasticity—the brain's ability to change its neural connections—we can influence our brains to perceive the world differently. So if, for example, we mostly focus on the things we're grateful for, our brains will naturally direct our attention toward the things we enjoy in life.

We're creating our reality all the time, in reaction to the way the neurons in our brains are firing. The experience of reality is slightly different for each person based on our individual perceptions. Our thought patterns influence everything from what we notice in our environment to the micromovements and choices we make in each moment. What we think becomes amplified in our reality whether we like it or not; what we focus on becomes what we experience. Our thoughts turn into beliefs, our beliefs inform our actions, and our actions create the results in our lives. We get what we expect. So if we want to manifest specific experiences in our lives, we have to develop thought patterns that will support those experiences. This is the Law of Attraction as it takes place in the brain.

From a pragmatic point of view, whether the Law of Attraction works because of some spiritual energy or simply as a mechanism of the brain—or a combination of the two—the outcome is the same. So even though it sounded like some "woo-woo" thing that my Age of Aquarius mom would have told me to try, I could see the merit in Niko's proposed crazy idea. Consciously forming new neural networks and, eventually, new neural pathways associated with feelings of joy, could open up more than my brain; it could open up my world. If I could just manage to feel good for thirty days, perhaps I would attract wondrous things into my life. Although changing my entire life in thirty days just by doing whatever "felt good" seemed unlikely, despite my skepticism, something inside me said, *It's worth a try. You don't have a better plan, do you?*

And then I realized this could be a plan for me to grab on to: the Joy Plan.

"What do you think will happen after thirty days?" Dan asked when I told him about Niko's suggestion. Luckily, my husband is incredibly patient and accepting and isn't easily shocked. He knew how bad I'd been feeling about the collapse of the business and how eager I was to get my life back on track.

"I don't know. A miracle?" I replied. It sounded even crazier when I said it out loud, but I somehow wanted it to be true.

"Do you think thirty days is enough time to give you the perspective you need to see things clearly for the future?" Dan gently probed.

I thought that was an interesting way of looking at it. Not that I should expect anything in particular to change in my circumstances during those thirty days, as Niko had implied, nor should I have expectations of miraculous opportunities falling into my lap. But rather I should enter into this with the hope that thirty days might be long enough to give me the perspective to see my way through to the next step.

"I don't know, honey," I answered. "But it seems like just as good an idea as any. And if nothing changes after thirty days, I'll start applying for jobs."

"I trust you," he asserted. "Like my mom always said, the most important thing in life is to be happy—nothing matters more."

Happy seemed like a tall order. But I would do my best.

In the days that followed my conversation with Niko, I decided to take on the Joy Plan as an experiment. I would be scientific about it and try to measure my joy and the amount of things that were going well in my life compared to my sadness and the things that were going wrong. And I would keep track of how it all changed over the course of thirty days by writing everything down. If it worked to turn my life around, it would happen faster than I could probably get hired for a new job—and it would be more fun. But if it didn't work, it would only be one month that I had wasted, and I could take the first job I was offered after the Joy Plan ended.

I had received a small buyout payment from the business, so one month was just about the amount of time I had before I really needed to produce an income and help cover our expenses. *Maybe this buyout—as small as it was compared to the calculations of millions of dollars in profit I had made in my head—was enough to buy me the time I needed to completely change my life*, I thought.

My kids were in school from 8:30 a.m. to 2:30 p.m. every day, and my husband was at work until about 5:30. This meant I had the house to myself and an open schedule to focus on my own joy for at least six hours every day. I could do this. Maybe it would actually work. But how would I even get started? Unlike a lot of the self-help books I had been reading, this plan was based on joy, not happiness, and I was pretty sure I had neither at the moment.

I'd never really thought about the difference between happiness and joy; I'd previously used the terms interchangeably. But they are quite different. According to scientists, happiness is a cognitive experience, a state of mind that exists in our conscious awareness, while joy is an emotion, a subconscious feeling that occurs without thought.[8] We experience happiness in our neocortex—the largest and also the newest part of the cerebral cortex to evolve—where analytical thinking, planning, and decision making take place. Happiness creates a sensation of satisfaction, primarily related to physical needs (like hunger and thirst), but it's temporary and fleeting.

Joy, on the contrary, appears to originate in the brain's limbic system, the part of the brain that controls emotion, behavior, and long-term memory. Unlike happiness, joy involves little cognitive awareness—we feel good without consciously deciding to—and it's longer lasting. Whereas happiness is usually induced by and dependent on outside conditions, joy is something we experience more deeply; it's a state of being that's not necessarily tied to external situations. While happiness is a state of mind based on circumstances, joy is an internal feeling that disregards circumstances.

In fact, joy is often associated with spiritual experiences, a feeling of being connected to a higher power, and a state of inner peace and contentment that's sustained throughout varying experiences. As Craig Lambert, PhD, wrote in *Harvard Magazine*: "The mystics have linked joy to connection with a power greater than themselves. Happiness activates the sympathetic nervous system (which stimulates the flight-or-fight response), whereas joy stimulates the parasympathetic nervous system (controlling rest and digest functions)… Happiness is a place to visit, not a place to live."[9] I didn't want to just visit happiness; I wanted to live in joy.

When I thought about the most joyful people I'd ever met, they were in

Bali and lived in abject poverty. They weren't necessarily happy with every aspect of their lives, but they embodied joy. My goal was to figure out how I could do the same, despite the current state of affairs in my life. I would make that goal my top priority for the next thirty days.

So now, armed with a free month and the luxury of time and space, I set out to see what would happen to my life if I made my own joy my top priority. This was a luxury I knew most people would never have, and I was determined to make the most of it. If I could intentionally cultivate positive thoughts and experiences and feel joyful long enough, would the universe provide the means for my continued joy? Or would my brain start firing in new ways that would lead me toward a joyful life? I was about to find out.

JOY PLAN TIP #1

According to the theory of the Law of Attraction, when you pay enough attention to something, you'll get it—whether it's something you want or something you don't want. From a pragmatic point of view, we're creating our reality all the time, in reaction to the way the neurons in our brains are firing. Neural connections are strengthened when thought is combined with an emotion, like joy. Whether the Law of Attraction works because of some spiritual energy or simply as a mechanism of the brain, either way, the outcome is the same.

CHAPTER 2

THE BITCH IN MY HEAD

"Recognize the ego for what it is: a collective
dysfunction, the insanity of the human mind."
—ECKHART TOLLE

I decided I was going to start my month dedicated to joy on November 1, which was about a week away. I felt a bit ludicrous, setting aside a whole month to do something as simple as find joy. Why didn't I have it already? Yes, I'd failed in some work endeavors. But I had a lot going for me still. If you could assemble the ingredients for "joy" in a stew, it would seem that I had them all in my pot.

But regardless of how joyful I looked from the outside, I rarely felt joy—even with all the blessings in my life. I had happy moments, for sure, but true, sustained joy had always eluded me. I experienced most of my life through a filter of worry and anxiety, against a backdrop of negative thoughts and self-criticism.

Home alone in bed, while my kids were at school and Dan was at work, I stared at the stack of self-help books I'd unsuccessfully turned to for inspiration teetering precariously on my nightstand. I perused one book, written by a Buddhist monk, which said the "self" we perceive as our true identity is merely an illusion. I thought about this universal concept, which has pervaded so many schools of thought for centuries: humankind's mental construct, which many call the "ego," often leads to our downfall. I was feeling pretty despondent but still trying to get psyched up to start my Joy Plan.

Come on, Kaia, you can do this, I thought. *How hard can it be to find joy?*

Well, actually, it could be pretty hard. In fact, even though I could've pondered myriad reasons for my lack of joy, I didn't really need to. It has already been explained and measured scientifically, and it turns out that my lack of joy has more to do with a neural mechanism in my brain than the circumstances of my life. In 2008, in between nighttime breastfeeding sessions with my younger daughter, I edited a book called *The Evolutionary Glitch* by Dr. Albert Garoli.[1] This insightful book explains scientifically why most people aren't joyful most of the time.

The Evolutionary Glitch details how most humans develop a mental defense mechanism in response to the various experiences of rejection that we all inevitably go through at different points during our childhoods. For some people these early, pivotal experiences involve a feeling of being rejected by their own parents; for others it's an experience of being rejected by other children or adults. But all of our brains compensate for this rejection by creating a coping mechanism calculated to keep us safe. Psychiatrists, spiritual teachers, and many other sages and scientists over the centuries have talked about this aspect of the ego as the "pain body," "monkey mind," or "inner critic."[2] I call it the "bitch in my head."

Dr. Garoli has worked with the world's top neuroscientists since the 1990s and has mapped hundreds of his patients' brains using EEG and other technologies. His research indicates that most people adapt one of six main mental defense mechanisms, which he equates to a "mental virus." Garoli calls these defense mechanisms "personas," a term coined by Swiss psychiatrist Carl Jung, referring to the masks worn by Etruscan mimes. Jung called the persona "a kind of mask, designed on the one hand to make a definite impression upon others and on the other to conceal the true nature of the individual."[3] Garoli's persona is more than an outward face we present to the world, however; it's a coping mechanism gone rogue in the brain.

Studies have confirmed that the same area of the brain is activated when we experience social exclusion or rejection as when we experience physical pain.[4] But Garoli took his research further to look at the actual physical changes that take place in the brain in response to social rejection and the defense mechanisms, or personas, that form as a result. When a persona is formed, there is an explosion of electrical and emotional output in the brain, which changes the brain's physical and psychological structure from that point forward. This results in acute psychological pain and causes actual physical furrows, or ridges, to form in the brain. (According to Garoli's findings, this phenomenon is visible in PET, or positron emission tomography, scans.) In other words, when social rejection is experienced, the brain conditions itself to restructure its natural tendency to one that it perceives will be more socially accepted.

Garoli describes this phenomenon as an "evolutionary glitch" because, once formed in the brain, the persona then evolves as its own separate mental identity whose primary objective is to keep itself alive. And since the persona only thrives when its host organism feels stress, it actually creates the mental impression of danger or fear of rejection even when it's not relevant to external circumstances. The persona becomes a mask we wear much of the time, especially when interacting with other people. The persona also initiates negative self-talk, doubt, and repeated habits aimed at hiding a person's true nature—because the true nature was at one time rejected.

It's all one big mental overreaction. And the crazy thing is that most of us don't even recognize our personas, because they're so ingrained in us that we can't see them as a separate identity. But the persona is *not* who we truly are!

Personas vary in their strength in different people, depending on the intensity of the rejection that originated it. The six persona types are like six different villains in various classic tales; their methods vary, but all of them are wicked. Dr. Garoli gave them names based on the temperaments, or humors, in classical Greek medicine: Sanguine, Lymphatic, Nervous, Melancholic, Bilious, and Phlegmatic.[5] The descriptions of each of them are awful, but it's important to remember that the *persona* and the *person* are not the same.

Of Garoli's six persona types, my internal villain is Nervous, the controlling persona. She's the bitch in my head. Her goal is to stay safe by maintaining control and to prevent others from getting too close because they could potentially do emotional damage. She isn't just critical and controlling toward others; most of her condemnation is directed toward me. When I think I'm writing something brilliant, she tells me it's stupid drivel. When I look at my husband with love, she tells me he's lazy or that he could leave me high and dry someday. She is harsh, unforgiving, and tireless in her mission to make me feel that I am worthless and no one can be trusted.

She does this because the persona has one objective: to make its host feel that *it* is the only thing that they can count on—and in that way, protect itself. The last thing that my persona wants is for me to have joy. Because if I have joy, then I don't need her anymore. Without a clear mind, free from the overriding control of my persona, it's difficult to figure out what my true path to joy really is. I know my persona will intentionally steer me off my natural course, in a direction where I'm more likely to encounter problems and stress.

Even though I had studied this research for years, I had never really applied it to my own life. And I decided it was about time I did. I needed all the help I could get so that my Joy Plan would have the best possible chance of succeeding.

I found my copy of *The Evolutionary Glitch* on the bookshelf and dusted it off. I walked over to the full-length mirror on the back of my bedroom door and saw a tired-looking, slightly disheveled woman staring back at me. The critical voice of the bitch in my head kicked in immediately with the list of faults she saw in my reflection: *body too fat, complexion too splotchy, hair too thin*. I crawled into bed with the book and a notebook, determined to uncover and expose the bitch for the imposter that she was.

I went back and performed the exercises detailed in *The Evolutionary Glitch* designed for loosening the grip of the persona, something I hadn't done since I edited the book. Through these exercises—which involve identifying which of the six persona types you have and then delving into childhood memories to determine when it was formed—you can start to recognize when the persona is active. Recognizing the persona is the first step to short-circuiting this "mental virus." With practice and dedication, you can create new neural networks that override the persona and rewire the brain's pathways. The persona only continues to exist if the neural networks that form it are frequently used. But just like muscles will weaken from lack of use, the persona will wither away if it's no longer perpetually confirmed.

I knew if I could free myself from the persona's grip, even a bit, I could start to feel my body's natural inclinations and interests and replace the persona with who I really am. Because once we're in touch with who we really are, that's when joy comes flooding in. So how do we figure out who we really are?

The astounding thing, according to *The Evolutionary Glitch*, is that the key to our joy, direction, and purpose in life is written in our cells. Our bodies are the vessels for our goals and desires, but our personas hijack our brains and hide our true nature from ourselves, controlling our conscious minds and blocking our intuition. We each have a unique direction in life for which we're best suited; following that direction can lead us to a successful life of joy and ease. The trick is to see past the persona blocking our path so we can figure out what our true direction to a joyful life is.

What others might call "an instinct" or "a calling," Dr. Garoli has scientifically classified into eight different "resonant wave patterns" that lie beneath the persona in each of us. One of these eight resonant wave patterns is the primary true nature for each person, which points to his or her ideal direction in life (see exercise #1 in the appendix for descriptions of the eight resonant wave patterns). According to Garoli's theory, the activities we will enjoy the most and derive the greatest success from are determined by the natural predispositions of our individual brain functions as well as by the particular hormonal and physical profiles of our individual bodies.

As I reviewed *The Evolutionary Glitch*, I went over the eight resonant wave patterns and tried to figure out which one felt right to me. I thought I might relate to more than one of these waves, but according to Garoli's brain research, each person has only one that is primary. The key to figuring out which wave we resonate with—and then riding it all the way to Joy Town—is to learn how to follow our subconscious, rather than our conscious, minds.

The terms "mind" and "brain" are often used interchangeably, much like "happiness" and "joy." But according to scientists, the mind is actually *created by* the brain.[6] The brain collects cues from the environment, which it then uses to create our beliefs, desires, and goals.

The mind can be divided into three functions: conscious, subconscious, and unconscious.[7] The conscious mind is where we operate in the present moment. Conscious thought occurs largely in the prefrontal cortex, located behind the forehead. This is the smallest part of our brain, representing only a fraction of what our brains are doing at any one time.

The subconscious mind consists of information that is accessible but outside the realm of conscious awareness. Subconscious information is like a short-term memory: available when we draw our attention to it. It's located in the "reptilian brain," the part of the brain that evolved first, and is more concerned with survival mechanisms rather than logic.

But whereas we know where the conscious and subconscious minds are found in the brain, the location of the unconscious mind—if there is one specific location—is still unclear. The unconscious mind is made up of primitive instincts and deep, long-term memories that are rarely accessible to the conscious mind.

The key to finding our path to joy, however, lies in unlocking the subconscious mind, which is accessible to the conscious mind. The subconscious mind is the realm of intuition: knowledge or solutions that are available through very quick thought processes, or what we often call a "gut feeling." Intuition may seem mystical; it is often explained from a spiritual perspective as tapping into a "universal energy" or "higher power," perhaps through a collective subconscious to which we are all connected. In reality, intuition is simply the process of accessing information stored in the subconscious mind, which lies beyond conscious reasoning.

Intuition can often feel subtle, like an understanding or solution that gently appears without words. It may present itself as a sudden image or impulse that indicates a course of action. Intuition feels sure and certain, instinctual, even though it is often quickly overridden by conscious thoughts that doubt its validity. But it's imperative that we do follow these "gut feelings" and listen to our intuition, because the subconscious mind's impulses are the most accurate representation of our true nature—although they often go unnoticed—and they are usually quite different from the messages our persona is sending us. Tapping into this subconscious intuition is another way to bypass the persona.

Harnessing your intuition takes practice. We can practice listening to the quiet voice of our subconscious mind by paying attention to the feelings and reactions we have when different events and circumstances occur. This process can be likened to tuning into your own radio frequency, or your own inner voice. If your persona's voice is loud, your inner voice will be harder to hear. But when you *are* listening to that inner voice, you'll see signs appear in your life, showing you the right path to follow.

"Signs" may sound like something supernatural, but they are a well-documented phenomena. Carl Jung referred to "synchronicities," or meaningful coincidences, that happen all the time.* Jung believed that our lives aren't merely a series of random events, but rather that there's a larger spiritual picture that we're all a part of.[8] Do signs come from the universe or from God as a way of spiritual communication, or are they simply your brain's attention to specific clues that were always present but outside your field of awareness until you brought them into focus? Either way, recognizing signs is an important element of intuition. Of course, we all interpret our observations differently, and signs have a unique significance to each person. What matters when seeing a sign is what it means to you.

Although I understood signs and the subconscious intellectually, I didn't feel connected to my intuition, purpose, or calling at all. And even though I'd had years to soak up knowledge about the mechanisms behind

---

*   Jung gives an example of a sign, or synchronicity, in this description of an experience he had in a session with a particularly challenging patient:

       She had an impressive dream the night before, in which someone had given her a golden scarab—a costly piece of jewelry. While she was still telling me this dream, I heard something behind me gently tapping on the window. I turned around and saw that it was a fairly large flying insect that was knocking against the windowpane from outside in the obvious effort to get into the dark room. This seemed to me very strange. I opened the window immediately and caught the insect in the air as it flew in. It was a scarabaeid beetle, whose gold-green color most nearly resembles that of a golden scarab. I handed the beetle to my patient with the words, "Here is your scarab."

the persona, it was still daunting to tackle my own mental virus, knowing it would be contending with me in my quest for joy. I hoped thirty days would be long enough to change what was happening in my mind as well as in my life.

I knew that to truly achieve the joyful results I wanted from my month-long experiment, I would have to remove the barriers to my joy—including my persona. I was ready to finally quiet the bitch in my head, if not take her out completely.

About five days before I planned to officially start my Joy Plan, I followed Garoli's advice from *The Evolutionary Glitch* and started paying close attention to the content of my thoughts, so I could recognize when my persona was active. This was surprisingly hard, because it was so frequent. It was almost easier to recognize the times she wasn't active—those rare moments when I felt calm, peaceful, caught up in a pleasant moment, or distracted enough to temporarily forget my troubles.

When I really started noticing the near-constant chatter in my mind, it was like shining a spotlight on a thief in the shadows. Suddenly I could see her for all she was trying to steal from me: my confidence, sense of worth, trust in others, and hope for the future.

I wrote down the most repetitive messages my persona hammered me with daily:

1. I am a failure.
2. I am stupid.
3. I am old and ugly.
4. No one truly loves me; I'm really on my own in this life.
5. I suck at pretty much everything.
6. I have nothing of value to offer the world.
7. None of this is ever going to change; it's only going to get worse.

Seeing it on paper, I felt the blow of these words like a kick in the stomach. But I also felt some relief. At least now I knew what I was dealing with and could pay better attention, so that when those thoughts flooded my mind, I would recognize them as my persona's agenda and not my own. I knew this would be critical in my Joy Plan.

I decided to give the bitch in my head a name: Chatty Patty. I started thinking of her as my mind's annoying, negative roommate who rarely shut up. And I decided that—since Chatty Patty would likely be cohabiting with me for quite some time still—I would practice tuning her out. I imagined the sound of Chatty Patty's negative droning fading into the indiscernible sounds of the teacher in Charlie Brown cartoons: "*Wah, wah, wah,*" I said out loud when I caught her in the act of telling me I was a failure yet again. She really was quite repetitive.

And when she tried even harder to get my attention by reminding me about all the time and money I'd wasted on my failed business, instead of joining her rampage of negativity, I loudly said, "SHHHHHHHHHH!" Mostly, I wanted the bitch in my head to be quiet long enough for me to hear what my subconscious mind might be trying to tell me about my true nature and the means to finding my joy.

By going through the exercise of slowing down my life, quieting my thoughts, and focusing on my own joy for a month, I planned to get in touch with my elusive true nature, which I suspected was actually both very different from my persona and very different from my chosen livelihood. I would be keeping a close eye out for any signs along the way.

JOY PLAN TIP #2

The subconscious mind lies just beneath conscious aware-
ness and is the realm of feelings and intuition, providing
more general sensations rather than precise input. You can
practice tuning out the negative voice of your persona, or
ego, and listening instead to your subconscious mind by
paying attention to the reactions you have when different
events and circumstances occur in your life. This process
can be likened to tuning into your own radio frequency, or
your own inner voice.

CHAPTER 3

KNOW THYSELF

"There came a time when the risk to
remain tight in the bud was more painful
than the risk it took to blossom."

—ANAIS NIN

The beginning of November, my month of joy, was just a few days away. As a planner, I wanted to prepare for my Joy Plan with an agenda, schedule, spreadsheets, and checklists. But how could I prepare and plan for a month of spontaneously following joy and tapping into my subconscious intuition? The objective was clear but fuzzy at the same time: find ways to feel good; let my true nature rather than my persona lead; keep making joy my top priority; wait and watch for miracles.

While I prepped myself for the challenge of a one-month Joy Plan, joy was already the focus of my children's lives. Kira was eight, Nava was six, and they were occupied with the things that occupy most eight- and six-year-olds: toys, friends, school, their dog, and mostly, having fun. They played, they asked a lot of questions, and for the most part, they didn't notice what was going on with me. They'd never understood much about my business anyway, except that Mommy worked all the time. So they figured whatever happened to pull me away from the near-constant attachment to my laptop was a good thing. While I moped about, they fluttered like butterflies around me, a flash of brilliant color against my backdrop of gray.

One afternoon, in a quiet moment at home after school, I asked the girls if they'd noticed anything different about me since I'd stopped working.

Kira answered, "You're more open-minded when you're not stressed."

I wondered if she meant I said yes to more things when I wasn't stressed, but regardless of what she meant, "open-minded" was totally accurate. Stress activates the amygdala, the brain's danger sensor, and impedes the prefrontal cortex, where logical thought takes place.[1] Under stress, the mind is literally less open; the path to clear, solution-oriented thought is blocked and survival instincts run the show.

"When you're stressed, you're *eeeevillll*," Nava said with a scowl and then laughed like a classic villain from a movie.

She was right too; when the bitch in my head took over, I was a mean dictator, demanding that my subjects obey or face my wrath. Perhaps I seemed less stressed to the kids because lately my stress had taken on a more desperate, longing quality.

Meanwhile, Dan was wrapped up in his own job situation, which seemed to be getting worse by the day. Usually an avid surfer and the most consistently cheerful person I knew, my husband had become quieter and less active than usual. Dan wanted to leave his job, but the applications and inquiries he'd put out for other positions weren't getting him anywhere. At forty-seven, he was twice the age of many of the employees at the companies where he applied, and he was feeling discouraged, old, and stuck. Despite this, he was supportive of my Joy Plan and excited for me to start. But I could tell he wasn't all there; he had other things on his mind.

I had other things on my mind too. Now that I was on a diligent lookout for Chatty Patty, I was paying closer attention to my thoughts, and it was disturbing how repetitive they were. According to the research of Dr. Fred Luskin at Stanford University, the average person has sixty thousand thoughts per day during waking hours, and ninety percent of them are repetitive.[2] If my Joy Plan was going to work based on the positive content of my thoughts, I needed to find a way to shift them toward the other end of the spectrum.

To better understand my headspace, I decided to classify my thoughts into categories. I found that the content of my thoughts primarily fell into four groups: the past (usually with a feeling of sadness or anger), the future (dominated by worry and fear), judgment (mostly about myself but sometimes others), and the present (something that captured my immediate attention or engaged one of my senses, such as eating or feeling tired).

I wrote these categories down and made check marks next to them throughout the day whenever I noticed corresponding thoughts. This was an interesting process. I found that as I noticed and classified my thoughts, I started to see them as separate from myself, primarily generated by my persona. And since I'd started referring to Chatty Patty as a separate entity, the power those thoughts had over me lost a bit of their grip. I felt a little like a crazy person, writing down the voices in my head, but I was willing to be crazy for this plan to work. I came up with a simple mental exercise of imagining my thoughts turning into bubbles and floating away. I hoped I could train my mind to let thoughts slip in and out just like bubbles, instead of jerking me along on an emotional journey that I hadn't signed up for.

Noticing how many negative thoughts I had throughout the day made me realize I really needed this Joy Plan. I thought it would do wonders for my mental health, but I knew my physical health would benefit as well. In fact, I thought the Joy Plan might just save my life.

Over the past couple of years, I'd learned quite a bit about epigenetics, the study of how the environment affects genetic expression.[3] Epigenetics explains why identical twins raised in different environments or with different health habits develop completely different health profiles decades down the road, despite having the same DNA. We all carry genes—a predisposition in our DNA—for different diseases, but that doesn't mean every disease will necessarily be expressed.[4] When genes are expressed, they're turned on like a light bulb, and there's usually something that's triggered the flip of the switch.[4] Often the trigger is stress. But it's entirely possible to carry the genes for certain diseases that never get switched on.

I have had severe psoriasis, an autoimmune skin condition, since I was four years old. In 2009, after undergoing a course of UV light treatment to help the worst psoriasis flare-up of my life, I developed hundreds of *multiple dysplastic nevi*—a spontaneous eruption of numerous "pre-melanoma" moles. My dermatologist and several other doctors informed me that I was at the highest possible risk for developing melanoma, one of the fastest progressing—and most deadly—forms of skin cancer. Along with telling me to avoid sun during the harshest hours, cover up, and wear sunscreen, my dermatologist told me that the most important thing I could do to prevent future cancer was avoid stress.

Although I always knew stress was "bad," it wasn't something I had considered deeply as it applied to me. And I definitely hadn't expected to hear from a dermatologist that stress could activate genes that cause disease. While I was busy worrying about deadlines, money, and getting it all done—feeling stressed most of the time—I had never considered what that stress was doing to my body. It turns out stress creates inflammation, which promotes the growth of cancer cells.[5]

I'd thought about my dermatologist's advice a lot since that appointment, but I hadn't really followed it. I spent so much of my life being stressed out, I hardly knew how to be any other way. I remember being four years old, in a diner with my mom and a guy she was dating at the time, who happened to be a professional clown. He had just gotten off work and was in his clown costume at the diner. We were having my favorite meal, and the clown was doing all sorts of silly tricks to entertain me. I should have been happy. But I just couldn't stop worrying about everything.

"Kaia, just relax," my mom had said.

"I'm trying as hard as I can!" I exclaimed, the juxtaposition of which was so funny to my mom and the clown that they burst out laughing. But it was true. I have tried "as hard as I can" to relax for years—and most of the time have not succeeded. This is the story of my life. Chatty Patty has often been the one holding the reins inside my head.

At twenty-five, while traveling through Europe by train, I met a white-haired Catholic priest from India late one night, somewhere in Spain. His name was Ephraim, and I swear he emanated wisdom from every pore. He even smelled wise. We ended up talking all night about life, death, and everything in between. And as we were approaching his train stop, I quickly asked him, "By the way, I've been wondering, how do I stop negative thoughts and worry? I seem to have them all the time. I know that worry is like praying for what you don't want, but I don't know how to stop."

Ephraim looked at me with his kind, brown eyes and smiled so that his face wrinkled all the way from his mouth to his forehead. In his grandfatherly Indian accent and with his head bobbing from side to side he said, "Leave your front door and back door open. Let thoughts come and go. Just don't serve them tea," and then he exited the train. I later realized he had quoted meditation guru Shunryū Suzuki, and I did my best to remember those wise words. But I usually didn't succeed.

However, this month—on the Joy Plan—I was determined to keep my thoughts positive. I would recognize Chatty Patty's chatter and do my best to let it pass right on by. Meanwhile, I would set the table for gratitude, optimism, and joy, and welcome them to come in and stay for tea.

In preparation for this "tea party," the next thing I did to get ready for my Joy Plan was brainstorm ideas on how to actually create the conditions for joy. How could I make joy my top priority if I didn't know what it felt like?

I considered what I enjoyed. My life had been primarily focused around work, so I focused on that first. I thought about my skills. I was good at getting media attention for people, projects, and products, and I'd been doing it for twenty years. I was good at making marketing plans, and I was pretty good at planning events. I really loved writing and thought I was okay at it, especially the blogging I'd been doing in the past year for the start-up.

The more I thought about it, actually, the more I realized that— although I had achieved good results in the media relations and event planning aspect of public relations and marketing—it was the writing that I really enjoyed the most. Writing press releases, newsletter and magazine articles, even emails—the sheer act of stringing words together—was really fun for me.

I'd never considered myself to be a writer, even though I'd done lots of writing in my life. As a child, there was nothing I loved more than writing and illustrating my own books. I would spend hours a day slowly writing out the words and carefully drawing the pictures to stories I'd either made up or put my unique spin on—like my own version of classic fairy tales. Making those books are some of the happiest memories of my childhood, but somehow I never considered that I could do that as an adult. I thought of making books as "play time," and when I decided on a career path, I chose marketing—something I knew would bring me a steady paycheck.

However, as I took the time and space to reflect on what I truly enjoyed, I realized that the aspect of all the work I'd done that really lit me up was the writing. And the part that drained me the most was a lot of interaction with other people. And then, for the first time ever, I acknowledged something that I think I must have been fighting against my whole life: *I am an introvert.*

I thought back to the resonant wave patterns in *The Evolutionary Glitch* and realized I had been primarily engaged in the activity of the Soothing Wave (taking care of others as a mom) and the Expanding Wave (bringing people together through publicity), when I actually most resonated with the Yielding Wave (research, writing, problem solving).

When I was working with my team to build the personal health software, I'd studied quite a bit about brain activity and learned that the brains of introverts and extroverts work very differently. Extroverts' brains rely on external stimuli in order to engage and activate, whereas introverts' brains generate so much internal stimuli that external input can feel overwhelming.[6] Being an introvert isn't the same thing as being shy or reclusive; rather, introverts need alone time to process their thoughts, while extroverts rely on the energizing force of others to stimulate their thoughts.[7] The more I thought about it, the more I realized I've always been a natural introvert— but I've tried hard to fit into an extrovert's world. And that's probably why I've often felt overwhelmed and mentally exhausted.

With the time and space to actually think through what brings me joy, I finally started to recognize and accept my inner introvert. All of a sudden, I was seeing myself in a different light, as if I was meeting myself for the first time. Given this new realization, I decided that my personal Joy Plan would probably be very different from the Joy Plan of an extrovert. Instead of seeking joy in social environments, I would find comfort in retreating into my own mental space, with long periods of quiet and delicious hours of solitude.

I had never done this before. In fact, I'd spent most of my life being super social. In my twenties, as a public relations executive in San Francisco, I had a huge wall calendar posted next to my desk with time slots by the hour, and I filled up every single slot from morning until night with other people and activities. If an hour was blank, I quickly made plans to fill it. I didn't take the time to consider whether all this social activity was filling my cup; I just assumed that was what I was supposed to be doing, because that's what everyone around me did. Then I met Dan (a hard-core extrovert). We got married and had kids, and life had been, well, busy. Too busy for me to notice my true nature, I guess, which I was now quite relieved to discover.

I felt liberated. Like I was acknowledging something that my inner voice had been trying to tell me for years, begging for some solace, but that I continually shushed: *I don't have time. I have to get ready for another dinner party.* But now I was embracing my life as an introvert, and I needed to put some new procedures in place to make sure I would listen to that inner voice from now on.

Figuring out that I'm an introvert gave me a sense of direction for my Joy Plan. Whereas an extrovert's Joy Plan would likely involve lots of time with others—and probably multiple parties—I knew my joy would have a better chance to thrive if I had plenty of time alone. It was time for me to tell Dan about my discovery. But I was nervous.

Dan and I had always been very social together—as a couple and as a family—attending parties, group camping trips, and community events on a regular basis. I was worried that having an introverted wife would be hard for him to accept. In an attempt to break the news gently, I started by explaining brain waves and inner equilibrium to him, but I wasn't really getting my point across.

"I'm realizing that I'm an introvert. I've kept it hidden well, but I'm coming out of the closet now," I explained. "I love you, I love the kids, I love our friends and family. But I need time alone to recharge. Too much time with other people—even the people I love most—is draining to me. I've always felt this way, but I'm finally admitting it. Does that freak you out?"

It didn't. He was totally cool with it and called me his sexy librarian.

We discussed a plan of action now that I was going to be social less often than Dan would like to be. We agreed that we would both spend time doing what we love, even if that meant spending time apart. I assured him that my being an introvert was nothing personal and didn't mean I loved him any less; I just needed to be quiet more often. Logistically, this meant he would go out with friends in the evenings more frequently than I would. It meant I would take time to be alone on the weekends. I suggested that I could drive separately to events where I might want to gently excuse myself early.

I'd always tried to go along with Dan's social preferences. However, I wanted my Joy Plan to work, and for that to happen, I had to stop pretending to be an extrovert. Dan and I decided we'd focus on the things we do best together: getting out in nature with our kids, traveling to new places, and spending time between the sheets. And he could take over the management of our social calendar, leaving me the option to bow out gracefully when I wasn't up for whatever he had planned.

JOY PLAN TIP #3

The brains of introverts and extroverts work very differently. Extroverts' brains rely on external stimuli in order to engage and activate, whereas introverts' brains generate so much internal stimuli that external input can feel overwhelming. While an extrovert's Joy Plan would likely involve lots of time with others, an introvert's joy will have a better chance to thrive with plenty of time alone. Which are you?

PART 2

Strategy

THE PLAN!

The "Strategy" section of a business plan outlines the nitty-gritty details of how the plan will be put into action. For my initial thirty-day Joy Plan, I focused on fostering joy through four main techniques: simple pleasures, gratitude, mindfulness, and joyful body. Since this is a practical memoir—think of it as a memoir with benefits—the chapters that follow can also serve as a guide to create your own Joy Plan (and there are more tools in the appendix, "Create Your Own Joy Plan").

CHAPTER 4

DOES THIS FEEL GOOD?

*"I learned to be with myself rather than
avoiding myself... I started to be aware of my
feelings more, rather than numb them."*

—JUDITH WRIGHT

November 1 had arrived: the first day of the Joy Plan. *Okay, this it*, I
thought. *Project Joy: Day One*. It was a cool and cloudy day, with a
slight drizzle in the air. Not a great day to be outside, so I decided to start off
in the sauna. After I dropped the kids off at school in the morning, I picked
up a juice and went to the gym.

The Joy Plan is based on this directive: feel good first. So I spent the day
doing what felt good to me. I sat in a hot sauna, read a good book, wrote
in my journal, had a quick chat with Niko, and took our dog for a short
walk in the redwood forest before I picked the kids up from school. *Is this
going to do it? This doesn't seem earth-shattering*, I said to myself. I felt like an
unemployed loser.

But that evening, I walked to the beach with Dan and the kids to see the sunset. I'd consistently worked through the evenings, so this was the first sunset I'd seen in months. As the shades of pink and orange filtered through the clouds, I could sense my own joy longing to peek through the haze as well.

Because I need a plan to be simple in order to follow it consistently, I boiled down my approach to the Joy Plan to one question, which I would ask myself repeatedly throughout each day: *Does this feel good?*

My persistent questioning reminded me of one of my favorite books as a child, *Are You My Mother?* by P. D. Eastman.[1] In the story, a baby bird hatches alone in his nest while his mother is out finding food. Determined to find her, the small bird embarks on an earnest quest, asking every animal and inanimate object he comes across, "Are you my mother?" He asks a kitten, a hen, a dog, a cow, a car, a boat, and even a plane, until he and his mother are reunited at last.

Of course, I had a multitude of experiences every day in which the answer to "Does this feel good?" was a definite *no*. But that's when my work began. On the Joy Plan, my goal was to do whatever it took to switch things up so that I did feel good. Sometimes that meant changing the thoughts I was currently thinking or taking a break from what I was currently doing, and sometimes that meant I needed to end a conversation or walk away from an uncomfortable situation. My goal was to make "feeling good" my number one priority—and to that end, to make adjustments throughout the day, all day long. Simple. Not always easy, but simple.

When feeling good was out of the question, I simply tried to feel better. I remembered something I'd learned about many years ago, under rather unusual circumstances, called the Emotional Tone Scale.

Let me back up. You see, I didn't exactly have a "normal" childhood. My parents split up when I was two years old, and I moved back and forth between them over the next fifteen years, attending eight different schools in four states. I always felt like I had a double life: one in which I went to public school and tried to fit in and be "normal" and one in which I was anything but normal. In my "normal" life, I just did my best to survive. But in my other life, I sometimes got to experience pure magic.

For most of my childhood, my dad worked as an intensive care unit nurse, with a keen interest in the mental and emotional side of illness. He had witnessed many of his patients have transformational emotional experiences, often on their deathbeds, and he yearned for a deeper understanding of the connection between feeling and healing. Now he's a psychotherapist, and he wrote a book about the connection between emotion and illness called *Deep Feeling, Deep Healing: The Heart, Mind, and Soul of Getting Well.*[2]

In the mid-1980s, my dad connected with a group of people in Atlanta, Georgia, who were experimenting with a new therapy technique called Body Electronics.[3] This modality is based on the discoveries of Dr. John Ray, who found that acupuncture/acupressure points, as well as joints and injury sites in the body, contain tiny deposits of crystals. When Dr. Ray photographed these crystals with an electron microscope, he saw that they are made up of mineral deposits and bound with melanin protein, a structure similar to electrical resisters in a wire.

The premise of Body Electronics is that these crystal deposits impede the flow of energy along pathways where energy flows through the body, based on the meridians in traditional Chinese medicine. Dr. Ray discovered that under certain conditions, when emotional blockages are released, these crystals can be made to melt, thereby reducing resistance and increasing the flow of energy again. This freeing of blocked energy is the goal of Body Electronics, and when it happens, medical miracles can often occur.

Even at twelve years old, I found the concept of Body Electronics fascinating, and I begged my dad to let me come along to his weekend workshops. There I was, a child of the 1980s—with big hair, neon clothes, and jelly shoes—spending my weekdays attending a middle school that was plagued with violence and most of my weekends hanging out with adults, doing deep, emotional healing work. It was an odd combination, but I lived for those weekend workshops.

I personally witnessed—in just a few hours—people's eyes changing color, a bone spur dissolving, a sprained ankle mending, a person with lifelong asthma having it totally clear up, a woman's congenital heart condition completely disappearing, and my own medical miracle: the straightening of my spine and reversal of scoliosis.

I had been diagnosed with scoliosis when I was in sixth grade at one of those mortifying public school spine checks. All the girls in my grade were lined up in the gym locker room, made to take off our shirts, and—one by one—told to bend over while having our spines inspected. First of all, this was horribly embarrassing because many of the girls my age had already developed breasts and I most certainly had not, and there we all were, shirtless and on display, for everyone to see. It was also horribly embarrassing because I was the only one, among all the girls in my school, who got the positive—and very public—diagnosis of scoliosis. X-rays at a chiropractor confirmed the diagnosis, and I was looking at a likely treatment of back braces and potential surgery.

At that time, there was a Body Electronics weekend workshop taking place in North Carolina that focused on spinal acupressure points, and I convinced my dad to take me. I wanted to heal my scoliosis naturally, and I had seen enough remarkable healings take place that I knew it was possible. When we arrived at the workshop, everyone's height was measured and marked on a chart on the wall. When it was my turn to have a "session," I laid down on a massage table, in this case on my stomach, while four or five people pressed firmly on acupressure points around my body, mostly on my back.

My session lasted about two hours, during which time the acupressure points along my spine got very hot. According to Dr. Ray, the incredible heat that's produced in these points during Body Electronics sessions is caused by the crystals melting, leading to an electrical rewiring of the body. And the trigger for this melting is intense emotional release.

For me, at twelve years old, the emotion that came up as my session facilitator asked me leading questions (similar to how a therapist works) was one of being pulled in two different directions between my parents. For those who aren't familiar with scoliosis, it looks like a spine being pulled in two different directions. After a lot of crying and emotional release on the table, my points cooled down, and I felt incredibly peaceful. I slowly got off the table and made my way to the height chart on the wall. I had grown one and a half inches in two hours! And X-rays the following week confirmed that my spine had straightened. My scoliosis was gone.

One thing I learned from that experience that has stayed with me all these years is Dr. Ray's concept of the Emotional Tone Scale.[4] This is a series of emotions that is often experienced during a Body Electronics session in a particular order: apathy, grief, fear, anger, pain, and enthusiasm. After going through each emotion on the Emotional Tone Scale and pushing through the pain, there is a calm sensation of peace. That's when the final state of enthusiasm is reached, which is characterized by a state of awareness and vitality.

Moving through the Emotional Tone Scale in a Body Electronics session is a powerful experience. But the truth is, we're all moving through it regularly. Every day, we each go through a range of emotions. And although we don't have people pressing on our acupressure points all day long, we can easily tell which emotions feel better than others. Apathy feels terrible, and so does grief—but at least there's emotion in grief, while apathy is nearly numb. Fear is terrifying, but it's usually motivating, whereas grief has lost all motivation. Anger is awful, but it's more proactive than fear. And pain—although we all naturally want to avoid it—is a powerful catalyst for change. Enthusiasm feels fantastic, but we aren't likely to feel enthusiastic all the time. What I committed to do on the Joy Plan all day, every day, is to reach for a better feeling, a higher emotion on the Emotional Tone Scale, and to continually move onward and upward.

An analogy I discovered that worked well to help me put this theory into practice came from one of my favorite inventions of the modern world: free, streaming music. Pandora is a website and an app that streams music based on the preferences you set. If you like a particular artist, you set a station for that artist, and Pandora will not only play you songs by that artist but also songs by similar artists it thinks you might like. It's all based on complex algorithms of what Pandora calls the "music genome project," software that's trained to receive feedback about your musical preferences and adjust to your desires continuously.

The coolest feature of Pandora is the "thumbs." Each time Pandora plays a song, you can give it a "thumbs up" or a "thumbs down," and Pandora will log your preferences. If you give a thumbs up, Pandora will play that song for you, along with similar songs, in the future; but if you give it a thumbs down, Pandora will never play that song again. Back when I started using Pandora, I did this with my favorite station—Alison Krauss—and chose either a thumbs up or thumbs down with every single song for a couple of weeks. This took dedication, but the payoff was worth it. My listening experience improved dramatically! I heard all my favorite songs and none that I didn't like.

When I started the Joy Plan, I decided to apply Pandora's technology to all facets of my life. Thumbs up for seeing dolphins on my morning drive to take the kids to school! Thumbs down for getting stuck in traffic. Thumbs up for an unexpected check arriving in the mail! Thumbs down for having an argument with my husband.

I started seeing every experience as an opportunity to provide feedback, to log my preferences, and to ask for more of what I liked. I wasn't exactly sure why, but I felt that somehow my feedback would be registered, my preferences would be noted, and life would respond accordingly. That was the idea behind the Law of Attraction and the objective of the Joy Plan— and I was going with it. Who or what was responding to my feedback remains one of life's great mysteries, but I do have my own theories. I believe science and spirituality are two sides of the same coin, each inform-ing and shaping the other.[5]

I know that many people believe that the way their lives unfold is predetermined by a higher power, and they approach their trials and tribu-lations as tests or lessons beyond their control. Others believe that every-thing they experience—the good, the bad, and the ugly—is entirely their own creation, whether they create it consciously or not. Then there are those who believe it's all up to chance. I prefer a middle-path approach. Perhaps that's my inner control freak, who wants to have a say in things, combined with my inner child, who believes in magic and miracles.

I know that I experience reality through the filter of my mind, which is housed in my brain. I realize that each person's mind operates slightly differ-ently, and thus we're all experiencing our own version of reality. I under-stand enough about neuroplasticity to know that my thoughts and behaviors, which shape the way I perceive and act in the world, are moldable and can be influenced to change my experience of reality. From this perspective, I can see how stating my preferences would simply be giving feedback to my own mind as a way to shift my focus from what displeases me to what pleases me. By looking for opportunities to give a thumbs up throughout the day, I'm training my brain to notice positive experiences. Eventually seeing the positive will become a habit, and I'll notice more pleasing things in my life, even though they may have been there all along. That's one explanation.

But I also believe in something bigger, greater, and wiser than the confines of my own mind and brain. I believe that I'm connected to a higher power through a bigger, greater, wiser part of myself. And I like to believe that part of me—call it my higher self, my source, my soul, or my inner being—is the *real* me. The "me" I hang out with every day is caught up in the petty concerns of my conscious mind, often dwelling in negativity. But the *real* me feels good *all the time.* That "me" is made of pure, positive energy. And whenever I feel emotions that are negative in any way—be they sad, scared, angry, annoyed, or overwhelmed—it's just an indication that my positive energy flow is blocked.

I like to believe that my source, or soul, is more beautiful, positive, and loving than I can describe or even imagine. And if I feel good, alive, excited, clear, free, and joyful, then I'll be closer to that source. My hope was that the more I consciously found ways to feel good, the more my source would do what it does best: create magic and miracles in my life.

Some look to God to create miracles—and of course people all over the world have different names for God—but I believe we're all talking about the same thing. Whether God is an outside force, separate from us, or an integrated source that we're all a part of, it is amazingly awesome and powerful. I believe the power of God is available to everyone and so are miracles, and *feeling good* is the key to creating them. At least that's the hypothesis I went into the Joy Plan with.

The idea behind the Joy Plan is that free-flowing, positive emotion opens the floodgates for miracles—just like releasing energy blockages opens the pathway for physical healing. And just like my Alison Krauss Pandora station, life responds favorably to positive feedback. Whether the response comes from a higher spiritual power or from the power of the brain, the result is the same.

I set out on the Joy Plan as a grand experiment to test this theory, to think of my life as a menu, with taste testers: "Laughter, oh that's nice. I'll take more of that please" (thumbs up!), or "That project was a real strug-gle, I don't want that experience again" (thumbs down!)—all based on the question, *Does this feel good?*

When I told Dan about my method, he said, tongue in cheek, "If the Joy Plan is based on just doing whatever feels good, then I'm not going to go to work, and all I'm going to do is have sex, watch sports, drink beer, and eat junk food all day long."

I tried to explain to Dan that the Joy Plan isn't just about being hedonistic.[6†] It's about learning how to use the Emotional Tone Scale to our advantage and our feelings as a feedback system. I wanted to create lasting joy, not a temporary feeling of satiety. And I didn't want to cloud my awareness with alcohol or drugs, even if they could give me a temporary high, because I wanted to be fully present to notice the signs, opportunities, and changes I was looking for.

I don't think you'd have to have an entire month to do whatever you want to be able to practice this. Even within my month on the Joy Plan, I had certain responsibilities that I had to tend to. I wasn't advocating irresponsible behavior; I simply wanted to train myself to feel good more often, and that started with noticing what feels good and what doesn't.

---

†   A series of studies looked at blood samples of different subjects and correlated them with their "happiness style," as determined by a questionnaire. The researchers rated participants' happiness on a scale, placing *eudaemonism* on one end of the spectrum and hedonism on the other.

      Eudaemonia is a Greek word most directly translated as "human flourishing." Barbara Fredrickson, a psychologist at the University of North Carolina at Chapel Hill and one of the researchers involved in the original study, defined eudaemonia as "…those aspects of well-being that transcend immediate self-gratification and connect people to something larger."

      The study was replicated multiple times by different researchers and always found the same thing: those participants who tended toward eudaemonism, rather than hedonism, showed the greatest positive aspects in their gene expression. Inflammation was lower in these subjects and their antiviral performance was higher. The researchers claimed that lacking eudemonia could potentially be as damaging as smoking or obesity. Could *eudemonia* simply be a fancy Greek word for joy?

When something felt good, I may not be able to do it all day, every day. But I could access the memory of the feeling it gave me and play it back in my mind when I needed a pick-me-up. If something didn't feel good but others were counting on me to do it right then, I could find a different way to think about it in order to make it feel good. If feeling good seemed totally out of reach, I could at least try for a better-feeling emotion on the Emotional Tone Scale. The point was to feel good as often as possible, and to be able to accomplish this, I had to pay more attention to my feelings than I ever had before. Ultimately I wanted to become so accustomed to feeling good that I could do it regardless of my circumstances or activities. But first I needed a lot of practice.

When I made feeling good my top priority, I started evaluating every single experience I had in my daily life as either contributing to or taking away from my joy quotient. I quickly realized that the images coming through my various screens (smartphone, computer, TV) were, for the most part, making me feel bad.

I like Facebook, because I have friends all over the world and it's such an easy way for all of us to keep tabs on each other. However, whenever I looked at Facebook, I regularly saw images, petitions, warnings, and articles about various tragedies. My friends posted these out of love—their love for others, their love for the earth, and their desire to make the world a better place. But it was creating the opposite reaction in me. With every one of these posts I saw (about shootings, kidnappings, war crimes, environmental destruction, animals dying brutally), I felt fear, horror, and hopelessness.

It was also distorting my view of reality. According to Steven Pinker, professor of psychology at Harvard University, violence of all types has actually been on the decline for thousands of years. Pinker crunched the numbers in his book, *The Better Angels of Our Nature: Why Violence Has Declined*, which shows that in reality, we're living in the most peaceful era since the existence of our species.[7] We usually don't see it this way, though, because of the nature of news. With the rise of social media and the ability to hear about atrocities in real time, we're often exposed to more bad news than good news. That—coupled with our inborn cognitive bias that predisposes us to remember negative input more readily than positive—creates a formula for hopelessness.[8] As Pinker says, "News is about things that happen, not about things that don't happen. If you base your beliefs about the state of the world on what you read in the news, your beliefs will be incorrect."[9]

This created an existential dilemma for me: How could I stay informed and active in solutions and peace for the planet while also maintaining my own inner peace and joy? I decided I would allow myself to stick my head in the sand for a while, in the name of joy and for the sake of my experiment. Studies that utilize eye tracking have shown that optimists pay less attention to negative visual images and thus actually view the world differently.[10] I needed to do the same—at least for a month.

I took some time to dig deep into the mysterious functions of Facebook and learned how to be selective with what I saw. This simple, albeit laborious, process actually had a huge impact on my daily experience going forward. With that clean sweep, I eliminated a large amount of negativity that I had been willingly engaging in at least once a day for more than seven years. I also stopped looking at most news online.

Did this mean I was less informed about what was happening in the world? Yes. And I decided I was okay with that. I decided I'd be informed about the things I felt inspired to know, and I'd take action from a place of hope rather than guilt, from love rather than fear.

Don't get me wrong, I do care about what's happening on the planet— very much. I majored in sustainable living in college; I wrote a thesis on renewable energy. I'm well aware of the challenges facing the earth. But it's as simple as this: What feels better—focusing on problems or focusing on solutions? It feels much better to me to think about, talk about, and take action for inspiring solutions. And I believe I'm much more effective at creating positive change when I'm feeling hopeful, empowered, and inspired.

Once I had cleared my Facebook account of all less-than-joyful content, I went through the same exercise with my email and other electronic messages, as well as TV, books, movies, and other forms of news and entertainment. Now that I was on the Joy Plan, I constantly screened all input—and if it wasn't increasing my joy quotient, then it got the boot.

This process of clearing the visual clutter in my life wasn't just about ignoring what felt bad; it was about creating the space for what feels good. I found that once I cleared that opening, inspiration had a doorway to enter through that had been too crowded before.

I just kept asking myself multiple times a day, "*Does this feel good?*" and turning my attention away whenever the answer was no.

It wasn't ignorance or denial that I was reaching for, but rather the selective and intentional focus on what felt good—or at least better. Better and better is what I was reaching for, moving my way up the Emotional Tone Scale every chance I got.

And those chances came along pretty frequently every single day. *Do I feel good in these clothes? Am I enjoying this conversation? Do I want to say yes to that invitation? Is this thought bringing me more joy?* There were constant opportunities to give a thumbs up or thumbs down.

If I create my own reality, then I'm doing it all the time through my thoughts, words, and actions. And on the Joy Plan, small moments that occurred all day long were opportunities in motion to create my life.

JOY PLAN TIP #4

Every day, you go through a range of emotions. And you can easily tell which emotions feel better than others. Just ask yourself, Does this feel good? When it doesn't, reach for a better feeling—a higher emotion on the Emotional Tone Scale—in order to push yourself onward and upward. This is the core practice of the Joy Plan.

CHAPTER 5

REBOOT: FROM STRESSED TO BLESSED

"Almost everything will work again if you unplug it for a few minutes, including you."
—ANNE LAMOTT

One week into the Joy Plan, I was paying close attention to what felt good so that I could seek more. I was taking an honest look at my life through the lens of joy and asking, "What is bringing me joy, and what isn't?" I had read that having a "gratitude practice" is a good way to increase joy, which makes sense. If you take the time to consider all the things you're thankful for, you'll probably realize you have a lot to feel joyful about.

I certainly did have a lot to be grateful for: a wonderful husband who adores me and who works hard to provide for our family; two healthy and energetic children, full of vitality and zest for life; our sweet and adorable Maltese/toy poodle, Lovey, who was, like her name, an absolute love. I had a close relationship with my parents and two younger brothers whom I knew had my back and who knew I had theirs. I had the greatest girlfriends I could have ever asked for, including my women's circle, a group of five friends I'd been meeting with every month for the past fifteen years. And I had my health, mostly. I'd had some challenges in that department but could have been much worse off. I also had some skills—although they hadn't led me to wild success in the business world yet, I knew I could probably still land a decent job. From an outsider's perspective, I had it all. I wanted to feel that way too.

While I underwent my attitude adjustment, I reflected on what I had witnessed during a year that our family spent living on the small Indonesian island of Bali. Dan and I had worked at an international school there before I started my latest business.

Everywhere you look in Bali, there are offerings of gratitude. Temples, beaches, home and business entrances, and even vehicles are adorned daily with tiny baskets woven from palm fronds that are filled with flowers and incense to represent thanks and praise for the world's peace. Balinese people spend a great deal of time in prayer and gratitude to the gods for everything that they have. And yet, much of the time, what they have is very little. In spite of this, they are some of the kindest, funniest, and most joyful people I have ever met. It seemed they really practiced staying in joy despite their external conditions.

I knew I had a lot to learn from the Balinese. Although our family had participated in numerous Balinese ceremonies during our time on the island, we hadn't kept those traditions alive in our life back in America. So I decided to bring back a little bit of Bali and make it part of our daily lives once again. I created a small gratitude altar in one corner of the living room, where everyone—kids and Dan included—could leave offerings of gratitude and say a little prayer of thanks. I placed some family photos and drawings the kids had made on the altar, as well as a large glass jar, a stack of paper scraps, and a pencil. Whenever anyone thought of something they were grateful for, they could write it on a scrap of paper and place the paper in the gratitude jar. This practice became a fun focus for our family.

Researchers have found that thoughts of appreciation trigger the parasympathetic nervous system, the system responsible for calming our bodies.[1] The parasympathetic nervous system slows the heartbeat, contracts the pupils of the eyes, sends blood from the muscles to the organs, and slows activity in the intestines. Feelings of gratitude have also been shown to release dopamine, a neurotransmitter in the brain that induces a feeling of reward and satisfaction.[2] This happens because, when you think about what you're grateful for, the brain registers it as something you've earned and sends you a hit of dopamine for doing a good job. Dopamine plays a key role in motivating us to attain our goals by rewarding our achievement with a sense of pleasure and an elevated mood. Experiments have demonstrated that people who keep regular gratitude journals or lists feel optimistic more often and progress more rapidly toward their goals.[3]

In his book, *What Happy People Know*, Dr. Dan Baker explains that fear and appreciation cannot exist in the brain at the same time: "During active appreciation, the threatening messages from your amygdala [fear center of the brain] and the anxious instincts of your brainstem are cut off, suddenly and surely, from access to your brain's neocortex, where they can fester, replicate themselves, and turn your stream of thoughts into a cold river of dread. It is a fact of neurology that the brain cannot be in a state of appreciation and a state of fear at the same time. The two states may alternate, but are mutually exclusive."[4]

Determined to harness these neurological benefits, I pulled out a beautiful handmade notebook from my closet that a girlfriend had given me for a birthday years ago. I'd been saving it for a special occasion and this seemed like one. Notebook in hand, I set out to cultivate an "attitude of gratitude."

But it didn't work. Every time I thought about something to write down, I picked up that gorgeous notebook, with its handmade paper embossed with pressed flowers, and it looked just too pretty for my mundane musings. So instead I went to the dollar store and picked up a notebook that was small enough to fit in my purse and plain enough that I felt comfortable writing even my most trivial thoughts in it. And I started writing.

I wrote a lot in that notebook about Santa Cruz—the perfect weather, the lovely beaches, the pristine redwood forest, the beautiful sunsets, the fantastic food, my favorite fish taco place, my other favorite fish taco place, my beloved Trader Joe's supermarket. I wrote about my home—small, cozy, and close to the beach, with a dishwasher that made my life so much easier.

By simply taking a gratitude inventory of my life, I'd already discovered what I suspected would be a major key to my joy. So now I grabbed on to gratitude like a life raft. I was making gratitude lists every day, on general topics that I was grateful for as well as specific lists whenever I was feeling stressed about a particular subject or person in my life. Instead of focusing on the negative aspects that were bringing me down, I would make a list of the positive aspects of the situation or person. I practiced finding the silver lining like other people practice learning a new language.

For example, I had been feeling down about the car I drove. It was Dan's mother's car before she died, and it was twenty years old and pretty banged up. The engine was solid, but just about everything else was falling apart. Considering my uncertain financial future, it wasn't the right time for me to buy a new car. However, I found myself mentally bashing the car every time I drove it. So I decided to write about the car in my gratitude notebook:

I am so grateful to have a reliable car. It never lets me down. The fact that it's old and beat up means that I don't have to worry about it getting messy or ruined. I also don't have to worry about it being stolen. We've made a lot of great memories in this car, and it's a reminder of Angela that lives on. What a blessing that I haven't had to buy a new car for several years. This car has served our family well.

Later in the week, after I'd written that journal entry, an elderly woman hit my car in a parking lot while she was pulling into her space. It was more like she scraped the car, making a scratch that barely stood out among the many others. She was very apologetic and gave me her insurance information. She told me she was a retired insurance agent and hoped I'd be able to receive a cash settlement for the damage, explaining that the body shop contracted with her insurance company would likely issue me a check on the spot to cover the cost of the repair.

So I went to the body shop to have the damage inspected but was disappointed when the mechanic told me he couldn't give me a payout immediately because my car was in such poor condition. I figured the insurance company would decide not to pay me anything since my car had clearly seen its share of bumps and scratches and this new one really didn't make a noticeable difference. However, later that day, I received a phone call from an insurance agent who said they'd like to offer me cash for the total value of my car—$2,300! They didn't need to fix the car, they didn't want to buy the car, they were just going to give me $2,300. I couldn't believe it! I now had yet another thing to write about that terrific, beat-up old car in my gratitude notebook: it was making me money.

To me, this seemed like evidence that gratitude was working to enhance my joy and that joy was creating miracles in my life. And with evidence like this, I was determined to become an optimist—something I had once teased Dan about when he posted *The Optimist Creed* by Christian D. Larson on our refrigerator years ago.‡ I thought it was cheesy at the time, but reading it now, it was exactly what I aimed to embrace:

The Optimist Creed:

Promise Yourself

To be so strong that nothing can disturb your peace of mind.

---

‡   "The Optimist Creed" was originally published by Christian D. Larson in 1912 as "Promise Yourself." In 1922, it was adopted as the official manifesto of Optimist International.

To talk health, happiness, and prosperity to every person you meet.

To make all your friends feel that there is something in them.

To look at the sunny side of everything and make your optimism come true.

To think only of the best, to work only for the best, and to expect only the best.

To be just as enthusiastic about the success of others as you are about your own.

To forget the mistakes of the past and press on to the greater achievements of the future.

To wear a cheerful countenance at all times and give every living creature you meet a smile.

To give so much time to the improvement of yourself that you have no time to criticize others.

To be too large for worry, too noble for anger, too strong for fear, and too happy to permit the presence of trouble.

Optimistic thoughts are actually observable in brain scans.[5] Optimism has been shown to regulate levels of the stress hormone cortisol and increase dopamine and other pleasure-inducing neurotransmitters in the brain.[6] Optimistic thoughts also calm the amygdala. This is important, because when the amygdala is triggered by stress, it inhibits the prefrontal cortex and suppresses our ability to make clear decisions. Studies have shown that optimists are happier, more creative, faster at solving problems, and have increased mental alertness compared to pessimists.[7] Just like any other habit that our brains learn through repetition, when we have frequent positive thoughts—such as thoughts of gratitude—our brains are primed to keep them coming, thanks to the formation of neural pathways.

Inspired by the wave of gratitude I was riding, I decided to write letters of appreciation to people I was feeling thankful for. I went on a total thank-you-letter-writing spree. I wrote to my kids' teachers, friends I hadn't been in touch with in a while, business colleagues who had been important mentors and collaborators throughout my career, as well as to each of my family members and close friends. It felt good to share my gratitude with others, and they responded with gratitude in return. Gratitude feels good, whether you're the giver or the receiver.

I've always enjoyed giving gifts more than receiving them, and giving appreciation was feeling really good. Perhaps it was the dopamine rushing through my system, but research suggests that gratitude also affects our hearts. The Institute of HeartMath has found that gratitude and appreciation induce a smooth, even heart rate, while negative emotions like anger and frustration create an erratic, chaotic rhythm.[8]

And while my heart was feeling full, I knew my gratitude was having a positive effect on others as well. Scientists at the National Institute for Physiological Sciences in Japan measured the effect of receiving a compliment and found that the same area in the subjects' brains, the striatum, was activated when they received a compliment as when they received a gift of cash.[9] (This gives "paying someone a compliment" a whole new meaning!) Moreover, in this double-blind study, participants in the group that received compliments performed significantly better on a manual task than those in other groups.

Personally, the more I focused on gratitude and sharing it with those around me, the more relaxed I felt. The same situations or thoughts that were stressful to me only a few weeks earlier now felt manageable—enjoyable even. My attitude of gratitude and intentional optimism were working; I could feel the joy bubbling up inside of me. When worry showed up, I was more deliberate than I had ever been about opening the doors and ushering it out. If I started worrying, I busted out my well-worn gratitude notebook and made a list. I quickly realized that I have way more to be grateful for than to worry about, and it helped to put my mind at ease.

I was pressing the "reboot" button on my life. The Joy Plan was well underway.

JOY PLAN TIP #5

Keeping a regular gratitude journal or list will help you feel optimistic more often and progress more rapidly toward your goals. Thoughts of appreciation and optimism reduce stress, increase pleasure-inducing neurotransmitters in the brain, and trigger the parasympathetic nervous system, which calms your body.

CHAPTER 6

MINDFULNESS OVER MATTER

"I have so much to accomplish today that I
must meditate for two hours instead of one."
—MAHATMA GANDHI

Two weeks into my Joy Plan, I was already feeling better. I'd been more intentional about choosing positive thoughts and experiences than I'd ever been in my life. I was looking for opportunities to give a thumbs up and feel grateful all day long. I felt like I was doing what I set out to do—making joy my top priority—and it was working. But I wanted to amp it up. I needed more than to just feel better; I needed to turn my life around.

I had read over and over how important having a regular meditation practice is to joy and success, especially when you start the day with it. Many of the world's most successful—and wealthy—people have a daily meditation practice and claim it has a profound effect on their ability to achieve results.[1] I'd tried meditating before and never felt like I was doing it right. I treated meditation like a contact sport: I'd get dressed in my uniform of loose-fitting clothes, enter the arena of a designated quiet space, and sit quietly with the best intentions of reaching peaceful nirvana. But inevitably I would spend the whole time wrestling with my thoughts, straining to clear them from my mind, while more and more would flood in. I usually emerged from my attempted meditation sessions exhausted, frustrated, and with no more inner peace than when I'd started.

I'd heard the term "mindfulness" batted around, and although I had a vague sense that it was something that could be helpful in my life, I wasn't entirely sure what it meant. The more I looked into it, though, the more I realized that mindfulness is simply the act of paying attention, on purpose, to the present moment. This includes observation of one's own thoughts, feelings, and sensations. It sounded easy enough. Although at first mindfulness seemed to me to be ethereal in nature, I came to understand that it's mostly about how to best utilize your brain.

If you make two fists with your thumbs tucked inside and hold your fists together, you'll see a rough representation of the size of your brain. The thumbs can be likened to the amygdala: a small area in the middle of each hemisphere that acts as the brain's alarm clock. Triggered by any stressful situation, it responds with the primal protection reactions of fight, flight, or freeze. Each person's amygdala reacts slightly differently to stress, with some hair-triggered to the slightest upset and others fairly blasé about danger.

I figured, with my tendency toward anxiety, my amygdala must be pretty tightly wound. And because the amygdala is housed in the limbic system of the brain—the same area that generates joy—I thought it would help my Joy Plan if I could train my amygdala to be less reactive. The amygdala is critical to our survival because it alerts us to danger. The problem is, it doesn't know the difference between a stressful conversation and being chased by a tiger. All it knows is that you're threatened. And when the amygdala senses a threat and reacts with fear, it hinders the performance of the prefrontal cortex, the part of the brain that's responsible for higher reasoning.

In a stressful situation, higher reasoning is rather handy to have, since we're likely to want more options available than fight, flight, or freeze. One of the main tenets of mindfulness practice is an intentional focus on the breath. The science behind this shows that deep breaths flood the brain with oxygen, and oxygen acts as a signal to the amygdala that it's okay to stop sounding the alarm. Deep breaths literally help us think more clearly by calming the amygdala and freeing access to the prefrontal cortex.[2]

Of course our amygdalae aren't likely to be active when we're sitting in meditation, but the practice of regularly taking deep breaths can become a habit just like any other action that we repeat frequently. The benefit of cultivating this habit is that hopefully it will kick in when we need it most, in times of stress. We've all heard "just breathe" a thousand times; this is the brain mechanism behind that common advice. Being able to separate our panicky thoughts and amygdala-based reactions from the less dramatic reality of a situation is a skill that can be mastered with practice. Ultimately, the practice of mindfulness can help us feel more empowered and in control of our life experience.

The act of meditation, or sitting quietly and breathing deeply, also affects our brain waves. Brain waves are measured in cycles per second and classified into delta, theta, alpha, or beta waves. Most of the time, our brains are hard at work in fast-churning beta waves. All this brain activity takes tremendous energy and requires rest and recuperation to keep going. When we sleep, our brains recharge in the slowest frequency waves, theta and delta. When we meditate, we're awake, and yet our brains are able to slip into slower alpha waves, which is incredibly relaxing for them. Meditation is like a soothing massage for the brain, and studies show that doing it regularly has multiple health benefits, including calming anxiety, reducing inflammation, and decreasing the signs of aging.[3]

Knowing how beneficial it was, I wanted to find a way to incorporate meditation into my Joy Plan—in a way that was actually joyful instead of strenuous. This is how I did it: Rather than gearing up, going into a sacred space, lighting candles and incense, and generally making a big deal of it, I just committed to spending the first fifteen minutes of the morning in bed sitting quietly. Since clearing my mind or repeating a mantra felt too hard to me, I instead used those fifteen minutes to focus on things I'm grateful for while taking deep breaths. I used the snooze button on my alarm clock to help me keep time, and because I was sitting up in the bed, I was less likely to fall back to sleep.

I would start by appreciating my bed; I'd nuzzle into my blankets and pillows and appreciate how cozy they were. Then I would begin a gratitude incantation in my mind, thinking about my precious children, my loving and generous husband, my wonderful family and friends, my health, the beauty of my home, the delicious and nutritious food in my refrigerator, and on and on. It went like something this:

I'm waking up to another beautiful day. Here in this comfortable, soft, warm bed, I know that I'm perfectly safe and cared for. I'm so grateful for my healthy body. I'm thankful for my eyes that allow me to see beauty, my nose that can smell the delicate aroma of a flower, my ears that hear the birds chirping and my children laughing, and my mouth that lets me taste delicious things. I'm thankful for my sense of touch, which brings me so many sensations of pleasure, like the silky feeling of these sheets against my legs. I'm grateful for my arms, legs, and muscles that give me movement and strength. I'm grateful to my brain for allowing me to think and feel and work and learn. I celebrate the wonder of being here, in my body—it is truly a miracle.

I'm so grateful for the ones I love. My sweet husband, lying in bed next to me, and my children in the next room. They fill my heart with joy, and I'm so thankful for everything that they bring into my life. I'm grateful for my friends, my parents, my brothers and extended family, and for all the people whom I know and interact with. I'm so thankful for their contribution to all that I experience.

I love my home, my community, my town, my country, and my planet. I give thanks for all of it and feel so blessed to be here. As I prepare for this day, I give thanks and recognize it as a fresh start. Today I will see my life anew. I will look for opportunities to appreciate the many blessings in my life, knowing that as I appreciate those blessings, more will come.

If my mind wandered while I practiced this gratitude meditation, I would just do my best to direct my thoughts back to gratitude while also focusing on my breath as a stabilizing force. This was a form of meditation I could actually do, and I found that my mind drifted less off-topic with each day that I practiced. I also tried using a few different meditation apps and timers on my phone, which I found useful at times.

Many people believe that the objective in mindfulness or meditation is to stop all thoughts. But that's actually not the point at all. Meditation isn't about stopping thoughts; it's about releasing the grip they have on you. Like Shunryū Suzuki said, it's about letting thoughts come and go without serving them tea. Through regular practice, meditation becomes a form of mental exercise that trains the brain to observe thoughts while not engaging in them. The benefit isn't so obvious when you're sitting in bed counting your breaths or your lucky stars, but the practice pays off when you can react calmly and clearheadedly in moments of stress or conflict.

I found that starting my day with thoughts of appreciation really carried those thoughts forward into the rest of my day. I was training myself to look for things to appreciate all around me and then mentally bookmarking them for my morning practice. I also continued to write in my gratitude notebook every day. I wrote "Joyful Thoughts = Joyful Life" on a Post-it and put it on my bathroom mirror as a frequent reminder.

Meanwhile, I looked for opportunities to engage in simple pleasures that would nourish my body as well as my mind.[4] I had been so focused on mental stimulation because of my work that I hadn't really been in touch with my body in a long while. Taking time to intentionally hone in on each of my five senses allowed me to connect with my body, notice sensations that were happening in that very moment, and practice mindfulness. Our five senses are how we experience our world and are therefore an excellent way to tap into the present moment, especially when our minds are anywhere but here and now.

Although anxiety can be a powerful force to reckon with, it exists primarily within the construct of the mind. The body is rarely anxious without input from the mind, unless it's missing what it needs for survival. To calm my mind and find more joy, I shifted my attention to my body.

I started with taste. I love papaya so much that my nickname as a child was Kaia Papaya. During the year we lived in Bali, I ate papaya every day. There is just nothing more delicious to me than a ripe, sweet, juicy papaya. But papaya doesn't grow in Northern California, and thus it is much more expensive than it is in Bali, which meant I hadn't had my favorite fruit in a long time.

I know it sounds simple, but I decided I would stop buying other unnecessary food items so I could spend the money instead on papaya, which I could get from the local Mexican market. The small indulgence of having a bit of my favorite fruit every day brought me so much pleasure. I made up different papaya smoothies each morning, which became another simple part of how I started my day with something I could appreciate. There's a reason for the term "comfort food": these foods trigger feelings of well-being, and papaya does that for me.

Next, I focused on my sense of smell. Smell is a potent carrier of memory, even more so than the other senses, because of the direct connection between olfactory receptors and the brain's limbic system. To take advantage of this, I picked jasmine and Cecile Brunner roses from our yard and placed them around the house, in my car, and even in my hair. I wore these particular flowers in my hair on our wedding day, and their smell still carries that delightful memory. I surrounded myself with sweet-smelling fragrances every day and made sure I took the time to notice their delicious aroma. I was training my body and mind to recognize and appreciate pleasure again and using smell to anchor the memory.

For sound, I had my beloved Pandora Alison Krauss station, which was trained to give me exactly what I wanted all the time; bluegrass music makes me tap my feet and feel like dancing. However, in my "normal" life, I hadn't really listened to bluegrass music all that much. In fact, I had been so focused on work that I didn't really listen to music of any kind all that much. So now I started listening to music a lot more often and giving in to my impulse to dance and sing along. I even started having regular dance parties with the kids in our living room after school. You know how certain songs remind you vividly of different times in your life? Music is a powerful trigger for memory and emotion. The Alison Krauss Pandora station was becoming the soundtrack to my joy.

Sight was an easy sense to experience joy through because I live in such a beautiful place. But the crazy thing is that I had barely taken advantage of it—rarely walking on the beach, watching the sunset, or visiting any of the numerous gorgeous parks and hiking trails in Santa Cruz—because I was constantly attached to my computer. So I got out and walked with our dog, Lovey, every day. And I really made the effort to notice and appreciate my natural surroundings. It's amazing how much beauty there is in the world! And how easy it is to miss it when you're constantly looking at a screen. I started noticing the stunning cloud formations in the sky, the majesty of the trees, the patterns on flowers, and the brilliant colors of the ocean. I trained my eyes to be on the constant lookout for beauty that I could revel in and appreciate.

For the sense of touch—since I was really going for it on the Joy

Plan—I even indulged in a couple of massages. I allowed myself to relax and be pampered. I also started carrying a small, silky pillow around with me, something Nava had made in sewing class, and rubbed it on my cheek several times a day. Of course I also enjoyed the sense of touch with Dan—but more on that in chapter 7. In addition, I started spending extra time petting, brushing, and snuggling with our dog. Lovey had an endless capacity for attention, yet when I was working so much, she got very little. But now I could cuddle her whenever I wanted to. Again, it was such a simple thing, but those cuddles brought me (and Lovey) immense pleasure. In fact, scientific studies have shown that contact with a pet increases oxytocin levels (the hormone associated with love, trust, and bonding) as well as significantly increases mental, emotional, and physical well-being.[5]

When I focused on my five senses, I wanted what they were experiencing to be pleasurable. To facilitate this, I started keeping props around my desk, car, and purse that helped me take a quick "five senses break" throughout the day. Occasionally, I would stop what I was doing, slow my breathing, and focus in on each of my senses, one at a time. The props I kept on hand were aromatherapy oils for smell, yummy treats for taste, a few beautiful cards and photos to look at for sight, my small, soft pillow for touch, and my favorite playlist for sound. The key was to take in each sensation slowly, with nonjudgmental attention.

Even when I didn't have my props available, I made more of an effort to seek beauty in my surroundings throughout the day. Sometimes the best moments of my day were when I was walking across a parking lot and got a whiff of sweet jasmine wafting through the air, or I noticed the delicious sensation of breeze on my cheeks. I experienced deep gratitude in those moments, as if my senses were a gateway to my heart.

Another simple indulgence that I discovered gave me an enormous amount of pleasure is a hot bath. Something visceral happens when I immerse my body in hot water—the hotter the better. It's like the heat activates all of my body's sensations while shutting down the chatter of my conscious mind. Although soaking in a hot bath has always been one of my favorite things to do, I've done it very little since becoming a mom. So once I gave myself the luxury of taking baths again—even in the middle of the day—I discovered something marvelous.

When I lie down in hot water, close my eyes, relax my body, and let go of worry or guilt about what I should be doing instead, I get inspired ideas. They don't come because I'm ruminating about something or trying to solve a problem; they just pop into my head as soon as I relax into the hot water. And when these ideas come, they're fast and furious and full of detail. Many times I had to run—dripping across the house—to find something to take notes with. I quickly learned to keep a pad of paper and pen near the bathtub, because I know those inspired thoughts are my subconscious mind's impulses and the ticket to the miracles I've been waiting for.

Thoughts are habits, and habits can be changed. By focusing on my body, senses, aesthetics, and tactile sensations, I was actually changing my thoughts. Although they usually feel like they're beyond our control, thoughts are in fact self-generated. They often come from the persona, or the ego, and tend to be focused on lack, fear, or regret—all the antithesis of joy. When my inspired thoughts came—such as the ones that formed the basis for this book—I recognized them as a sign I could follow to more inspiration.

I was treating my thoughts just as I treated my Pandora station—giving a thumbs down when I didn't like what I was hearing and tuning into a more pleasant thought instead. I developed a mental list of go-to joyful thoughts I could always switch to when negative ones were trying to dominate— easy things like loving thoughts about my children, fun thoughts about the characters in a novel I was reading, wishful thoughts about trips I'd like to take in the future, or even sexy thoughts about my husband.

When I started to worry about something—and I couldn't change the current situation immediately—I would imagine a different scenario in my head. Brain scans have shown that imagining actions stimulates the same parts of the brain that are activated when you actually perform them.[6] Knowing this, I did my best to harness the power of my imagination to soothe myself when negative thoughts got me down. I would conjure an elaborate fantasy, if necessary—whatever it took to flip the switch on my worry. I did my best to turn my thoughts to how I wanted things to be instead of how I didn't want them to be.

With each day that passed, in addition to being really choosy about my thoughts, I was also more selective with my time. If doing something felt like an obligation or drudgery, I either didn't do it or found a way to feel good about it. My daily schedule went from long hours attached to my laptop, phone, and iPad—often all three at once while juggling multiple projects and staff in several countries—to leisurely days of exercise, walks, baths, and healthy food. I went from barely interacting with my family to relishing hours of time with them every day.

As luxurious as this sounds, it wasn't easy for me at first. I was so used to accomplishing things and working toward goals. I sourced my self-worth from my career and was driven to succeed, to make both an income and an impact. With this new schedule, what was I achieving? Where was my income? I worked hard to turn down my feelings of guilt, as I knew I needed to fully immerse myself in joy to give the experiment a chance to work.

And when my endless to-do lists were gone, my internal chatter was quieted, and I was actively gobbling up joy in every way that I could, the space opened up for my inspiration to bloom. At first, the ideas that came to me—most often in the bath—were for new businesses I could start. I just wrote them down, bought domain names if they weren't taken yet, and kept focusing on simple pleasures. And then I had one surprising impulse that I couldn't set aside.

An idea popped into my head to write a blog post about my women's circle. For the past fifteen years, I've been gathering with five remarkable women in San Francisco once a month (as long as I was in the country, or otherwise virtually) to support each other in creating the lives we want for ourselves, our families, and the world. I feel incredibly blessed to have this powerful support network. So while I was driving one day, I thought about how much joy these five women bring into my life and how awesome it is that we've managed to stay committed to meeting every month for fifteen years. I was focusing on my gratitude for these women when a random thought came to me.

I regularly read blog posts on the popular well-being website mindbodygreen and noticed that the site had never covered the topic of women's circles. I had this spontaneous thought that maybe other women would be inspired to start a women's circle of their own if they knew what it was and how wonderful it could be. I felt moved to contact mindbodygreen's editor about my idea for a blog post. It was a fun and frivolous—but strongly compelling—impulse.

The editor liked my idea. The blog post took me about an hour to write and was live within a few days of the initial thought popping into my head. That simple blog post opened a floodgate within me, and before I knew it, I was brimming with ideas to write about. The editor invited me to blog weekly for mindbodygreen, which receives fifteen million visitors per month. All of a sudden, I had a potential audience of millions.

JOY PLAN TIP #6

Thoughts really are the key to joy. A mindfulness practice can help release the grip negative thoughts have on you. By focusing on your body, senses, aesthetics, and tactile sensations, you can shift your attention to appreciation and actually change your thoughts. Thoughts are habits, and habits can be changed. When inspired thoughts come, recognize them as a sign you can follow to more inspiration.

CHAPTER 7

EAT, PLAY, LOVE

"Everybody needs beauty as well as bread,
places to play in and pray in, where nature
may heal and give strength to body and soul."

—JOHN MUIR

Our bodies rebuild themselves constantly. In fact, our cells are regenerating at such a rapid rate that 98 percent of our atoms are replaced within one year.[1] Through neurogenesis, our brains produce a fresh supply of neurons—approximately 1,400 per day during adulthood.[2] We are literally building new bodies all the time.

Although emotions, like joy, are experienced in the brain, emotional memory is also stored in many places throughout the body.[3] The cells that make up our organs, muscles, skin, and glands contain peptide receptors that carry and store emotional information. What this means is that by following the Joy Plan, I had the opportunity to rebuild myself from the inside out, down to the cellular level.

I'd realized I didn't only want to change my thoughts and shift my

mind; I was going for a new, joyful body. I wanted the improved feelings
I was experiencing to imbibe my newly regenerated cells with joy and
deeply anchor that elated memory into my body. My goal was to build
joy-based emotional muscle memory—to replace my stressed-out cells with
new, joyful ones.

Based on my work in personalized health, I knew there were certain
lifestyle choices that have been scientifically proven to increase the brain
chemicals associated with joy.[4] I was already doing some of them and
decided to improve my chances as much as possible by trying them all:
vegetables, laughter, nature, sex, exercise, and sleep.

Because I have an autoimmune condition and a lot of allergies, I've
tried many different diets to figure out which one makes me feel best. I've
done everything from being a vegan for seven years to trying a diet where
all I could eat was chicken, rice, pears, and cabbage. But I now knew what I
needed—what really keeps my symptoms at a minimum and my energy at
a maximum—is lots of vegetables and lean protein, a bit of fat, and limited
carbs. I knew from trial and error what works for me, but I didn't always
follow it—especially when it came to my greatest vice, sugar.

On my Joy Plan, I wanted to pay more attention to the food I was eating
and feeding my family. We're blessed in Santa Cruz to be at the epicenter of
a huge organic agriculture region, but we also have every other unhealthy,
yet delicious, food option easily available. And truthfully, I'm not naturally a
very inspired cook. On the other hand, Dan is great in the kitchen, which
is something we both recognize. He had never really expected me to cook
for him all these years, and when I did, it was just a bonus. I usually only
cooked simple meals for the kids and ate something premade and on the go
for myself. We rarely shared family meals together.

As my Joy Plan progressed, I actually felt inspired to start cooking. I
played around with food for hours, making up new recipes. I came up

with a number of ways to sneak vegetables into pancakes. I blended, chopped, baked, and actually created some pretty delicious things. It was late November and pumpkins were in season. I baked a huge pumpkin and made pumpkin soup, pumpkin cake, pumpkin muffins, and pumpkin curry. It was like a pumpkin festival in my kitchen.

I also put more intention into enjoying food. I started sitting down to eat—plating the food and sitting at the table—rather than eating out of a container at the countertop while looking at my phone or eating at my desk while working on my computer, which had been my modus operandi for years. I practiced mindful eating by slowing down during my meals and really noticing the aroma, texture, colors, and taste of my food, while consciously appreciating everything about it. I turned off all screens and technology while I ate and paid closer attention to the actual sensations of eating. I found that since I was eating more slowly, I ate less and enjoyed my food more. I took pleasure in setting the table for family meals when Dan came home from work. I also started saying a regular blessing at each meal with the family and asking everyone to share something that they were grateful for.

In my new commitment to having a more joyful relationship with food, I cleared the kitchen of all foods containing white sugar. If they were there, I would eat them, so I made my kitchen sugar free. And then I started having a full-on love affair with kale. I couldn't get enough of it and kept finding ways to eat kale at almost every meal. I made the most delicious smoothies for breakfast, packed with kale. I ate kale salads for lunch and stir-fried kale with cranberries and almonds for dinner. I felt like I could actually feel the minerals and vitamins from the kale infusing my body, and I craved it voraciously.

I was curious why kale was making me feel so good when I discovered that kale, along with other vegetables in the cruciferous family (such as broccoli and cauliflower), are high in tryptophan, an essential amino acid that our body converts into serotonin.[5] Serotonin is the "hormone of happiness," the neurotransmitter that antidepressant medication primarily targets and increases. Research has found that a higher intake of tryptophan-containing foods, relative to other foods in the diet, can increase serotonin production in the body.[6] So kale was literally making me happier. Another benefit of my love affair with kale was that once I started taking the time to prepare and really enjoy vegetables—kale and others—my cravings for salad and fresh soups overtook my cravings for sugar.

In addition to nourishing my body with healthy food, I wanted to feed my soul with the ingredients for joy. I knew that I was happier, but I was going for a lasting state of joy. And that meant I needed to embrace actually being a joyful person.

They say laughter is the best medicine—and for good reason. Laughing releases endorphins, the brain's "feel good" hormones that activate the body's opiate receptors and reduce pain while increasing pleasure.[7] Endorphins are behind the light-headed, giddy feeling you can get from laughing. They reduce the body's stress response and relax the muscles. Full belly laughs, in particular, also release oxytocin, which bathes our nervous system in a warm, fuzzy glow.

I am quite a serious person in all honesty. I like to ponder and discuss deep and meaningful topics, geek out about science, learn new things, and solve problems. Those activities aren't exactly humorous unless, of course, you have a great sense of humor. Which I actually think I have. I crack myself up all the time. But the only people that usually witnessed my comedic side were my children.

I was often silly with my kids, so I knew I had it in me. To laugh more, I just had to start being silly with other people too. I set a goal to make at least one person laugh every day, and so I started joking around with the teachers and other parents when I picked the kids up at school. Dan came home from work a couple of times and asked, "Have you been drinking?" when he found me trying to juggle oranges in the kitchen or only speaking by singing—but I told him I was just trying to lighten up. My kids were also surprised to see me joking around more with other people besides them, and they loved it.

I rented some funny movies to watch with Dan; I steered the conversation more often to humorous topics when I was with my girlfriends, and I did my best to stop taking myself so seriously. I even tried laughing along to "laughter yoga" videos on YouTube. I found that laughter became kind of a habit. When I cracked jokes and was lighthearted in my conversations with others, almost everyone met me there in response. It was a challenging way to be as an introvert, but I liked it.

I did another thing that was entirely superficial but made a big difference in my joy quotient: I whitened my teeth. Over the years, my teeth had developed a definite yellow hue, and it bothered me every time I saw them in the mirror. So I picked up an inexpensive teeth-whitening gel, and it worked like a charm.

The funny result of whitening my teeth was that every time I looked in the mirror, I smiled so I could check out my teeth. Scientific studies have shown that the act of smiling triggers the brain to release endorphins, even if the smile is fake or forced.[8] This even happens when you place a pencil between your teeth and form the shape of a smile with your mouth. In fact, in studies where subjects' faces were placed into different positions with electrodes, facial expressions were found to strongly affect emotional states.[9] So although I was going for a cosmetic result, I ended up experiencing an emotional one. This simple act helped me to be kinder to myself when I looked in the mirror, focusing immediately on something I could appreciate.

It may have been only skin deep, but my whiter teeth made me feel more beautiful. And feeling beautiful sends soothing messages of self-love and well-being throughout the brain and body. If whitening my teeth is what got me there, *hallelujah!*

Once I had incorporated more laughter and smiling into my life, I moved on to the next challenge. As part of my Joy Plan, I was already taking more walks outside. I worked it into my routine to take Lovey for a walk on the beach, around the block, at a park, or on a path in the nearby redwood forest every day. On these walks, I did my best to pay attention to the smells, sights, and sounds, to really take in and appreciate my natural surroundings.

Almost all my best memories have taken place outside, yet I had fallen out of the habit of going outside. How is that even possible? When we lived in Bali, I was walking for probably two hours a day, on long paths through rice fields and around the enormous school campus where we worked. And we drove a car a lot less in Bali, so we walked more. But back in Santa Cruz, I had gotten into the habit of driving everywhere. So when I made it a priority to spend time outside every day, I started to feel like I was experiencing Santa Cruz in a new way. Everything was more beautiful than I had noticed before. When I took the time to truly observe with mindfulness and my five senses, the air in Santa Cruz smelled sweeter to me than anything I had ever smelled.

We lived near a cliff where Lovey and I could walk to the edge and watch the seals and otters in the ocean below. Lovey often barked at them, like she wanted to play with them. It was the time of year when anchovies fill Monterey Bay, bringing a feeding frenzy of harbor seals, dolphins, sea lions, sharks, and lots of whales. And now that I was looking, I was seeing the whales breach more often, jumping majestically close to shore. Scientists don't know why they do it, but I liked to think that they were jumping for joy.

I fell even more in love with Santa Cruz as I spent more time outside.

I appreciated the striking coastline, perfect surfing waves, redwood forests, gorgeous beaches, blue skies, puffy clouds, monarch butterflies, and sea animals. Soon even the parking lots started looking pretty to me.

Spending time outdoors is scientifically proven to be good for our health. Studies have consistently shown that exposure to plants and outdoor environments raises white blood cell levels, boosts immunity, and lowers cortisol—that stress hormone we don't want to have too much of.[10] Fresh air and sunshine also provide important vitamin D, health- and mood-boosting negative ions, and energizing oxygen. Studies utilizing mobile EEG brain-measuring devices found that urban dwellers became less frustrated and more relaxed when they entered green spaces.[11] Even if, like me, you need to avoid excess sun exposure, you can still receive the benefits of the great outdoors while covered up.

As I was appreciating the natural world around me, I started to feel more connected to it. I once interviewed a father-son duo of Huichol shamans, spiritual leaders trained by the indigenous Huichol Indians of Mexico. I saw firsthand a number of miraculous healings seemingly brought on by a little bit of drumming, chanting, and incense. The shamans revealed some of their methods to me, and their connection to nature was a central theme. They told me that the Huichols believe humans are not separate from nature, but rather they are an extension of it. The shamans told me, "When you connect with nature, you connect with your true nature," and I think I was finally figuring out what they meant.

As I became more and more inspired by my surroundings, I decided it was time to buy a wet suit. The ocean is very cold in Santa Cruz, and without a wet suit, I never went in the water. I found a purple wet suit at a thrift store that fit me perfectly. And one Sunday afternoon, just before sunset, I spontaneously said to the family, "Let's get in our wet suits and run to the beach!"

When we reached the sand, I witnessed one of the most incredible scenes I had ever seen. Not more than fifty feet offshore, there were hundreds of harbor seals bobbing up and down in the water, surrounded by larger seals, pods of dolphins, and even a breaching whale. The anchovies were thick in the water, pelicans were diving amidst the sea creatures to get their fill, and the whole scene was unfolding directly in the lineup of perfect, clean, right-facing waves at a beautiful beach break. There were about ten surfers catching rides right in the middle of it.

I grabbed a boogie board and paddled out, straight into the middle of hundreds of harbor seals. The seals just kept right on swimming and feeding around me, unfazed, while I caught wave after wave. Meanwhile, a picture-perfect sunset put on an award-winning performance above me. It was one of the most joyful experiences of my life—like a full-on *life orgasm*.

And speaking of orgasms, as my Joy Plan progressed, my libido drastically increased. The thing about sex for me is that the more I have it, the more I want it. But when I haven't had it for a while, I forget how much I like it.

Dan and I are friends with a fabulous couple, David and Tracy Wikander, who are, respectively, a relationship coach and a marriage and family therapist. They each have a busy private therapy practice, and together they lead weekend couples retreat workshops and write a lot on the topic of sex. After many years of working with couples, the Wikanders have found that most people fall into one of two camps: either they need to feel emotionally connected before they want sexual connection, or they need to have sexual connection before they open up emotionally.[12] These distinctions are not necessarily gender specific, although it tends to be women who want to talk first and men who want sex first. I always thought I fell into the first category, but I started reconsidering this. When Dan and I have built-up sexual tension between us, no amount of talking makes me feel any closer to him, but as soon as we get down, more than just my legs open up; I actually feel more open to him emotionally. So the key for me was to keep a steady stream going. And Dan was more than willing to oblige.

Orgasms are amazing phenomena. They flood our brains with endorphins, reduce our cortisol levels, and induce a feeling of relaxation. Studies have shown that regular orgasms can even regulate the menstrual cycle, due to a balancing effect on female hormones. Orgasms increase dehydroepiandrosterone (DHEA) levels in the body, improving memory, brain function, and even the appearance of skin.[13] Yes, studies have actually shown that orgasms can make us look younger.[14] Orgasms, as well as the skin-to-skin contact in sex, increase oxytocin, which regulates heart function, reduces cell death and inflammation, and increases feelings of love, trust, peace, and well-being. Mothers may be familiar with oxytocin, as the hormone is produced in abundance during pregnancy and breastfeeding.

Sex had become a key ingredient in my Joy Plan. But if I hadn't had sex, I would have still had exercise, which is almost as good. Exercise actually induces the same endorphins in the brain as sex. It also reduces cortisol and adrenaline in the body, reducing stress.[15]

Endorphins are released after both aerobic and anaerobic exercise, creating a powerful effect on mood. According to research from the University of Vermont, the mood benefits of just twenty minutes of exercise can last for up to twelve hours.[16] In one study of clinically depressed subjects, as little as thirty minutes of walking on a treadmill for ten days in a row was sufficient to produce a significant reduction in depression.[17]

Since starting my Joy Plan, I had been going to the gym almost every day. Before my business collapsed, I maybe made it to the gym twice a month for a yoga class or a session on the elliptical machine, but I never enjoyed it. I watched the clock constantly in classes; while I was on the elliptical, I read gossip magazines, with their photoshopped images of impossibly gorgeous celebrities, and I always left feeling even worse about myself and my shape than when I went in.

With this month I was giving myself to focus only on joy, I thought I'd try to lose both some physical and emotional weight. It wasn't easy at the beginning. I really had to make myself go to the gym, and I felt incredibly guilty for spending so much time there. But I kept telling myself it would just be for one month, and then I would go back to being a good little worker bee.

I had been to Alli's Pilates class a few times before, but it was always so hard that I often left early. After a few classes in a row where I actually forced myself to stay all the way through, I started to feel different. I began to feel my abdominal muscles, deep under the layers of softness, engaging again—and I got excited. I stopped looking at gossip magazines during my sessions on the elliptical, which always made me feel bad about how I looked, and brought juicy novels to read instead. I kept my routine simple and pushed myself until I was sweating each time. I also sat in the sauna every time I went to the gym. As the sweat poured out of me, I thought of it as negativity and depression clearing out of my system.

Sleep was the last item on my list of well-being boosters to embrace. While we sleep, our thoughts suspend, our organs recuperate, our cells regenerate, and by the time we wake up, we are each, in fact, a new person. This gives us a chance to leave behind any less-than-joyful thoughts or experiences from the day before and start afresh each morning. Sleep has also been shown to reduce cortisol levels—decreasing inflammation, reducing stress, and preventing disease.[18] Maintaining a regular sleep pattern sets our internal circadian rhythm, which signals our bodies to pump out the right hormones at the right time of day.[19] Our bodies are wired to sleep at night, with the deepest levels of sleep occurring between the hours of 11:00 p.m. and 3:00 a.m.[20] Going to bed later than eleven can mean we miss out on the most restorative functions of sleep, which I usually did.

Before the Joy Plan, I was in the habit of often staying up until two or three o'clock in the morning and frequently going without more than four hours of sleep a night. Over the years, I had developed difficulty with sleep—both in falling and staying asleep. My mind was often occupied with thoughts running wild in my head, and whether I was worrying about my children, something work-related, or another problem I was trying to solve, sleep often felt more like a battle than a rest. I tried sleeping visualizations, deep breathing, eliminating computer and tech time before bed, sleepy music, herbal remedies, and even sleeping pills, but nothing had worked for me consistently. I had decided I just wasn't a good sleeper.

But once I started going to bed earlier and staying in bed for eight or more hours each night, I started sleeping. In fact, I became a champion sleeper. I can only guess that all the sex and exercise I was doing—along with the changes in my diet and state of mind—contributed to my improved sleep. Before long, I was sleeping like a teenager again: deep, restorative, uninterrupted sleep. With a sleep history like mine, it's incredibly exciting to wake up in the morning and realize that you haven't been awake since you laid down in bed eight hours ago. This was something that I hadn't experienced in more than ten years.

I also came up with a new trick to help me fall asleep with gratitude on my mind. Instead of counting sheep (yes, I'm embarrassed to admit I had actually been mentally counting sheep hop over a fence for years in an attempt to fall asleep each night), I mentally went through the alphabet and thought of one item per letter that I was grateful for: Avocados. Back rubs. Compliments. I rarely made it to *z*.

I really felt, and saw, the difference. We've all heard that sleep is the best beauty product, and I could see a visible difference in my face when I started sleeping more. My eyes were brighter and less bloodshot, and I swear my wrinkles smoothed out a bit too. I was now excited to go to sleep every night and wake up refreshed and enthusiastic about each new day. I was taking better care of my body than I had in a long time, and I was appreciating it more than ever.

I'd be turning forty soon, and for the past five years or so, I'd been struggling with accepting my aging body. The damage from my sun-worshipping days was really showing, I didn't lose weight as easily as I used to, and I was sprouting gray hairs. But while I was taking the time to intentionally nurture my body, something clicked, and I found myself feeling a new appreciation for aging. Because really, if I wasn't aging, I would be dead. And since I'm going to get older anyway, I might as well do my best to enjoy it.

I thought about "aging well" and how it's not just about taking care of my body but also about taking care of my mind and spirit. Nourishing my emotional body with thoughts, people, and experiences that bring me joy is just as important as eating healthy food and exercising. And so is steering clear of those that don't. This month, I'd noticed the plethora of tiny stressors all around me in a new way and realized it was my responsibility to navigate my reaction to them in every moment.

With each day of my Joy Plan that passed, I felt better emotionally and healthier physically. And about three weeks into it, I realized a miraculous thing was happening—I was starting to feel at peace with who I was and where I was in my life. I had gone into the Joy Plan with a near-constant barrage of self-loathing and defeatist thoughts—a problem based primarily in my mind. Yet in addition to the effort I'd made to change my thoughts, I believe my joy finally came through taking care of my body. As my body blossomed and gained strength, my mind started to ease. I was no longer in despair over the collapse of my business and my lack of a clear plan for what to do next. I was enjoying the moment.

I discovered I could drape my iPad cover over the top of the elliptical machine at the gym, put a wireless keyboard on the elliptical's magazine shelf, and type while I worked out. That's how I realized an awesome personal benefit of endorphins—they inspire me to write. In fact, aerobic exercise has regularly been shown to inspire ideas; Albert Einstein claimed he thought of E=mc^2 while riding a bicycle![21] A few times a week, I would get on the elliptical machine for an hour, type whatever I was thinking about, and then email it to my editor at mindbodygreen.

The inspired ideas that started coming to me quietly when I was in the bath were now screaming at me in Pilates class and coming out in blog posts about growing old gracefully, finding inspiration in nature, and making joy a top priority.

As the end of November approached, my life didn't look too different on the outside. I had lost a few pounds and my teeth were whiter, but I still lived in the same place, had my same family, and my same bank account balance. However, on the inside, everything had changed. My negative thoughts and worry were greatly diminished. I was appreciating my surroundings, my family, my body, and my life more than I ever had. I was experiencing joy almost all the time. My friends said I looked ten years younger. My family said I was a lot more fun to be around. Instead of feeling like the Joy Plan was coming to an end, I felt like it was just beginning.

Thanksgiving was in a couple of days, and I was particularly looking forward to a holiday dedicated to gratitude. I was in the grocery store shopping for ingredients when I ran into an old boss of mine, the president of a prestigious university of traditional Chinese medicine in Santa Cruz. I hadn't seen him in over five years. He said he'd been thinking about me lately because I'd produced an important anniversary event for the university ten years prior and they were in need of an event planner for a similar gala coming up in a few months. Right there in the baking aisle, he offered me a high-paid, low-hours consulting gig that would last for the next three months.

I now knew how I would pay the bills for the next few months, and I hadn't gone looking for it at all. It seemed like Niko was right: by making my own joy a priority for thirty days, I had successfully changed my thoughts and behaviors, and miracles were starting to happen in my life. I began to wonder what would happen if I could sustain the Joy Plan beyond this initial month, and whether the insights and skills I had gained in just thirty days really would be enough to change my life.

JOY PLAN TIP #7

Certain lifestyle choices have been scientifically proven to increase the brain chemicals associated with joy. Give them all a try, and create the best possible conditions for a joyful body: vegetables, laughter, nature, sex, exercise, and sleep. Falling asleep with gratitude on your mind and waking up with thoughts of appreciation will help you feel enthusiastic about each new day.

PART 3

Challenges

I THOUGHT THIS WOULD BE EASIER.

In the "Challenges" section of a business plan, the inevitable barriers to success are presented, along with their proposed solutions. Every plan has challenges, and often they are unexpected. The Joy Plan is no exception. As uncomfortable as trials and tribulations can be, they are powerful catalysts for change. Challenges provide an opportunity to improve, refine, and strengthen the plan.

CHAPTER 8

THE QUEST FOR HAPPY HORMONES

"When the brain perceives that you are no
longer reproductive because your hormones
are out of balance, it tries to get rid of you."

—SUZANNE SOMERS

It was hard to believe that only one month had passed since I decided I
would test out the Joy Plan. That month felt languid, long, and luscious—
like it contained an entire year—and I didn't want it to end. Since I was
feeling so good, I decided to keep up with my new joy practices. As I entered
my second month dedicated to joy, I didn't think I could ever go back to
where I had started. I felt like I was high all the time. But I wasn't using any
illicit substances to bring on my joy (Pilates, papaya, and bluegrass music
were my drugs of choice); I was getting there all on my own.

And my joy was pretty consistent now. I felt incredible! That is, until this
one day when I realized I was crazy and everything in my life was a disaster.

It started out like any other day in early December. The sun was just
rising as I walked outside in my pajamas to put the garbage on the curb

for collection. The brisk air was a shock to my system, as I'd just recently emerged from my warm, soft bed. As I dragged the recycling bin to the front of the house, I caught a glimpse of our neighbor's Christmas tree lights twinkling in the living room window. That's when it hit me. That Christmas tree stood proudly in the living room of a three-bedroom home that my neighbors owned, like *real* grown-ups. My neighbors would soon be getting in their *new* cars and driving to their *real* jobs, while I, nearly forty years old, was there in my pajamas in front of our rented town house—with no stable job, no new car, no home that I owned, no Christmas tree, and no real plan. *What was I doing with my life?*

In the days that followed, I felt even more horrible than I had before the Joy Plan. And now that I knew how good it was possible to feel, I desperately wanted to get back to feeling good. But getting back there felt absolutely impossible; I was stuck. I wrote this in my journal:

I have fallen into a terrible place. It's dark and scary and lonely, and I don't know how I got here. I feel like everyone who I love has left me here to rot because they don't give a shit about me. And I don't blame them, because I'm not really a very nice person and I don't have much to offer anyone. Since I can't seem to make it in the professional world, I should be doing a much better job of taking care of my family, but I can't stop snapping at them. I'm a bad wife and a terrible mother, and I keep thinking they'd be better off without me. I know these thoughts are wrong, but I'm powerless to stop them. I feel like screaming, crying, and breaking things all at the same time. I'm doing my best to pretend I don't feel this way, and because no one sees or understands, I feel utterly alone.

This disastrous feeling had been with me for days, and boy, was it awful. Nothing worked to get me to shake it: I couldn't meditate; I barely noticed papaya; bluegrass music didn't sound good; Pilates just felt hard. Every single thing Dan said either annoyed me or made me sad. And then it dawned on me that I would be bleeding soon; my period was due in about five days.

If I hadn't been focusing so much on feeling good for the past month, I don't think I would have recognized this dip in my emotions. I would have just blamed my hopeless, irritated, and fearful feelings on the circumstances of my life. But once I noticed this totally out of place feeling of mental torture and knew that nothing in my life had actually changed that week, I realized something was wrong. This had probably been happening to me every month since I started puberty, except when I was pregnant, breastfeeding, or on birth control that suppressed my ovulation.

It's estimated that 75 percent of women of childbearing age experience some form of premenstrual syndrome (also known as PMS, *pretty miserable shit*). And 3 to 8 percent experience a severe form of PMS called *premenstrual dysphonic disorder* (PMDD), which can disrupt a woman's ability to function normally.[1] In both PMS and PMDD, symptoms begin seven to ten days before menstruation. While PMS can include mood swings, PMDD is characterized by extreme mood shifts—particularly hopelessness, anxiety, and anger. These symptoms can become worse during perimenopause, which can begin as much as ten years prior to menopause. And with the average age of menopause at fifty-one, I realized I could already be experiencing the effects of perimenopause.

The contrast between that week of agony and the past few weeks in my month of joy was so stark that I could see it clearly for the first time, and now I could do something about it. I decided I should just go into the "red tent" until I was past my period. Now, of course, I have two children, so I couldn't actually go into a tent with the other menstruating women in my community and sit on straw and drink tea for a week, like I would have thousands of years ago. But what I could do was minimize the interactions I had with others and spend more time nurturing myself so that I had fewer opportunities to get upset.

Dan was a great sport about this, especially since it required a lot of extra childcare time on his part for the week. I think he was relieved, because he'd been telling me for years that I had PMS and it only ever made me mad. (Of course, he'd only ever told me when I was in the midst of it, so I couldn't see or think clearly enough to realize he was right.) Now I was admitting I had a problem, and that meant he had been right all these years. But I don't think Dan cared about being right; he cared about avoiding my drama. When I have PMS, I can be distant, weepy, snappy, easily annoyed, and terribly pessimistic.

So that week, I was going to avoid Dan like the plague. Not because I didn't love him, but because I did. I wanted to spare him my wrath and learn how to control and minimize my PMS so I could stop spending 25 percent of my life in turmoil. Here's what I did.

The kids were in school during the day, so I just had to get through the mornings. Dan left early for work, and I let the girls watch a video during breakfast to minimize the possibility of them getting into a sisterly squabble, which might spur me to lose my cool with them. After I dropped them off, I either went immediately to the gym or home to take a bath, depending on what felt most nurturing to me that day. Because I was working part-time now—on the event planning gig I'd landed—during my workday, I emailed instead of speaking with people. I canceled all my in-person meetings for the week. I didn't call my friends or family members. As an introvert, talking with others doesn't feel soothing when I'm emotional. While an extrovert might want to take the opposite approach and sched-ule extra time with supportive friends and family, I prefer to process my emotions myself and then reflect with others later.

Dan and I split the evenings; I took two nights of dinner, homework, bath, and bedtime while he spent time with friends, and he took the other two nights while I went to the gym to sit in the sauna or take a Pilates class or to a coffee house to sit quietly and write until he and the girls were all asleep. For four days, Dan and I saw each other only in passing and kept our interactions brief, sweet, and mostly nonverbal. When I was with the kids, I let them watch more videos than usual and gave them lots of art projects to work on that would keep them happily occupied without asking too much of me.

And it was an improvement: the less I talked to people, the fewer triggers I encountered that might spin me out of control. My internal anxiety engine was still churning away, but it had less fuel to add to its fire. Unfortunately, my "red tent experiment" did not go so well for Dan. Even though he had been supportive of it in theory, Dan is an extremely social animal, and I felt too cold and distant for him to believe that it was nothing personal. He became so convinced that I was mad at him that the process of trying to convince him that I wasn't mad made me mad. And when I got mad, I decided to leave.

It was Saturday and my state of mind was pretty negative, so I decided my family would be better off if I just went to a hotel for the weekend. I had never done anything like that, but I wanted to continue my red tent experiment until I felt better. So I checked into a cheap motel around the corner from our house, went to the health food store to stock up on organic chocolate and salty chips, and retreated into my hotel room for two days.

It was pretty fun, actually, and if it wasn't so expensive and stressing on my husband, I would gladly do that every month. But in the end, I decided that although my red tent experiment did make my week of mental hell feel easier, it wasn't a sustainable solution. I would contact my friend Susanna, who's an herbalist in Italy, and ask her to recommend some supplements I could try for the next month.

I knew I needed to get my hormones in check so I didn't get physiologically hijacked away from my Joy Plan every month. Now that I'd had a taste of sustained joy, I never wanted to feel bad again—especially not as bad as I felt right before my period. So I made it my goal to learn as much as possible about hormones so I could boost them in every way.

I started learning about the wonderful world of hormones when I was trying to get pregnant. Getting pregnant didn't "just happen" for us. We tried for more than two years, and during that time, I learned all about my cycle and the complex chemical cocktail of hormones that affects not only conception and pregnancy but so many other things about our health and sense of well-being.

From my multiple blood tests during that time, I learned about the bell curve of hormones a typical woman experiences in a month. Estrogen and progesterone signal our bodies when it's a good time to reproduce; they give the green light that all systems are in well-enough working order to replicate. When estrogen and progesterone levels are high—around the time of ovulation—our hormones are doing their best to make us feel vital, healthy, and sexy so we'll procreate.

Evolution has designed us this way. When we aren't ovulating, those hormones aren't necessary to put us "in the mood," which is why our estrogen and progesterone levels are at an all-time low right before we bleed. When estrogen and progesterone drop, so does serotonin, which affects mood, appetite and digestion, memory, sleep, and more. For me, that means I spend a week every month feeling ugly, angry, and crazy.

Estrogen, progesterone, testosterone, and serotonin all reach their lowest levels each month when a woman's period starts and a new cycle begins and then gradually climb until they peak around ovulation in the middle of her cycle.[2] When estrogen and testosterone reach their peak toward the middle of a cycle, many women become chattier, more confident, and feel—as well as actually look—more beautiful. Estrogen increases the collagen in our faces and gives our hair more luster, while prolactin plumps up our breasts and makes them perkier. Hormones also give us a sharper memory and the ability to speak more eloquently at this time of the month. Higher testosterone levels increase our sex drive as well as our desire to take risks.

But the high doesn't last for long. In the third week of a woman's cycle, progesterone levels keep rising while estrogen drops. This can make us sleepier, more forgetful, and impair our ability to speak articulately. I often can't remember simple words during this time of the month—which is very embarrassing in work meetings. I also have cravings for sweet, salty, and fatty foods around this time. The hardest week is the last one. The six or seven days before a woman's period starts is when all the good-feeling hormones plunge—and during this week I often can't even remember that I ever once felt joy, regardless of how good I may have been feeling only the day before. For many women like me, the mood swings we experience usually start about a week before we get our period and level out by the second day of our cycles.

Without suppressing my ovulation, I thought that serotonin was a hormone that I might have a better chance of controlling than estrogen and progesterone, so I looked into how I could increase my serotonin levels naturally. Serotonin is a neurotransmitter—a hormone that communicates between areas of the brain—that is responsible for maintaining mood balance. Low serotonin can lead to feelings of depression and hopelessness. While estrogen and progesterone levels affect serotonin levels, they aren't the only things that do.

It turned out my instinct to have a "red tent week," during which I minimized my social interactions, was a good one, since, as an introvert, I can find social interactions stressful, especially when I'm premenstrual. Whereas extroverts would want to be with others when they're premenstrual, keeping to myself for the week lowered my stress. And stress raises cortisol levels, which lowers levels of serotonin.

On the other hand, studies show that certain dietary elements can help boost serotonin production, as I'd discovered by accident in my own diet by adding in more foods that are high in tryptophan.[3] I also learned that exercise, sunshine, loving touch, and remembering happy events can raise serotonin levels.[4]

I'd already made positive changes in my diet and exercise and was getting enough sunshine and loving touch, but I was most intrigued with happy memories. This seemed like it should be the easiest of the serotonin-boosting options, since I didn't have to go anywhere or do anything difficult to conjure a happy memory. Like I said, when I was feeling really low, conjuring anything except despair felt nearly impossible, but that's when photos were helpful. I did have photographic evidence of happier times, and I kept my favorites on my phone. So in an attempt to increase my serotonin levels, I looked at photos and videos of good times and did my best to mentally transport myself back to those moments.

When I talked to my gynecologist to get her insights, she suggested I use an app on my phone to keep track of my cycle—at least that way I wouldn't be so surprised when the mood swings hit me. I also asked my herbalist friend Susanna for her advice. She responded that in her experience with patients, 80 percent of the time, emotional distress is caused by low levels of hormones—in both men and women. She also said that hormones can be thrown off balance when our bodies are either not stimulated enough through physical activity or our brains are stimulated too much with stressful thoughts.[5] Knowing how much I'd been working and stressing lately, Susanna was concerned that my lack of balance had knocked my hormones out of whack.

She gave me some recommendations for foods to eat and supplements to take to improve my hormonal balance. She also suggested that I get eight to ten hours of sleep a night so that my hormones could regulate properly.[6] (Luckily, I could already check sleep off the list.) Susanna also told me to exercise more to induce endorphins and cuddle more with Dan and my children to increase my levels of oxytocin.

With that quick prescription—take these herbs, stop thinking so much, exercise and cuddle, go to sleep, and call me in the morning—Susanna had to go. But I now knew my task: find my happy hormonal balance, and 25 percent of my life would instantly become a whole lot easier.

JOY PLAN TIP #8

Hormones have a powerful effect on mood, in both men and women. To help keep a healthy hormonal balance, get some sunshine and think of happy memories to boost your serotonin, exercise for endorphins, cuddle more in order to increase oxytocin, and do your best to sleep at least eight hours every night.

CHAPTER 9

LET IT GO, LET IT GO

"The path of least resistance is nonresistance."
—I CHING

After my period passed, I was back on track with my continued Joy Plan. It had been almost two months since I decided to try this crazy experiment, and overall I was definitely feeling better. I had started blogging; a chance encounter in the grocery store had led to a profitable consulting gig; and now I was feeling clear that my passion was in writing. Dan mentioned to a buddy from his beach volleyball team that I was writing a lot these days, and that resulted in another serendipitous opportunity for me. Dan's friend worked at an environmental consulting firm and asked if I could rewrite a large amount of the organization's website and marketing materials.

When I started the Joy Plan, I thought I'd be charting my progress, creating measures to gauge my success, and looking for visible evidence of changes in my life—but all of that was completely unappealing to me now. I knew that I had changed tremendously and that I was clearly more joyful much more of the time than I had been two months prior. But I no longer had an interest in analyzing my joy; I just wanted to enjoy it.

I felt like my persona, Chatty Patty—the aspect of me that usually controlled, justified, and criticized every action—was slipping away. And in its place, a new me was emerging—the true me—as if waking from a long sleep. She was relaxed and peaceful, introverted and introspective, spontaneous and goofy.

I didn't have as much free time as I had in the previous month since I was working now, but even work felt different to me than it had before. Everything felt easier, lighter, and more fun. I was pretty sure that I was rocking this Joy Plan and things would just continue to get better and better. I was taking Susanna's recommended supplements and felt confident that my PMS woes would be greatly diminished the next time my period came around. In fact, my optimism was so high that I felt almost unshakable in my joy—like nothing could ever get me down again. *Boy, was I wrong.*

It was a lovely, sunny afternoon on December 21, the winter solstice, and we had the front door open to allow the breeze in and to welcome friends who would be arriving soon from out of town. Our sweet dog, Lovey, who was always eager for fun, often ran up to other dogs to play. On that fateful afternoon, Lovey saw a dog walking on the other side of the street in front of our house. Before we could stop her, she ran through the open door and was hit by a car. She was killed instantly.

Before we got Lovey, I wasn't a dog person. I wasn't a cat person either—or any kind of pet person for that matter. I used to say that I already had two pets—my daughters, Kira and Nava—and plenty of mouths to feed, hair to brush, and poop to clean up. But my children were relentless in their pleas for a dog, and it was Nava saying, "I will *die* if I don't have a dog," that pushed me over the edge. Lovey was the perfect dog for us: low maintenance, nonshedding, with infinite patience and adoration for kids. And she loved snuggles, bubble baths, and cute outfits.

It didn't take long before I fell completely in love with her. Although we got Lovey for the kids, I was the one she spent the most time with. I often worked with Lovey cuddled on my lap or at my feet, and she was my walking partner when I embraced spending more time outside. I had no idea how much I could love—and grieve the loss of—an animal until we lost Lovey. Even though she only weighed six pounds, we felt a huge empty space in our family's life when Lovey was gone. And I definitely took it the hardest.

The kids helped us bury Lovey in the backyard. They decorated her grave with flowers and pictures they drew for her; they sang her a good-bye song as we placed her in the ground. They cried, and they let her go. They handled it really well. But I felt her loss profoundly; I was overcome with waves of sadness, crying regularly. I had come to love Lovey as a third child, something I had never understood about pet owners before. I realized what a huge source of joy Lovey had been in my life, and I missed her deeply.

Lovey—like all dogs and probably like all animals—was pure, positive energy. She never had a bad day or a bad mood, and it was never a bad time for a cuddle. She was a constant reminder of joy in my life—a role model, in a way. Without effort, Lovey was the embodiment of unconditional love, and she reminded me of the joy and love within my own heart. And now I felt like a piece of my heart was gone with her, never to be the same.

I imagine it's this way with all types of loss. The ones we love leave an indelible imprint on our hearts, and we're never really the same after they're gone. The memories of Lovey's gentle kisses on my nose, her cute squeaking noises, and the sound of her skidding across the hardwood floor in our living room when she chased a ball were like a phantom limb I could still feel. An undercurrent of sadness filled our Christmas celebrations, and Lovey's small presents remained wrapped under the tree.

As New Year's Eve approached—a time when I usually wrote a long list of resolutions and wishes for the new year—I had only one this year. We have a tradition in our family that everyone writes their wishes for the new year on a piece of paper and then seals them in an envelope to open on the following New Year's Eve to see if they've come true. As I sealed my envelope this year, I prayed to the powers that be, *Please just let me feel good— or at least know how to get back to feeling good when I don't.* I simply wanted joy this year, nothing more. I had experienced joy before Lovey's death, but when we lost her, I felt like I had lost it too.

I thought about the line from Kahlil Gibran's *The Prophet,* "The deeper that sorrow carves into your being, the more joy you can contain," and I desperately reached for joy again.[1] But I couldn't find it. I felt guilty that I hadn't been more cautious and saved Lovey's life. I was still crying every day, weeks after her death. It was the most my children had ever seen me cry, and they were concerned. They suggested we get a new dog, but I couldn't imagine replacing Lovey. And as my sadness continued, it spread to other areas of my life.

When neurons fire in our brains, they set off a chain reaction of sorts that lends itself to replication. Our brains classify thoughts, feelings, beliefs, emotions, and sensations together into a database of similar items that form clusters of neurons, or neural networks. When we think about something repeatedly, our brains respond by grouping related data together to support and reinforce those thoughts with more clusters of neurons.[2] This process is strengthened when strong emotion is involved, especially negative emotion. And when thoughts are repeated frequently enough, activation of the neural networks they've formed in the brain becomes habitual. So when we think thoughts and feel an emotion about one subject, our brains will seek to connect similar thoughts and emotional responses from other areas of our lives as well. When it rains, it pours.

For me, sadness and desperation seemed to pour out all over my life after Lovey died. The floodgates were opened, and my persona came back with a vengeance, pounding me with reminders of what a failure I was. Even though I had picked up some consulting work, I was hardly supporting the family. Maybe I'd been kidding myself all along that the Joy Plan was actually working. I certainly hadn't attained unshakable joy. The joy I'd discovered in the previous months now felt totally out of reach.

I felt guilty that I didn't make enough money for Dan to quit his job and do something he loved. I felt guilty that we were throwing away thousands of dollars a month on rent when we should own a house. I looked at job listings online, and it made me feel worse. All the jobs sounded hard, boring, or uninspiring. As much as I wanted to free Dan from work he didn't like, I dreaded having to do work I didn't like. I looked at real estate listings and felt even more hopeless and dejected by the home prices that were way out of our range.

Even my regular blogging, which had been making me so giddy, now seemed self-indulgent and superfluous. I started having a regular stream of thoughts along the lines of *Who in the hell do you think you are that anything you write would be of interest to anyone? Or that you have the authority to write about any subject with sufficient knowledge to back it up?* As soon as I pressed "send" on a new blog post for my editor at mindbodygreen, I would start doubting the content.

And then, as if I had mentally written a letter to myself and transmitted it telepathically into the ether, I received this email through the feedback form on my website:

Kaia,

I read your bio on mindbodygreen and looked through your website and noticed you missed a few things—didn't you discover the cure for cancer and weren't you the first woman to land on the moon? I think you and Brian Williams would make a good couple.

I was at first taken aback by this message. It was one of the first emails I had ever received through my website from someone I didn't know and I had no idea who Brian Williams was. But then, I laughed out loud. I found it hilarious that the barrage of thoughts I'd been hurling at myself physically manifested in an email from someone else. To me, this was *proof* that the Law of Attraction was as active in my life as ever. And I knew I could turn its flow in the other direction if I wanted to. That email snapped me out of my funk.

I decided it would be much more fun to receive fan mail than hate mail. I thought about the type of letter I'd really like to receive instead. And I thought, if I could manifest a message like that from my own negative thoughts, what could I manifest from positive thoughts? What if I could attract a letter from someone who enjoyed my blog posts so much that they encouraged me to reach an even greater audience? So I sat down and wrote this letter to myself:

Dear Kaia,

I have been a quiet fan of your blog posts on mindbodygreen for months now. I find your articles to be refreshing, relatable, and movingly honest. I believe you have a style that connects with readers without being preachy and offers practical action that many would be inspired by. Have you considered writing a book? It would be great if you could reach more people with your writing. If you ever do write a book, I'd love to help bring you to my town for a book signing. Please add me to your mailing list so I can follow your work.

Thank you,
Jenny

I sent the letter to myself by email and thought, *Okay, Universe/God/Source/Great Spirit, show me what you've got. Show me that this Law of Attraction stuff really works. I'll play your little game, but you've got to show me a sign so I know I'm on the right track.*

And the *very next day*—and keep in mind, I had not been regularly receiving messages from readers—I received this:

I just read an article of yours. I've never contacted an author before, or even so much as written a comment on YouTube. But I had to let you know that I felt like you were speaking directly to me. That probably sounds ridiculous and I bet you get letters like this constantly. Is there anything else of yours that I can read? Do you have other articles or perhaps a book? I appreciate and am so grateful that you do what you do. Thank you and take care.

I was amazed! I was thrilled that I had touched someone with my words and that they took the time to thank me, but more than that, I recognized it as a sign that the Universe/God/Source/Great Spirit had accepted my challenge and responded. And as if that wasn't enough, the next day I received this:

Hey Kaia,

I'm just dropping you a line because I really enjoyed your article and it came at a good time for me. I wanted you to know that you helped someone today. I wish you all the best and hope you keep writing. Thank you!

Another letter! I couldn't believe it! And *then*, I received this on Twitter:

@kaiaroman I keep clicking on MBG articles, really enjoying them, scrolling down to comment, and seeing you wrote them! Thanks yet again!

The letters kept coming. I had never received a fan letter before, and now they seemed to be arriving every day. But as this steady stream of messages poured in, I didn't receive a single negative letter since the one that referenced Brian Williams.

The fan letters definitely gave me a boost, and I started to feel light again. I dreamt about Lovey regularly and did my best to shift my focus from sadness over losing her to gratitude for having known her. Her unconditional love and pure, joyful presence in my life (and on my lap) had helped me tremendously as I embarked on the Joy Plan, and I was grateful that at least the fog of my depression had lifted enough by the time she died that losing her didn't drag me down so far beneath the surface that I couldn't make it back up again. I had gone down, but now I was coming back up for air.

I couldn't bring myself to get a new dog, but since Lovey had been a rescue dog, I thought it would be fitting for our family to honor her memory by fostering other rescue dogs. I signed up to volunteer for Peace of Mind Dog Rescue, a local nonprofit that finds homes for elderly dogs whose owners have passed away or can no longer take care of them. Dogs would come and stay with us while they were waiting to find their "forever homes." We also helped out at events where the organization brought dogs to meet potential owners. The dogs we cared for often had health problems, restricted diets, and special needs. Sometimes it felt like taking care of a new baby, getting up in the middle of the night to comfort a dog or give it medicine. But it felt good to be helpful.

In fact, volunteering has been shown to lower depression, increase one's sense of well-being, lower blood pressure, and extend life expectancy.[3] The social interaction from volunteering (as well as the doggie interaction, in my case) gives an oxytocin boost, and the increased physical activity helps lower cortisol. Interestingly, these health benefits are only seen in individuals who volunteer in order to help others rather than to help themselves—for instance, for personal recognition or to add an item to their resume. In my case, I felt like volunteering for Peace of Mind Dog Rescue helped me just as much as it helped those dogs. At one of our doggie adoption events, I saw a Chihuahua riding in her owner's bicycle basket, wearing a tiny pink shirt that said I RESCUED HER. I could relate.

I started to feel like I was back on the Joy Plan, once again turning regularly to my gratitude notebook, simple pleasures, and the healthy lifestyle changes I'd implemented as sources of joy. And as I felt better and better, I took stock on what had been happening in my life since I started making joy my top priority: Without hustling for clients, they were coming to me. By being more lighthearted with my kids and giving them more autonomy, they were actually begging to help with the household chores. I still had things to do, but I seemed to be getting them done more quickly and with a spring in my step that made everything feel fun.

I felt like the less I did, the more I accomplished. Work projects that would have taken me four hours before, I could now complete in thirty minutes. I was planning a trip to Miami in March to visit Susanna, who would be spending the winter there with her husband Gordon, and my travel plans fell into place with minimal effort. Often, things I wondered about showed up in my life through synchronistic events shortly after I thought about them. In addition to the two consulting jobs I'd gotten in the previous month, two more came along through word of mouth. And clients just kept offering me more and more money, more than I'd ever made per hour before. Despite my persona's efforts to convince me otherwise, I did think the Joy Plan was working.

Throughout January and into February, I started applying the Joy Plan in subtle ways with my clients, steering team members to work on the tasks that felt most joyful to them and delegating tasks that I normally would have done but now realized felt like a drag to me.

Niko hired me to help her and her husband with a new marketing plan for the career college they owned and operated in Southern California, and I traveled to Orange County to work with them for a few days. After our second day of tackling a number of challenges in the college, Niko came up with the concept of "handing it up." Handing it up is what you do when instead of handing an issue over to someone else to take care of, you "hand it up" to a higher power to deal with. Basically, if you get stuck on something, you set it aside and focus on something joyful for a while instead. After Niko and I came across a number of problems that we didn't know how to solve, we decided to hand it all up, and we left work and went to a yoga class. I think the biggest contribution I made to Niko and her husband's business wasn't their search engine optimization or improved website copy, but conspiring with Niko to bring in a bit of magic. Could the Joy Plan really work at work?

The next day, Niko's phone rang off the hook in a way she said was highly unusual. One after another, solutions showed up to every single problem we had handed up the day before: Three new employees appeared for positions she had been trying to fill. Two employees volunteered to take on work Niko previously had no idea how to cover. A talented marketing associate who had only been available part-time suddenly became available to work more hours. A slew of potential new students requested interviews. The building owners finally approved new outdoor signage Niko had been wanting to put up for a year. Even a mechanical problem within the school's air conditioning system was fixed. All in one day.

The Joy Plan had sounded too good to be true when Niko proposed it, and it presently seemed too good to be true now that it was actually working. Even though many things in my life were feeling almost effortless, I knew I'd laid the groundwork and put in the effort over the past few months. However, I was directing my effort differently now. By continually asking, "Does this feel good?" whenever I found myself pushing too hard and slipping into negative thoughts or emotions, I made the effort to feel better. This sometimes meant taking a bath when I had writer's block, for example—which went against my dedicated work ethic—but I was learning to let go of strain and embrace ease.

I was reading a small and poorly translated yet fascinating book, recommended to me by both my mom and Susanna, called *Reality Transurfing*.[4] The book details a process to "lean in" to our worst fears as a way to actually create what we want in our lives; finding a way to accept that which we fear most takes away the power the fear has over us. As Eleanor Roosevelt said, "You must do the thing you think you cannot do."

This philosophy reminded me of when Dan and I were trying to get pregnant. As months, and eventually years, passed, I became more and more obsessed. I charted my ovulation, regulated our sex schedule, and restricted my diet. The fertility specialists couldn't find anything physically preventing us from conceiving, and we were considering fertility drugs or IVF as our next option.

During this time, Susanna came to visit us from Italy. She had already decided that motherhood wasn't for her and said we should consider the freedom, opportunities, and adventures we could have, unencumbered, if we didn't have children. I resisted the idea at first, but then I started to imagine what I would do with my life if I never had kids. I thought about how many inspiring projects I could throw myself into without ever worrying about my schedule. Susanna and I began dreaming up a new business venture. And I actually started to get excited.

I was decorating our new home at the time, and I had my eyes on this gorgeous white couch. Immediately, though, I told myself it was a foolish buy. Soon we'll have kids, I thought. A white couch is a terrible idea with children around. But the day I gave up on getting pregnant, I bought that white couch. And I was thrilled with it. The next month, I got pregnant.

Our pregnancy was not timed, calculated, or scheduled. When my period was late and the pregnancy test came out positive, I felt the tiniest pang of disappointment that I wouldn't be following my new plan. Of course I was thrilled, and our kids are terrific. But would those kids ever have come along if I hadn't bought that white couch, which eventually turned a muted shade of brown from all the stains?

The book *Reality Transurfing* explains that sometimes we hold so tightly to the things we want that we prevent them from coming into our lives. Because along with all that desire is a fear that we might not get it—and it's pretty hard to attract good things into our lives when we're in a state of fear. Fear is generated by an active amygdala, which impedes our ability to do our best thinking.

It was hard to believe that I could let go of something that I *really, really* wanted—having children—but I did. I imagined my life without children and found a way to be okay with that, even for a short while. As soon as I released my grip on the desire, it came to me with lightning speed. I believe a critical element to the Joy Plan is to master this art of letting go. And I know I can't fake it; it has to be a true release.

So I thought about my current fears. What was I afraid of? I mean, what did I feel was the worst thing that could happen?

I realized my biggest fear was that I would float along forever, never being successful in my professional life and only mediocre in my personal life. I was afraid that I would never make much money and that Dan would be forced to continually do work he hated in order to support us and that he would resent me for that.

But then I thought about my *worst* worst case scenario: that I would be seen as lazy and selfish. One of my greatest fears for many years has been to be considered lazy. This fear has motivated me to be someone who hardly sits down and is constantly doing chores, relentlessly tidying up, and obsessed with being useful. This fear of being lazy had driven me to be a mom who was often too busy cleaning to play with my kids. But now, I wondered, what if being lazy—if it feels good—actually makes everything become easier? In fact, it seemed like that's what I'd been experiencing on the Joy Plan so far.

One night in early February, I had a vivid dream that I was alone in a big Victorian house, exploring the upstairs. I walked into an ornate bedroom with a four-poster bed, and in the corner of the room, I saw two small, furry monsters that looked like they were out of the 1980s movie *Gremlins*. They weren't the scariest things in the world, because they were small and furry, but they had scary faces and bared their sharp teeth at me. I ran out of the room, slammed the door, and yelled for help. But no one came.

So I decided to open the door and have one more look at the little monsters. As I walked closer to them, I saw that they did look pretty scary after all. They growled and hissed and gnashed their teeth. But the closer

I got—the more I faced my fear instead of running away from it—the monsters morphed into puppies, and they started wagging their tails. When I bent down to look at them more closely, they licked my face.

Perhaps Lovey was sending me a message from the great beyond? *Let go of your fear, Kaia, and let in the JOY.*

JOY PLAN TIP #9

When you want things so badly that the lack of having them is felt more strongly than the joy they will bring, your focus on lack can actually prevent what you want from coming to you. As soon as you release your grip on your desires, what you want can come at lightning speed. Mastering the art of letting go is a critical element to the Joy Plan.

CHAPTER 10

COMPLAINING VERSUS CREATING

"If you think you can, or if you think
you can't, either way, you're right."
—HENRY FORD

It was now the middle of February and just over three months since I had started my initial experiment with the Joy Plan. As the weeks passed, while I was feeling pretty great about my consulting work, my writing, and my continued Joy Plan, Dan was miserable. His job had reached an all-time low, and he really wanted to leave. Of course, I wanted Dan to do work that he loved, but I also wanted to have enough money for our family to live the life we wanted in Santa Cruz, where the cost of living is high. To do that, we relied on his income. And I was a little annoyed that, while Dan was supportive of my Joy Plan, he didn't really ask me what I was doing or why or if there was anything he could do to create a Joy Plan for himself.

Dan would come home every day and tell me about how hard his day was. I can't blame him; ever since we had children, Dan and I had been in the habit of complaining about our days, almost as if it were a competition. I think it was part of a subconscious strategy we both used to try to get out of washing the dishes or putting the kids to bed: if we could show that we'd had the harder day, maybe we'd get off the hook with the chores.

I knew he saw how joyful I had become, and I was sure he wanted joy too. But would complaining ever bring either of us joy? I didn't want to complain anymore, but Dan's complaints about his job were bothering me so much that I needed to complain about it to someone. So when I called Susanna and Gordon to discuss the details for my upcoming visit, I had a talk with Gordon about complaining.

Gordon is a university professor and mentor for high-level business people. He has a PhD in psychology—which means he is certifiably really smart. So I asked him for his take on complaining, and what he shared with me helped me see complaints in a whole new light. Gordon explained that whenever we complain about something, whatever we're complaining about just *is*, but our reaction to it is our choice. A complaint is us saying that something should be different than it is, but this is just a point of view.[1] We project our thoughts through words and actions, and that's how we create our lives. Our experience of life is shaped by what we say about it. Perpetual complaints become a way of thinking, and that way of thinking can become a way of life.

Complaining is the opposite of acceptance. Complaining about your day diminishes your day, and your days make up your life. Even when negative things happen, we don't have to react in a negative way. Complaining blocks a different experience. For example, if we complain that work is a trap, that complaint blocks our ability to see work as a vehicle for income, which allows for comfort and stability. Complaining doesn't solve problems; it blocks solutions.

Gordon didn't only preach to me about the virtues of not complaining, but he really practiced it. He was one of the most perpetually positive people I had ever met. And he encouraged me to pay more attention to how I communicate in my life and in my relationships. I can't change Dan or any other person's behavior, he told me, but I can choose my own behavior and then model for others what I strive to follow. I could complain about what I don't want, or I could focus instead on what I do want.

Gordon asked me to consider who I would be in the world if I were someone who didn't complain. How would I react when something happened that I didn't like? What impact would my reaction have on those around me? He also suggested that we could adopt a "complaint jar" like other families have a "swear jar." But instead of putting money in the jar every time someone complained, like a punishment, we could use positive reinforcement by filling the jar with a token for every day we went without complaining as a family. When the jar was full, we could take a special family trip to celebrate our accomplishment.

I was inspired to take this on as a challenge, and I decided to start by doing my best to go without complaining for one week. I even wrote a blog post titled, "Why You Should Stop Complaining for One Week and See What Happens," and invited my readers to join me in a one-week challenge. I was paying close attention now to all the times I complained, and I was surprised at how often I was doing it. In addition to frequently complaining with my husband, I often complained when I was nervous, especially when I was talking with someone I didn't know well.

Somehow I had fallen into the habit of complaining about the traffic, the weather, high prices, whatever, in an attempt to bond with others. But this habit never felt good, and—just like other habits—I knew this one could be broken through willpower and practice. For my one-week challenge, I vowed to keep my frustrations to myself and tend to my well-being by taking a bath, going on a quick walk, or doing some deep breathing whenever I felt the urge to complain.

I promised to do my best to see the object of my potential complaint from a new perspective and to look for the silver lining by changing my attitude. Gordon had pointed out that complaints highlight what we don't want, which helps us better understand what we *do* want. So during my complaint-free week, I would ask myself what I was longing to be, do, or have, rather than what I didn't want. Instead of dominating conversations with my complaints, I would ask more questions, and specifically, I would ask leading questions that would steer us toward positive topics.

I would ask Dan and others about what inspires them and then thank them for inspiring me. And if they complained, I would change the subject to something we could be grateful for together. I didn't know how my life would change after going a week without complaining, but I hoped that I could break the habit I'd become accustomed to and start a new cycle.

At the end of my blog post I wrote, "Who's with me? Let's do this together!" And then I held my breath, pressed send, and wondered if anyone would read it.

When I send a blog post to my editor at mindbodygreen, I never know what day it will appear online. And since I wrote in the post that I would begin my one-week challenge on that day, I waited patiently until it appeared, trying to get all the complaints out of my system in the meantime. The post ended up going live on the day I was leaving on a weeklong trip to visit my family in New Mexico with the kids. It was President's Day, and the kids had a week of school vacation. Dan had to work and wasn't joining us.

The response to the post was incredible. As soon as it was published, thousands of people on Facebook and Twitter pledged to join me in a week without complaining. And I knew that my upcoming week, with the potentially stressful trip I had ahead, could be one of the most difficult weeks possible for this challenge to take place. But I felt I had all these friends in cyberspace I didn't want to let down—and that made me hyper-vigilant about not complaining, which helped me take everything in stride when things went wrong.

We got on our flight smoothly in Oakland, but once we were about to take off, there was a mechanical problem with the plane. So we had to sit in the plane, on the runway, with no air circulation, for an extra hour and a half. Many people on the plane were complaining, but the kids and I just sat back, watched a movie, and imagined we were somewhere warm and tropical.

Once we arrived in Phoenix, our suitcase got sent to the wrong luggage carousel and then removed when we never retrieved it. So we had to wait an extra hour at the airport for someone to bring it to us. But we just broke out the food we had brought with us and had a picnic in the baggage claim area while we waited. Then the GPS didn't work in the car I rented, but no problem; I made the five-hour drive through the desert into rural New Mexico without getting lost.

Once we arrived, however, the kids got sick with fevers, one after the other. This was still fine; I could manage this. I had acetaminophen and Chinese herbs, and the kids each recovered quickly. But then I got sick, and I didn't recover quickly. I had a raging fever, along with hallucinations, chills, full-body aches, and a splitting headache. My stepdad took the kids during the day for several days in a row, and they even spent a night at my brother's house. The kids were thrilled about this. They got to play with their adorable cousin, Sophia, and her huge Tibetan mastiff dog.

Meanwhile, I felt incredibly guilty that I'd come to New Mexico primarily to help my mom, who was in very poor health and needed a lot of help, and ended up being sick in bed myself for all but two days of our trip. However, I never complained out loud—and my internal lament was less of a complaint than guilt. Instead, I did my best to accept what I could not change.

While I was lying in bed in a fever-induced haze, it occurred to me that perhaps being sick was actually the path of least resistance for this trip. I avoided having to juggle taking care of my kids and my mom at the same time, and I was able to help her with the one big task she needed most of all on the day I felt well, which seemed to be plenty for her. Everyone was content, so I decided I should be too, and I chose to be grateful for the extra time I had to sleep. I was all better just in time to travel home, and I was pretty sure I deserved a prize for completing my weeklong challenge without complaining. I had focused on solutions rather than problems and practiced acceptance even when things didn't go as planned.

Back in Santa Cruz, stocking up on food at the grocery store, I mentioned to the guy working at the checkout counter that I'd just returned from a trip to New Mexico and needed to fill my empty refrigerator. He then launched into a tirade about the high cost of rent in Santa Cruz, compared to more affordable places like New Mexico. The cost of rent was a subject I would have normally jumped on the bandwagon to complain about; I'd been complaining about it for years. But this time I just smiled and said, "Yes, but look where we get to live. There aren't many other places in the world where you can swim in the ocean and hike in the redwood forest in the same hour." And just like that, as if I had flipped a switch, he started telling me about his favorite hiking spot.

I had successfully gone a week without complaining, but I didn't go a week without feeling guilty. And guilt was a whole other beast I needed to tackle. The truth is, I've had tremendous "happiness guilt" for a long time—probably the majority of my life.

In Australia, where Dan and I lived for seven years, the usual or proper response when someone asks, "How ya goin'?" (Australian for "How are you doing?") is "not too bad," "good," or "pretty average"—but rarely "great," "wonderful," or "fantastic." You're not supposed to be having too easy or too good of a time or else you could be considered a "tall poppy" (rising above the other poppies in the field) and get quickly cut down to size.

My friend Eleonor from Israel explained it to me this way: "It's bad luck to be too happy. You should always complain, at least a little bit. If you're too happy, you're asking for trouble." My mom also gave me this pearl of wisdom when I was younger: "Your flaws are a gift that help others relate to you. When you're happy, beautiful, and successful, people will be jealous of you, so it's good to have at least a few flaws."

My happiness guilt has run deep for years, reinforced by cultural influences like these but carried like a burden that I could only put on myself. I've had this idea that if I'm not being productive—either head down working hard at a computer or cleaning or accomplishing something—then I'm being lazy and unproductive. This has meant that—even though I've lived a block away from a beach for years—I've seldom set my toes in the sand. It means I've rarely relaxed on the couch and watched a movie since having kids. And it also means I've regularly complained about my workload, just to make sure that everyone else knows how busy I am and doesn't think I have it too easy.

This dynamic played out the most with my husband. When Dan and I would see each other after work, I felt I had to justify my time each day by rehashing everything that was hard. And if I did something pleasurable, I felt guilty telling him about it.

It was time for the end of both complaining and guilt; these twin toxic habits no longer served me and certainly didn't bring me joy. I decided I would keep up my challenge of not complaining and add in the challenge of catching myself whenever I felt twinges of guilt. I needed to reframe the way I experienced life—especially the way I experienced stress—so that I could stop these habits in their tracks.

Stress appears in many ways in our lives—mental, physical, and emotional—but not all stress is bad. In 1975, endocrinologist Hans Selye coined the term *eustress* (*eu* means "good" in Greek) to describe the kind of stress that motivates our minds and bodies to work toward a tangible goal.[2] Rather than shutting down our bodies and minds or causing a fight-or-flight reaction, eustress inspires us to go after what we want.

By mentally reframing experiences that I would have previously complained about, I could see situations as learning opportunities rather than as problems. This distinction between *distress* and *eustress* would be my guide for seeing a challenge as a chance to learn and grow instead of letting it turn into a downward spiral of complaint and worry.

When it came to guilt, I remembered from my college studies in psychology that it's an emotional experience that occurs when someone believes—accurately or not—that they've done something they shouldn't have or haven't done something they should have.[3] Sigmund Freud once called guilt "the most powerful of all obstacles to recovery."

So if guilt was an internal experience based on my own judgment of what is right and wrong, it seemed like I could just change my mind and stop being so hard on myself. I was already seeing evidence that working less was producing more income in my life, that inspired ideas were coming to me when I took hot baths and went to Pilates class, and that synchronistic solutions were showing up more quickly to questions I lightly pondered compared to issues I worried about heavily.

Also I had no evidence that any negative consequences would actually occur if I took care of myself and did things that I enjoyed. In fact, it seemed that the more I enjoyed myself and the less I worried, the better my life got.

I decided I just needed to keep it simple and, whenever possible, say yes instead of no. If I was enjoying myself, I would say yes and keep doing it. If I wasn't enjoying myself, I would consider what I'd rather be, do, or have instead and say yes to that. Using my Pandora analogy, I would look for the thumbs up on the other side of every thumbs down.

I drove past a house in my neighborhood and noticed an eye-catching front yard decoration. It was a wooden replica of a cute, little white dog squatting and pooping. NO! was written on the dog's chest in red. When I first glanced at this lawn ornament, I glazed over the NO! and thought that it marked a designated place for dogs to go potty. How odd, I thought.

But once I realized the purpose of this decorative sign, I found it ironic that these people want so badly not to have any dogs poop in their front yard that they're willing to look at a fake dog pooping every time they look at the front of their house. And I thought, if I was a dog, I wouldn't notice the NO! either. I would see a nice-looking friend showing me right where to do my business.

This dog poop sign has become a playful metaphor for me when I think about the things that I don't want in my life. Do I want to erect a monument to them, write NO! all over it, and then shout from the rooftops to anyone who will listen that I DO NOT WANT THESE THINGS!? When I think back on my life, the times I've had the most of what I didn't want—the most physical pain or discomfort, the most emotional pain, the most problems with anything or anyone—it has always been when I thought and talked about those things ad nauseam. *Ad nauseam* translates from Latin as "until nauseated," which I think is highly appropriate in this case. Because every time I'm talking about the things I don't want, I'm sticking my finger down my own throat.

After I took on the challenge to stop complaining and started becoming more conscientious about releasing guilt, I realized one day that I felt different. I had this feeling that something was missing, and I wondered if I'd left it behind in New Mexico. I kept looking around to see what I was forgetting, but that wasn't it. It seemed like there was something I needed to do that I couldn't quite remember, but that wasn't it either. I felt lighter, like I'd removed a layer or put down a heavy item I'd been carrying. But what was it?

This feeling stayed with me for a few days until I finally figured out what was missing: my anxiety was gone. Even though I was experiencing joy most of the time these days, I was still accustomed to carrying around some level of anxiety with me like a weighted sack on my back, and I felt strange without it. The low-grade panic I normally felt throughout my day was just...*gone*. I still had plenty to do—my life circumstances, relationships, and conditions hadn't changed—but I was different. I had peeled away another barrier to my joy, without even realizing it.

Was it the intentional week without complaining? Was it my attentiveness to letting go of guilt? Whatever it was, it felt liberating. I was free, at least for now.

Dan noticed this change in me too, and I noticed that he was complaining less. He still didn't like his job, but the less I fixated on his complaints, the less he complained. People often show us the behavior we expect of them, and perhaps complaining about my husband's complaining had just been perpetuating the problem.

In our wedding vows, Dan and I pledged to always be honest with each other. But is there a line between being honest and being destructive with the truth? If I'm feeling anxious, overwhelmed, and stressed—and I know that I'll feel better after I go to the gym or have a good night's sleep—do I really need to tell Dan all the nitty-gritty details of my worries? Is that really helping either of us? Dwelling in negativity with no attempt to find a solution or a better feeling only results in two people feeling bad instead of one. And that negativity can spread like a virus, as I pass it on to him and he passes it on to the next person he speaks with and that person passes it on and so on and so on.

I do think it's helpful to "vent" occasionally, to open my mouth and just let all the gunk come pouring out. But it's not really fair to my husband to be on the receiving end of my purge unless I mentally prepare him and he knows that he doesn't have to respond, solve anything, or take on any of my pain. And I can do that for him too. In fact, our couples coach/therapist friends David and Tracy teach an exercise called "holding the basket," in which couples ask each other to "hold the basket" for their troubles when they just need to let off some steam.[4] Now that I was shifting my focus from complaining to creating, Dan and I started to put that exercise into practice.

And we agreed that after we tossed our worries into the basket, we would set them aside. And instead we would use our partnership to cocreate solutions, visualize an improved situation, or simply get back to something more pleasant—like love.

JOY PLAN TIP #10

Complaining doesn't solve problems; it blocks solutions. Perpetual complaints become a way of thinking, and that way of thinking can become a way of life. Your experience of life is shaped by what you say about it. Instead of complaining about what you don't want, focus your attention on what you do want.

PART 4

Team

THESE ARE MY PEOPLE.

The "Team" section of a business plan introduces the key players behind the business. These people make up the executive team, whose expertise and dedication are essential to the plan's success. We are social animals; we need each other to survive and thrive. Even introverts don't live in a vacuum. Other people are essential to the Joy Plan, especially those whom you share your life intimately with. These are my people. Who are yours?

CHAPTER 11

THAT'S TRUE LOVE

"A successful marriage requires falling in love
many times, always with the same person."
—MIGNON MCLAUGHLIN

A study in 2015 at the University of Birmingham in the UK showed that oxytocin, the hormone that floods our nervous systems when we fall in love, has the same effect on the brain as alcohol.[1] Both substances influence the release of gamma-aminobutyric acid (GABA) in the prefrontal cortex and limbic areas of the brain—the upshot of which is reduced stress and anxiety and increased trust and risk taking. That sure explains a lot.

Falling in love feels amazing. That floating on air, daydreamy, warm-fuzzy feeling is actually a chemical process. And like the effects of alcohol, it can wear off over time. The act of falling in love is very different from the act of staying in love. Getting drunk is fairly easy, but maintaining a healthy buzz over several decades—now that's a skill.

We toast newlyweds at weddings with wishes for a long and happy life together while knowing that less than 50 percent will actually stay married.

We hope with great optimism that these two people will grow and change in tandem over a lifetime but realize that the odds are stacked against them. As anyone who's been in a long-term relationship knows, marriage isn't always easy. So I don't take it lightly that Dan and I are here, after fourteen years, still choosing each other. These days, being together for fourteen years is considered by many to be a long time. To me, it feels like we're just start-ing to get the hang of it, finally growing up enough to do this marriage thing somewhat well. But we still have a lot to learn about each other.

As I noted daily in my gratitude notebook, I continue to be very much in love with my husband. But in many ways, since having kids, I hadn't been putting much effort into our marriage, and I knew I could do better. There were numerous ways I could be more supportive, generous, and fun with Dan, which he would certainly appreciate. I also sensed that in some ways, my marriage was a fairly untapped resource for tremendous joy. It certainly had been in the beginning.

For our first date, Dan invited me to a private wine tasting at Ravenswood Winery in Sonoma. The wine tasting was led by the owner of the winery, and we tasted wine directly from barrels that had not yet been bottled. It was one of the most fun days of my life. We strolled through rows of blossoming grape vines. We talked about travel, business ideas, music, food, philosophy—and we laughed all day long. Dan was handsome, smart, funny, and an absolute gentleman. He spoke five languages and had lived in multiple countries. I was charmed.

A few days after our date at the winery, I received a package from a one-hour delivery service in San Francisco. It was the Macy Gray CD *On How Life Is*, with a note from Dan that said, "I'm listening to this right now and thinking of you. Can't wait to see you again." I popped the CD on and listened to the first sultry song with my friend Dulcie, who was over at my house when it arrived.

"Who is this guy?" Dulcie asked me when she heard the lyrics. "He's really into you."

"I think I'm really into him too," I said. "Am I in trouble? Is he going to break my heart?"

"If it doesn't break your heart, it isn't love," she told me.

But Dan has never even come close to breaking my heart. He's never made me wonder if he loved me, if he would be there for me, if he was attracted to me, or if I was a priority for him. He made it crystal clear from the beginning of our relationship how committed to me he is, and he hasn't faltered. On an early date of ours in his hometown of Berkeley, Dan took me to the famous Berkeley Rose Garden that overlooks the San Francisco Bay, with breathtaking views of the city and the Golden Gate Bridge. He described a wedding he witnessed there when he was a teenager—how the bride, descending through the tiers of roses, looked like an angel floating on a cloud. "I hope to see you descend those stairs like an angel toward me someday," he said. He introduced me to a group of his friends from high school at a party later that night as "the last girlfriend I'll ever introduce you to." And two years later, I did descend those tiered, rose-covered stairs to say "I do."

We've been through a lot since then. We've had two kids, moved countless times—sometimes to other countries—and started and left numerous jobs and business ventures. We've both had surgeries, illnesses, and injuries, and Dan lost his mom, who was his best friend. And through it all, I think we've fared pretty well. Even when he's seen me at my absolute worst— and believe me that is very, very bad—he has stood by me, solid as a rock. Dan fell in love with a twenty-five-year-old party girl in a pink wig, but he continues to love me as a nearly forty-year-old woman with gray-speckled hair, whose idea of a party is a good book and a cup of tea. Despite my ups and downs over the years, Dan has been a true friend and partner and loved me no matter what. But I know I'm a lot more loveable—and fun—when I'm in a state of joy.

And I *had* gotten to a point now in my Joy Plan that I felt pretty solid in my joy, especially since I reduced my complaining and stopped dwelling in feelings of guilt about my happiness. But I could tell that Dan, even though he was trying to complain less, really wasn't happy. And while everything else can be totally great in my life, if things aren't okay with Dan, it all just feels off-kilter for me.

It was a beautiful day in early March when Dan's unhappiness reached critical mass. Niko was visiting us in Santa Cruz, and Dan, Niko, and I were having tacos at one of our favorite spots. Between bites, Dan declared, "I'm having a midlife crisis." I had two immediate thoughts about this. The first one was that if forty-seven is the middle of his life, then he's thinking he's going to live to about ninety-four, which is pretty good. That made me happy. I like to think about growing old and wrinkly with Dan and being alive to meet our great-grandchildren. My next thought was that this was when he'd want to trade me in for a younger wife and a red convertible.

But when I mentioned the trophy wife and the convertible, he assured me that was not going to happen. "I just feel like I've hit a plateau," he said, "Like up until this point I've been moving up this ladder, always reaching higher and higher points in my life, and now there's nowhere left to go. I'm unsatisfied in my job, but it supports our lifestyle, and I just don't know where to go from here."

"I think the thing is, Dan," Niko said matter-of-factly, "at this point in life, the journey isn't up. It's *in*." She suggested he could think of it—rather than as a midlife *crisis*—as a midlife *opening*.

I digested that comment for the rest of the day. A lot of us spend the first half of our lives trying to reach certain milestones—to "grow up" and support ourselves, maybe have a family of our own and figure out how to support them—and for most of us, it's an upward journey, a journey filled with hardships and struggle and hopefully, triumphs. Is that why forty is often referred to as "over the hill"? Not only do you reach your peak in physical condition around this age but you've also hopefully attained a certain stability that can be sustained for the long descent down the other side, when everything in your life declines.

But I know it doesn't have to unfold this way, especially for Dan. He is the most resourceful person I know—it's one of the reasons I fell in love with him, and something I still love so much about him. Dan can make anything happen, from free concert tickets to a dream job. But at the moment, he was feeling uninspired and past his prime. I knew Dan needed to find his own Joy Plan, but I didn't know how to support him in doing that without sounding preachy or judgmental.

Thankfully, Niko stepped in. She and Dan have known each other even longer than they've known me, since Niko's husband and Dan are friends from high school. As fellow extroverts and adventure lovers, Niko and Dan have always had a special bond. The day after the taco/midlife crisis incident, Niko sent Dan this email, which he shared with me:

Dear Dan,

I wanted to reach out because when I looked into your eyes, I could see that you were feeling some pretty hard stuff. And if nothing else, I just want you to know, you are on your path. You are so full of love and light and energy and brightness and smarts and delight and adventure and there is so much left to your incredible journey. You had a peak, YES, and this is a different turn on your path. This is an internal turn, this one will take you to a place where you need to look in and then you will find your way. And you will shine in new and even more brilliant ways than ever before! Trust me. The next decade is going to be filled with so much joy and adventure and creation. You'll see.

Keep on keepin' on, brother.

Your sister always,

Niko

What a friend. I believed that she was right and there were brilliant solutions just around the bend, a way Dan and I could both have joy at the same time and still enjoy the lifestyle we love. This whole dilemma could have already been solved, I thought, if we were both on the Joy Plan. But I kind of felt like Dan was on the *Oy Plan*.

And as much as I wanted to be supportive and loving, I was sort of annoyed that he wasn't just grabbing the reins to his own life, following his passions, and creating magic like I knew he was so good at doing. But when I really thought about it, I realized I was afraid he wanted me to give up my part-time consulting/writing/caring for the kids and get a full-time job in Silicon Valley. If I was truly being honest, then I have to admit that as much as I wanted him to follow his passions if they led him to become a teacher or a coach or a chef, I was so used to the financial stability that Dan provided for our family with his high-tech sales salary that I was scared of losing it. And I knew that was what was at the heart of his midlife crisis.

I talked to Niko about it. "It's painful to hear how miserable he is in his job, because I feel so responsible. If only I had been successful in my business, or if I was making more money now, he wouldn't be stuck there. But I can't help thinking that he should be grateful that he gets to go into a lovely office with intelligent people every day and be valued for his time with a nice salary. He has such a sweet situation in so many ways."

It's helpful to have a close friend who is very similar in personality to my husband, because she helps me understand him when I don't.

"What Dan wants most right now," Niko explained, "is to be heard, to feel appreciated, and to be adored. He needs to know that you understand—like really get it in your bones—how he is feeling. Not that you agree or are up for anything specific but that you totally hear how he feels locked in, that he feels so far away from his calling, that maybe he's afraid he'll die having never had the chance to fully explore his life purpose. He wants the person closest to him in the whole world to really, fully be in it with him. To want this for him."

As I heard her speak, I wanted that for him more than anything.

"And wanting this for him doesn't mean you have to give something up!" Niko continued. "But can you hear him, like really hear him? And then just see what comes when you listen from a place of love without being afraid that he's trying to take something away from you. Something amazing might happen. Something you can't even imagine. There is more money and time and freedom and joy in this world than we can fathom. And I know that you and Dan can both have that without sacrificing anything. So listen with love and trust your joy and this universe that provides so well, and smile and laugh about the situation. This one is a real doozy! This is a perfect time to *hand it up*, girlfriend."

After talking with Niko, I drove over to Dan's office and met him in the parking lot. I wanted to hold him and tell him that we could get through any challenge as long as we did it together. As we leaned against my car and hugged, a convertible Cadillac pulled up next to us blasting "Not Fire Not Ice" by Ben Harper—the song we first danced to at our wedding. I took it as sign, a message, and a wink from the universe that we only needed to focus on our love for each other and everything would work out just fine. "Thanks for the music," said Dan to the guy driving the Cadillac. "We needed that right now."

I love this man so much, I thought. In fact, he often still takes my breath away when I see him from across the room. And when he holds me, when I rest my head on his chest and feel his warm, strong arms around me, I have a primal sense of safety that I don't feel anywhere else. There's nothing better in the whole wide world than Dan and I having fun together. In fact, I fell in love with Dan because he was fun. He wasn't rich—he actually had very few possessions when I met him—but he was fun, kind, and generous, and he inspired me to be fun, kind, and generous too. Yet at some point we stopped being so much fun.

To bring back the fun in our relationship, we needed to spend more time together without the kids—time as *us*, not just as Mom and Dad. So we decided to start having a once-a-week date night. We offered to pay the kids one dollar each to "babysit each other." We gave them dinner, put on a movie, and went outside to have our dinner on a blanket in the backyard. It actually worked. Because the kids were motivated by the money and the opportunity to be alone in the house, they didn't bother us. And we could still keep an eye on them through the sliding-glass back door to make sure they didn't burn down the house. The worst thing we witnessed them do was sneak whipped cream out of the refrigerator and eat it straight from the can—a small price to pay for our precious time alone.

More alone time together was definitely key to us becoming light-hearted as a couple again. We laughed, we flirted, and we talked about our dreams for our future together. Dan expressed how pleased he was that my Joy Plan was making me so happy. He has always been my biggest fan, inspired and turned on over the years by witnessing me be excited and passionate about my various projects. And there is no bigger turn on for me than seeing him light up about something he's truly excited about. But I hadn't seen that in him in quite a while now, and I wanted it for him desperately.

I asked him what small things he could do to start bringing more joy into his life, even if he didn't leave his job right away. He said he knew more exercise would help him feel better. So I asked him to commit to either surfing or playing beach volleyball, his two favorite forms of exercise, after work or on the weekend at least three times a week. He also said he would do his best to focus on the positive at work while at the same time exploring other career options that felt more fulfilling. And to my surprise, he told me he was going to start a gratitude journal. I assured him that his joy was more important to me than his income, and I would support him in doing anything that brought him joy.

Later in the week, one of my blog readers wrote to me and asked for advice about a challenging time she was having with her husband. As I read her letter, I reflected on how it could have easily been written by just about any person in a long-term partnership, at least at some point in the relationship. The laundry list of complaints may be different for each couple, but the sentiment is the same: If you're with someone long enough, you're bound to see each other's "dark sides."

Marriage and other long-term relationships are probably the most challenging ones we ever experience because we share so much: space, sleep, money, sex, food, and often parenting. And all this happens with a person whose approval and love is of the utmost importance to us. This makes marriage the ultimate ripe environment for challenges to arise. But that means marriage also provides the ultimate opportunity for personal growth.

Psychologist John Gottman's well-known "magic ratio" (also known as the "Gottman ratio") is a formula he developed to predict the likelihood of divorce.[2] Because of the brain's built-in negativity bias, it's generally believed that it takes three positive experiences to outweigh the impact of one negative experience. However, according to Gottman, in marriage and long-term partnerships that ratio jumps from three to one to five to one. In other words, it takes spouses five times more positive interactions than negative to create a long-lasting, stable relationship. Couples who don't maintain this ratio are more likely to split up.

Research at the University of California–Berkeley showed that couples who are more appreciative of each other are more likely to stay together over time: individuals who feel appreciated by their romantic partners are more appreciative in turn and more attentive to their partners' needs.[3]

With these findings in mind, in response to my reader's letter, I wrote a blog post for mindbodygreen called "How to Fall in Love with Your Long-Term Partner All Over Again." My suggestions were as follows:

1. Do what brings *you* joy. Get yourself in a good mood however you can, as often as you can. Although it may seem that your partner is fully responsible for his own mood, you have a lot of influence on the harmony in your relationship. By filling your own cup, you'll have extra patience, acceptance, and joy to go around, and your good mood will likely rub off on your partner. When possible, do activities together that increase joy-inducing hormones, such as exercising, spending time outdoors, laughing, cuddling, and of course, getting busy between the sheets.

2. Every day, make a list of things you appreciate about your partner. Ignore for the moment the things that you don't like and write down all the things you're grateful for. Focus on the specifics that help you remember falling in love in the first place: his unique and sexy smell, the beautiful sound of her laughter, how your head fits perfectly in the crook of his arm, the sweet way she tears up when

she sees a rainbow, etc. Get specific, engage your senses, and look at these lists whenever you're feeling less than loving.

3. Praise your partner as often as possible, for whatever you see that's worthy of praise. This includes the little things: how he fixed that annoying squeaky door, the cup of tea she brought you while you were reading the paper, those dishes he put away, that pile of laundry she tackled and conquered. And of course the big things, too: what a devoted father he is, what a caring friend she is, how impressed you are by his accomplishments, and how in awe you are of her brilliance and beauty. Hold your tongue when you have the urge to criticize, and ask yourself if it's really that important. Make sure you're offering at least five times more praise than criticism.

I hoped that if I typed it, I could live it—over and over—for the rest of my life.

JOY PLAN TIP #11

Marriage and long-term partnerships are the ultimate ripe environment for challenges to arise. But they also provide the ultimate opportunity for personal growth. Keep in mind that it takes five times more positive interactions between spouses than negative to create a long-lasting, stable relationship and that partners who appreciate each other stay together longer.

CHAPTER 12

PERSONAL BOARD OF DIRECTORS

"Don't underestimate the power of friendship.
Those bonds are tight stitches that close up
the holes you might otherwise fall through."
—RICHELLE E. GOODRICH

It was mid-March, and I was headed to Miami to spend a week with Susanna on a rare child-free vacation just for me. I knew this trip would provide a huge infusion of joy into my life. I had been away from Dan and the kids only a handful of times in the past nine years, usually for business, so this girls' getaway was a big deal for me. And even though Susanna and I are very close, we hadn't had much time alone together since I had kids. We were giggling like teenagers from the moment I walked into her art deco apartment in the heart of South Beach. Gordon was there too, but he made himself scarce throughout the week to give us as much girly time together as possible.

Hanging out with Susanna was like a flashback to a time in my life I could barely remember—a time before children when I never had to look at the clock and could eat and sleep whenever I wanted to. She and I were both taking five days off work, and without kids or husbands to take care of, we were completely free. She zipped us around South Beach on her Vespa. We laid on the beach for hours. We got dressed up and went to see *Wicked* at the Miami Opera House. We ate whatever we wanted at odd hours, stayed up talking until four in the morning, and slept until noon. And we laughed the entire time. In fact, my face hurt from laughing so much.

At one point in the week she said, "I feel like taking a bath. I usually take a bath for like an hour every day, and since you've been here, I've only been taking quick showers."

"Me too," I said.

And so we took turns taking a one hour bath each in her bathtub, while talking to each other through the bathroom door the whole time. Susanna's bathtub didn't have squeaky toys and bath crayons like mine did; it had fizzy, colored bath salts, aromatic herbal oils, bubble bath for grown-ups, and candles. *This is a woman who knows how to take care of herself,* I thought. When I told her about the Joy Plan, it made complete sense to her. That's how Susanna lives her life already.

My love for Susanna, as well as my other close female friends, has produced the same light-headed, drunk-feeling oxytocin reaction throughout my life as my romantic relationships with men. And when I fall in love with a friend like I have with Susanna, I can go years without seeing them and when we get together again, we just pick up right where we left off as if no time has passed at all. I am blessed to have a number of friendships like this in my life.

These women help me keep a healthy perspective about my marriage and make me a better wife. They give me comic relief and a reality check when I'm struggling with the complexities of parenthood and make me a better mother. They inspire me with their brilliance, courage, and kindness and make me a better person. And the thing I find most amazing about my friends is that my issues—the ups and downs of my life—are as interesting to them as they are to me. They genuinely care about what's happening with me and want the best for me—and I feel the same way about them.

It's quite incredible when you think about it: friends are often people that we meet by chance. I've met some of my closest friends at a random party, a business event, a birth class, and in Susanna's case, on a farm in Australia when we were both travelers there. And these people become intricately woven into our lives. They have complete buy-in on our joy; they might even want it more than we do. They cheer for us when we're down, celebrate with us when we're up, and remind us of how competent and creative we are when we forget. Friends are the family we choose, and I count my lucky stars every day for mine.

There are numerous health benefits of having close friends. People with close friends are 50 percent more likely to outlive those who don't. In fact, close friendships increase life expectancy as much as quitting smoking and even more than regular exercise or maintaining a healthy weight.[1] In a study at the University College London, college students who reported having close friends were 50 percent less likely to catch the common cold than their peers who reported not having close friends, when all subjects had the same exposure to the virus.[2] In another study, when subjects were placed in a stressful situation, they rated their self-worth higher and produced less cortisol when a close friend was present.[3]

Other studies have confirmed that regular contact with friends makes us happier. In fact, findings indicate that people are twelve times more likely to feel happy on days they spend with friends.[4] Studies have also confirmed what we all know: a quick chat with an upbeat friend significantly increases our own optimism and reduces stress.[5]

I didn't need science to tell me how important my friendships were, but I did realize after spending a week with Susanna that I should make time for getaways like that more often. Quality time with friends is an essential element in the Joy Plan. I laughed more in that week than I had all year, and I knew that was good for my mental, physical, emotional, and spiritual health. And, as luck would have it, I had the opportunity to spend time with close friends again right away.

I flew back to California and headed straight to the annual weekend retreat with my women's circle. A women's circle (or men's circle, or simply "circle" for a coed group) is an intimate group of friends who gather to support each other on a regular basis. Different from a professional networking group or a casual meeting like a book club, both of which concentrate on a shared topic of interest, the focus of a women's circle is mutual support and personal growth. The important distinction between a women's circle and any other gathering of friends is the intention behind it: the group is there to support each individual unequivocally, without judgement. It's a safe haven for deep and confidential sharing and for personal dreams and longings to be held by a collective.

Some circles choose to meet weekly; our group had been meeting monthly for the past fifteen years. Even though five out of the six women in my circle had married and had children since we started meeting and we'd each moved various times and juggled jobs and multiple responsibilities, we all made it a priority to gather in a beautiful place for a weekend together once a year.

For this weekend, we'd rented a cabin at a coastal camping resort (more like a *glamping*—a.k.a. "glamorous camping"—resort) called Costanoa, about forty-five minutes north of Santa Cruz. I arrived first, after an overnight flight from Miami, and enjoyed a relaxing day writing in the sunshine. As each one of the other women arrived, I reflected on how fortunate I was to call these inspiring women my inner circle, each of whom had a successful and rewarding career and fulfilling personal life.

I thought about all the stars that had to align for me to become friends with these women. I had been lucky enough to meet them when I was twenty-four, soon after I moved to San Francisco, through a women's entrepreneurial organization.[6] As we all aged, most of us were progressing in our professional lives, and we realized that what we really wanted was to continue getting together outside of the structure of the organization—to support each other in our personal pursuits of passion. So Sara, Erin, Michelle, Julie, Niko, and I formed our women's circle, and to this day—as best as we can, sometimes virtually if we have to—we meet every month and have one full weekend together a year.

This circle is made up of my friends, but they're more than that; they're my personal "board of directors." These women help steer me in the right direction when I veer off course. None of them live in Santa Cruz, so mostly I don't see them outside of our monthly circle dates. And because of this, we aren't mired in the daily details of each other's lives. When we do get together, we see the big picture, the high-level view, and since we've known each other for fifteen years or more, we hold each other to a high standard of personal best. These women remind me of my highest self when I forget who I am. They focus in on my best qualities, whether they are clear to me or not. And by the time I leave our circle, I'm seeing myself through their eyes.

I also see that even these successful, powerful women experience ups and downs. Being wealthy, being beautiful, or having a dream husband, house, or job doesn't guarantee a worry-free life. Life transpires in our hearts and minds; we all experience challenges, despite the blessings we may or may not have.

When I was in college, one of my part-time jobs was as a research assistant to a psychology professor who was studying the phenomenon of endorphin release when people talk about themselves. Some claim that's one of the benefits of therapy. In our women's circle, we always start with a check-in, where each woman gets ten minutes to talk uninterrupted. She can use this time to talk about how she is in the present moment, relate any challenges she's faced over the past month, or share anything else she wants to share. The rest of the women give their full attention; we don't comment or problem solve during check-in. To be fully heard by a group of people who know and love you deeply and are nonjudgmental feels wonderful.

Each month we also share inspiring meditations, visualizations, and exercises with specific intentions, and we are consistently amazed at the power these have to create real results in our lives. Scientific studies have shown that focused group intention can amplify the results of individual thought—and this is what we do on purpose in our living rooms at each monthly gathering.[7]

Every month when I come home from my women's circle, Dan jokes, "Did you do some hardcore sharing and radical acknowledgment?" And he can joke all he wants; I know that what we do in our circle is powerfully effective. Although we're all different, each of the women in my circle serves others in some way, both professionally and personally. We use our circle time to fill our own emotional reserves so that we can continue to be our best selves with others. After each circle, we emerge more energized, peaceful, and confident—better poised to go out into the world and make a positive contribution.

Everyone should have this, I thought, as our weekend together unfolded into a delicious mixture of organized, intention-setting exercises and playful free time. Beyond just being my friends, these women are the stakeholders in my life. They view my wins, as well as my challenges, as their own. We combine strategy with support and create accountability with each other to help us stay on track to reach our goals. Just as support groups have been shown to increase the effectiveness of treatment programs, I know my women's circle makes me more effective in my Joy Plan.[8]

If you're so inclined, I highly recommend creating a circle in your own life. It could be a group you assemble from among your acquaintances—the ones you sense are longing for deeper connection and support. You may encounter an existing group locally that you could join. Or perhaps you could connect with a virtual group that meets online. If group gatherings aren't your thing, perhaps you can bring the practices of uninterrupted sharing and combined intention-setting to your individual friendships, if you aren't doing that already. Sometimes a sounding board is exactly what you need to be able to hear your own inner wisdom.

On our last night together at Costanoa, we headed to the beach to have a fire under the full moon—but the fog was too thick for us to see the moon. Bundled up in sleeping bags on a blanket on the sand, Sara led us in an exercise of sharing what "lights us up." We went round and round the circle; with every turn, each woman shared something that made her feel joyful, giddy, sexy, spunky, and alive. And with each thing that was spoken, we all took a moment to let it soak in, imagining that joyful thing in our own experience and allowing ourselves to catch the buzz from our friend's joy.

One by one we spoke: dancing around my kitchen; singing Katy Perry songs with my daughter; riding my bike through the city after work; watching sunsets at the beach; the way my husband kisses my neck; knowing I've just totally nailed something at work; the taste of a sweet and juicy papaya; receiving a compliment from a stranger. One by one, we imagined all of those joyful things, and while we were lighting ourselves up, we physically burned a hole in the sky. In a dark sky thick with fog, a perfectly symmetrical hole opened up right above us and exposed the full, silver moon, joining us in our joy. We all left the beach that night feeling completely euphoric.

On my drive home the next morning, still high from the divine week I'd just had, I saw a pod of whales breaching as I drove south along the coast.

I pulled over to watch them. Sitting in my car watching those whales, I was so overcome with gratitude that it brought tears to my eyes. I felt grateful that things are always working out for me, that magic is the natural course of things, and that there is nothing I have to do to make it happen except allow it. *The path comes to me*, I thought. I reflected on the people I've been blessed to know and love and be loved by, and I felt deep appreciation for them all. These are my people, the executive management team for my life—and I couldn't do it without them. I couldn't wait to shower my abundant love on my husband and children.

JOY PLAN TIP #12

Close friendships increase health and happiness in many measurable ways. But beyond just being your friends, your nearest and dearest are the stakeholders in your life. They view your wins, as well as your challenges, as their own. Having the support of loving friends—and being a loving and supportive friend to others—will make you more effective in your Joy Plan.

CHAPTER 13

KIDS AND OTHER SPIRITUAL TEACHERS

"Your children are not your children.
They are the sons and daughters
of Life's longing for itself."
—KAHLIL GIBRAN

I had been away from Dan and the kids for ten days, and I was excited to see them again. As I pulled into the driveway, I saw that my daughters had written "Welcome Home Mom" in chalk and decorated my parking space with hearts, flowers, and a family portrait that included Lovey.

Seeing the word "Mom" on the driveway and hearing them call me by that name over and over again felt surreal. I still don't feel grown-up enough to be a mother. Dan's mom, Angela, told me when she turned eighty that you don't ever feel older than sixteen. Your body ages but your spirit doesn't, she said.

My own parents were only twenty-four years old when my mom's astrological birth control method surprisingly failed (what were they thinking?) and they ended up pregnant with me. Now that I'm nearly forty—and still feel like I'm not a real grown-up yet—twenty-four seems painfully young. I know that my parents always did the best they could under the circumstances, but in a way, we really grew up together. I can see how I developed a prematurely adult role in my family and how, faced with instability, I compensated by always having a plan. While my planning abilities flourished as a survival response, I also felt frozen in a kind of arrested development, always waiting for someone to take care of me and never feeling like a true adult, regardless of the years that ticked by or the responsibilities I took on.

Now that I'm a parent, I realize how hard it is to make decisions when you know your choices will profoundly affect the course of these small people's lives. I often catch myself wondering if this moment *right now* will be a defining moment for my children, creating an indelible memory they can never erase. I second-guess myself all the time and worry that I'm scarring them for life. Most of the time I feel like I'm doing my best, but there are plenty of times when I know I could do better and I just don't. I let them have too much screen time, too much sugar, stay up too late, and stay home from school if they're tired. I lose my patience with them and yell sometimes. I'm far from the perfect parent. And yet my kids will become their own unique selves just like I did—thanks in part to my less-than-perfect parenting.

Kira and Nava still write me love notes and shower me with hugs and kisses every day, but I often wonder what they'll remember about me when they think back on their childhoods. Will they remember all the times I didn't have grace under pressure? Or will they think of me as a mom who mostly kept her cool and helped them navigate the ups and downs of childhood with love and joy?

Since I started the Joy Plan, I had noticed more than ever that my kids are greatly affected by my mood. When I'm stressed, grumpy, and frustrated, they fight with each other more, push against me more, and move more slowly when it's time to get out of the house. On the flip side, I noticed that the more consistently I am in a good mood, so are they. I told them about my Joy Plan from the beginning and asked them to help keep me on track with being happy and fun. Every few days, I would ask them, "So guys, how am I doing as your mom today?" Most of the time they said I was doing an awesome job.

But every once in a while they said, "Mom, you could say that nicer," when I barked orders at them, or "I'd rather you be messy than mean," when I was stressing about a messy house. They helped keep me in check. Although I'm their mother and the grown-up in the relationship, I trust Kira and Nava's feedback.

Kira was an "easy baby": she slept, she ate, she pooped, she grew. But Nava didn't do any of those things easily. She was awake for hours every night and rarely napped, was upset often, and was only comforted by breastfeeding. She refused to eat solid foods until I weaned her at seventeen months. If I hadn't been so sleep deprived, I probably would have noticed sooner that something was terribly wrong. I was very sick myself during that time, with near-constant headaches and digestive troubles, itchy rashes, perpetual sniffles, and other strange symptoms. No doctor seemed to know what was going on with either me or Nava.

Finally, one doctor saw in my blood test that the histamine level was off the charts. Histamine is a natural compound released by the body as part of the immune response, particularly in the presence of allergies. In normal amounts, it helps to fight invading substances. But this doctor said he had never seen so much histamine in a blood sample, and it was remarkable that I was even functioning. With that information, I was able to take the right diagnostic tests and figure out that I have histamine intolerance: I lack the enzyme diamine oxidase, which breaks down histamine when I have an allergic or inflammatory reaction. And since I suffer from multiple allergies, without this important enzyme, histamine sticks around in my blood stream, wreaking havoc on my digestive and nervous system and creating a number of uncomfortable symptoms. Right before Nava was born, we moved into an old house that triggered my severe allergy to dust mites. Poor Nava was getting all that histamine in my breast milk—which explains why she couldn't sleep and why things got better after I weaned her.

Even though my breastfeeding days are long gone, I can see how I still affect my children as strongly as when I was feeding them from my own body. How I feel flows through me and into them when we're together, which is why, as a mom, my emotional well-being is just as critical as my physical well-being. Our kids need to see us model healthy habits, because that's how they learn. And joy is a healthy habit just as much as exercise, eating vegetables, limiting screen time, and getting enough sleep.

There's a particular faraway, spaced-out look my kids get on their faces multiple times a day. When I see that look, I know it means that their brains are emitting *mu* waves, a type of electrical activity in the motor cortex that occurs when mirror neurons are active. Mirror neurons are specialized cells in the brain that transmit impulses related to imitation and allow the brain to register behavior as if it is being performed personally, in order to replicate it later.[1] In other words, that glazed-over look my daughters get means their brains are memorizing my behavior so they can repeat it themselves later. That's how children copy their parents. Mirror neuron activity is fully developed by age seven, and it's the way children learn everything from language and speech patterns to social skills and empathy.[2]

Knowing how mirror neurons work in children—and what an impressionable age our kids are at—is a huge incentive to be on my best behavior in front of them. This phenomenon explains why I've seen Kira and Nava copy our words and mannerisms exactly, including arguing in the very same way that Dan and I have argued in front of them. The more Dan and I can express our feelings in a loving way, manage conflict with grace, find solutions instead of problems, keep things lighthearted, and focus on love and kindness, the more our children will cultivate those skills as they grow up. In fact, improving our own behavior will probably have a much more profound effect on their behavior than instructing them on the multitude of ways they could improve.

As anyone knows who has been around a baby, joy is our natural state; it's how we all start out. And at seven and nine years old now, joy is still Kira and Nava's natural state. I can see that my children actually have way more to teach me than I have to teach them, especially when I let go of my impulse to control and see them as they truly are: miracles unfolding before my eyes. And when I'm on point, I can give a little nudge here and there to help them steer away from forming a strong persona (like my own Chatty Patty).

My oldest daughter, Kira, has every reason to feel confident; she is truly gifted. And I'm pretty sure I'm not just saying that because I'm her mother. The first time Kira tried to ride a bike, she just took off, never falling. After a few lessons in vowels and consonants from her kindergarten teacher, she picked up a book and read the whole thing without a problem. The first time she hit a baseball, she hit a home run and then continued to hit home runs one after the other. Soccer, surfing, Spanish, Indonesian, math, dance, gymnastics, violin, piano, sewing—every new thing Kira has tried she's completely mastered right away with barely an effort. I watch her in awe and wonder if her confidence contributes to her competence. Kira expects things to be easy for her, and they usually are.

Kira also sets an excellent example for me of how to shake things off that are unpleasant. Just like anyone, she has ups and downs throughout her day, but she never lets anything keep her down for long. There is just too much fun to be had to waste time being upset. Kira is on the constant lookout for good times, and she finds them everywhere. She hardly lets a second go by without finding something to be excited about, whether it's a game, a song, a new idea, or a yummy snack.

And she's always scouting for new friends to share her fun with. Kira is just as social as her extroverted dad, if not more so. When I told her that I feel shy around new people sometimes, she comforted me by saying, "You just have to think of something to talk about that you might have in common with someone, and then go talk to them," as if that's the easiest thing in the world to do. And for Kira, it is. Her confidence and enthusiasm for life bubbles over into everything she does.

When Nava was younger, I worried that she would feel like she was living in the shadow of her older sister. Perhaps because of her troubles sleeping and eating when she was a baby, Nava is small for her age. She is also often quiet, off on a journey in her own mind. These two differences between Nava and her sister can make it seem like she is much younger than Kira than she actually is. But in other ways, Nava is wise far beyond her years. The words that come from her mouth when she does speak are as profound as any guru's, as far as I'm concerned. One day, she told me that she often played alone on the playground at school because the other kids weren't including her in their games. My maternal instinct to shelter her from rejection was instantly activated. But when I asked Nava if this situation was bothering her, she simply said, "I could be upset about it, but I'd rather be happy." She went on to tell me about the imaginary games she plays by herself and said, "At least it's quiet and peaceful when I'm alone." It was clear to me that Nava values her own well-being too much to let playground politics get her down.

Nava once gave me a big, delicious hug, looked me right in the eyes and said, "Mom, I love you and Dad and Kira second best, because I love myself the most." I couldn't have been more proud. Nava has managed to master self-love—something that we grown-ups struggle with endlessly. I knew I had a lot to learn from her.

As wonderful as my daughters are, they do still get into a number of sisterly quarrels, and Nava doesn't shake off being upset quite as easily as Kira does. When I came back from my trip, I bought them a board game they'd wanted to thank them for being so good while I was away. They immediately opened it up to play, but their game quickly turned into a yelling match over who would get to use the pink car. Nava threw her game pieces on the ground, stormed off to their bedroom, and slammed the door, furious. However, she emerged a few minutes later with a calm and serene look on her face and exclaimed, "All better!" This wasn't the first time I'd seen her do this, and I was so impressed that I asked her to tell me how she does it. To my surprise, Nava explained that she has a five-step plan that she follows (that she invented!), and she listed the steps for me:

1. Take deep breaths.
2. Shut your mouth so the sound can't come out.
3. Tell yourself, "Feel better, feel better, feel better."
4. Close your eyes.
5. Think happy thoughts.

I wrote it down and put it on the refrigerator so we could all remember and marvel at the wisdom pouring out of our petite prophet. Nava's five-step plan to calm down isn't only wise; it's actually scientifically sound. Deep breaths lower levels of cortisol by activating the parasympathetic nervous system, our body's natural rest and relaxation regulator. And when we are upset and defensive, our ability to reason is greatly suppressed.[3] So by taking a time out, we can cool down, stabilize our acute stress state, and then communicate clearly and with purpose. Also, closing our eyes anchors us immediately to the sensations of our bodies; it's easier to focus on our breath and an internal calming mantra (Nava's "feel better, feel better, feel better") when external stimuli are decreased. And finally, happy thoughts have been scientifically proven to decrease cortisol while increasing serotonin and improving our ability to analyze—literally making us think more clearly.[4]

Kira suggested they could have a "peace talk" to work through their disagreement. *With confident and wise girls like these, I must be doing something right*, I thought.

Attending a small private school where individuality and self-expression are encouraged has certainly contributed to their confidence, and we'd been nothing but pleased with their school experience so far. But recently, a mom of one of the girls in Kira's class had been complaining about the girls in the class not getting along. Kira's teacher told me that their behavior was common for girls their age and assured me that they were working it out with their teacher's support. But this mom was upset—and pointing her finger at Kira. She sent an angry email to me, copying all the other girls' moms, and accused Kira of being "in love" with one of the other girls in the class, which was making her daughter feel excluded.

I could feel myself start to bristle with defensiveness when I saw the letter, but luckily I had just written a blog post titled "How to Deal with Annoying People." I had written about looking for the lesson when someone pushes your buttons and taking the path of least resistance. So I looked for the silver lining in this situation and suddenly had a flash of an idea. I remembered a friend once telling me about a mindfulness class that was taught in her daughter's school. Perhaps what the kids in Kira's class really needed was to learn how to better recognize and express their feelings. If they were shown how to use deep breaths to calm down when they were upset, how to practice empathy with their friends, and how to choose optimistic instead of pessimistic thoughts, they wouldn't only become better communicators on the playground; they'd become more effective creators of joy in their lives.

I could teach a mindfulness class, I thought, based on what I'm learning from the Joy Plan. And by planning my lessons using the myriad of official mindfulness curricula available, I would learn a lot too. Mindfulness education is growing in popularity in schools and for good reason. Research has shown that it increases optimism and happiness in classrooms, improves focus and concentration, helps students resolve conflicts, decreases bullying and aggression, and increases compassion and empathy for others.[5]

I sent a quick email sharing the idea with the school director, and he responded immediately with a resounding yes. He also offered to reduce our tuition significantly in return for me teaching the class to the whole school, divided by age into four groups, one afternoon a week. Just like that—from a complaint to a creation!

I asked Kira and Nava what they thought about me teaching mindfulness at their school, and they loved the idea. They even started giving me suggestions for class activities right away. I knew they would be invaluable teaching assistants for my new class.

I taught my first mindfulness class in early April. To prepare for it, I gathered several empty glass jars and made "mind jars" by filling them with hot water and glitter glue. The warmth of the water dissolves the glue, leaving the thick glitter emulsion suspended in the jar. The glitter represents how our minds can feel when they're swirling with thoughts and emotions, especially the ones that feel uncomfortable, like anger, worry, or sadness. When we sit quietly and take deep breaths, even for one minute, our amygdalae calm down and we start to feel better, just like the glitter in the mind jar slowly settles to the bottom. My goal for the mindfulness class was to give my students tools they could practice so that over time they could learn to respond skillfully to the stress they would inevitably experience in their lives.

During the class, I gave the children each a piece of paper and asked them to fold it in half once and then in half once again. They took their time lining up the edges and carefully making even folds. Then I asked them to unfold the piece of paper and fold it again along the same fold lines, noticing how quickly the paper folded the second time—almost as if it was folding itself.

The folds in the paper are like the grooves in our brains, I told them. The first time we have a thought or experience, it is novel and new. It may even take some effort, such as learning how to ride a bike or deciding if we like a new food. With each new thought and experience, nerve cells in our brains, called neurons, register the information as memory. But over time, with repetition, those neurons join with others to form neural pathways.

Neural pathways are like favorite roads that our minds travel on all the time, I explained. The more frequently we access these pathways through repetitive thoughts and actions, the more automatic they become. That's why the paper folds so easily the second time. This is neuroplasticity in action, I told them, and it's how our brains learn. Neuroplasticity is the brain's form of muscle memory. The kids thought that was pretty cool.

We're all learning all the time, but children take in and process new information at a much higher rate than adults, simply because they're continually having experiences for the first time. The neural pathways they form in childhood form the basis of their knowledge, opinions, preferences, and even personalities as adults. Most of the time, this is positive: they learn how to communicate, use their bodies effectively, and feel and express their emotions.

But what about habits of thought and action that are less likely to serve our children well as they grow into adults? Neuroplasticity can also work to our detriment. I've seen kids who spend more time interacting with video games than with people, and it's obvious in their behavior. Even a frequently repeated statement as simple as "I don't like vegetables" activates neural pathways that will be challenging to change later in life.

The good news is that our brains remain moldable throughout our entire lives. Though neural pathways may be well established by adolescence, they can always be changed and rerouted. Many of us experience a time in our young adult lives when we reexamine all that we've learned—and possibly rebel against it, making new choices and drawing new conclusions about life.

However, what if kids understood what was happening in their brains from an early age? What if they recognized that they were forming habits, such as being a helpful friend or an attentive student, and made those choices repeatedly because that's the behavior they want their brains to learn and remember? How many hours and dollars in therapy could our children save as adults? How many conscious, self-aware children could we raise? And what kind of world would those children create when it's their turn to be in charge?

I believe knowledge is power; understanding something as fundamental as how our own brains work seems to me like something all children should learn and be empowered by. With the simple metaphor of a piece of paper, I hoped my students would see that they always have a choice about where to place their folds.

After teaching my first class, I was hooked. I was already excited about all the mindfulness games, exercises, and craft projects I would do with my students each week. I wrote a blog post for mindbodygreen with some of my favorite ideas titled "7 Fun Ways to Teach Your Kids Mindfulness" and was flabbergasted when it was shared more than one hundred thousand times on Facebook! It was incredibly encouraging to see how many parents out there wanted to share these exercises with their kids.

Juggling the complexities of life with kids in tow can feel like a monumental task, and staying joyful in the process may seem impossible at times. But practicing mindfulness with our kids shows them that we're just as dedicated to being calm and peaceful as we'd like them to be.

The Dalai Lama once said, "If every eight-year-old in the world is taught meditation, we will eliminate violence from the world within one generation." I had a found a new passion and a new mission.

JOY PLAN TIP #13

Kids are greatly affected by our moods. How we feel flows through us and into them when we're together, which is why, as parents and caretakers, our emotional well-being is just as critical as our physical well-being. Children need to see us model healthy habits, because that's how they learn. And joy is a healthy habit just as much as any other.

PART 5

Projections

LIGHT UP THE FUTURE!

The "Projections" section of a business plan forecasts the future. At this point in the plan, with a solid background, sound strategy, solution-oriented approach toward challenges, and dedicated team, the future should be looking bright. I once saw a sign at the Pigeon Point Lighthouse on the Northern California coast that said, "Light Up the Future!" and I decided to adopt this phrase as my personal motto. Because with every thought, word, and action, we're creating our world and our future. Let's make it shine!

CHAPTER 14
WRITING A NEW STORY

"Imagine a new story for yourself
and start living it."

—PAULO COELHO

As my parents did with me, I've always told my kids to visualize what they want to create in their lives and to believe in their own magic. They wish on shooting stars and throw pennies in wishing wells. I make up bedtime stories with themes related to dreams coming true, and I encourage Kira and Nava to believe in their own power to create. I wasn't always sure it would work, but—with the kids as my guinea pigs—I figured we would eventually find out.

Nava's manifestation specialty is parking spaces, and over the past five years, her success rate has been 100 percent. Whenever parking is tricky and I've got Nava in the backseat, I ask her for "parking magic," and she waves her hands in the air and makes a swishing sound. It usually takes less than thirty seconds from that point for a perfect parking space to open up.

Kira tends to set her sights on more material manifestations. She'll ask me for something I find wasteful or too expensive, like plastic dolls with far too much makeup on or shoes with roller skates built in that she'll grow out of quickly, and I'll say no. And then I'll watch in amazement as she makes a wish for that thing to come to her, totally trusts that it will, and then either she finds the object of her desire randomly or someone ends up giving it to her for free. She's done this over the years with toys, books, clothing, shoes, and even services.

Kira's latest desire was that she really wanted to learn how to knit. I went so far as to buy her knitting needles and yarn, but I wanted her to teach herself how to do it by watching instructional videos on YouTube, because knitting sounded about as fun to me as cleaning. So Kira started asking everyone—and I mean everyone—we came across if they knew how to knit. She asked the other moms at school. She asked her teachers. She asked the librarian. She asked the lady at the checkout counter at Trader Joe's. But over the course of a week, she had no luck finding a good knitting teacher.

A short time later, around seven o'clock one Saturday night, just as the girls and I were watching the ending credits to *Into the Woods* and waiting for a fresh batch of kale chips to come out of the oven, my friend Grace paid us a surprise visit with a friend in tow. I hadn't seen or heard from Grace in at least six months, and I was delighted to see her. Kira immediately asked both women if they knew how to knit.

Grace and I met in a café in Byron Bay, Australia, in 2009 when she overheard me talking with some clients about an ecorenovation TV show we were working on. Grace came right up to me and asked if she could be my marketing intern. We became instant friends. Even though Grace is fifteen years younger than I am, she is wise beyond her years and a cool combination of fun, free spirit, and smart, practical achiever. After Dan and I left Australia and were living in Santa Cruz, Grace came to visit us. She was trying to find a place to call home, and I suggested she give Santa Cruz a try. She ended up staying.

But life is busy, and between her multiple jobs, boyfriend, and travel and my work, kids, and life in general, Grace and I rarely saw each other. So when she and her friend were driving past our house and spontaneously decided to stop by, I put the kettle on to make us all a cup of tea while Kira talked to the women about knitting. It turned out that Grace's friend, Annie, was quite the knitter and more than happy to sit with Kira and her knitting supplies and show her the basics. Meanwhile, Grace and I caught up over tea and kale chips.

"I'm working for these millionaire brothers," she told me. "They started a tech company in Silicon Valley and made all this money, and they want to use it to make the world a better place. So they started a foundation, and basically I'm in charge of recommending how to spend the foundation's money. They're really passionate about environmental issues and education, and for some reason they're partial to projects in New Zealand. So that's what I've been doing—funding environmental initiatives in New Zealand while teaching yoga to the employees of the tech company."

"That sounds amazing!" I said. "Can you find me a couple of millionaires who want to spend their money on environmental issues and education too?"

By this time, I had been on the Joy Plan for over five months, and I really was feeling joyful the majority of the time. I had a new bag of tricks—a reliable set of tools to turn to whenever I felt my joy start to wane—and most of the time they worked. I was getting great pleasure from writing, and I was actually making money as a writer. That said, Dan still wanted to quit his job; I still worried about our finances; and when it came to money, it was still the same old story: Dan felt like he had no way out of the job he hated because we doubted we could make enough money to support our chosen lifestyle if both of us did something we were passionate about.

It seemed like I had always been effective at making other people's ventures financially successful, but never my own. Was that because I believed in other people more than myself or because I just doubted them less? I had no reason to believe my clients wouldn't succeed, so when I took on their marketing campaigns, I had no resistance and my clients experienced wild success. So why was I still blocked when it came to my own success?

I was reading Suze Orman's *The 9 Steps to Financial Freedom* and surprised myself by shedding a tear every few pages. As I read her descriptions of various clients who'd realized that their stumbling blocks around money had originated in their childhoods, Orman's approach struck me as a mixture of therapy and financial planning. Orman believes pivotal early-life experiences often create blockages around money—such as one client of hers who had broken her grandmother's valuable plate as a child and then never trusted herself with something valuable again, or another client who'd had his piggy bank money stolen by his sister and subsequently never trusted others with his money.[1]

I reflected on how my parents had always struggled with money and how my mother's entrepreneurial endeavors had never worked out financially the way she wanted them to, and I thought about my own mirror neurons as a child. With all the repetitive thoughts and neural pathways I'd formed over decades regarding money and scarcity, it was no surprise this still felt like a blockage for me. If I kept stressing about money, afraid there would never be enough, I wouldn't be open energetically to the abundant solutions that could be waiting right around the corner. And in a state of stress, I also wouldn't do my best thinking and problem solving. It was time for a new story about my past—one that didn't portray me as always falling short. I needed a new story in which I was the heroine—daring, brave, and successful.

At a business workshop I once attended, we did an ice-breaker exercise in which we were asked to walk around the room and introduce ourselves to others by talking about the movie we were currently starring in. The movie was meant to be the metaphor for our lives, and the exercise was meant to be a light and easy way to tell new people our abbreviated life story. Was it a drama? A romance? An action flick? A musical?

This exercise threw me off guard, because the movie I was starring in at the time felt more like a tragedy than the movie I would rather have been starring in, which was an epic adventure filled with romance, intrigue, and discovery. I struggled with how to answer this question and eventually settled on presenting my movie as a comedy, because at least I could laugh at how miserable I was. Later in the workshop, we cut out magazine clippings and glued them on poster board to make movie posters for our life's feature film. For that exercise, I decided to tell the story of my life the way I wanted it to be—not necessarily the way it was at the moment. I created a movie poster worthy of the most glamorous Hollywood stars.

I've thought a lot about that exercise since then and how the stories we tell about ourselves really do shape our lives. We're all the stars of our own movies, but how often do we seize the opportunity to give our very best performance and be the hero? And when we tell others about our movie, how often do we make it sound like a box office hit? Every time we talk about our problems, we're weaving a story that has energy and power to reconfirm what we believe, and thus what we create, in our lives.

I've spent most of my life telling my story as it currently is and—even if it happens to be good at the time—minimizing the happy parts and emphasizing what has been hard or challenging. Why? Perhaps I've wanted sympathy or understanding, or perhaps I've been reluctant to embrace a truly fabulous life story because I felt I didn't deserve it or because I worried it would make other people uncomfortable if I was better off than they were. But has this practice of telling my story, or presenting my movie, as less than brilliant really served me—or anyone else, for that matter? If I was tired of hearing my same old sob story about money, I'm sure everyone else close to me probably was too.

So, knowing what I know now about the power and creative energy of thoughts, I decided I would rather encourage thoughts about what I want to be, do, and have instead of how I happen to be, what I happen to be doing, and what I happen to have in this moment. I didn't really need other people to think about me struggling. Instead, I'd prefer to harness the power of other people's positive thoughts on my own behalf. I decided I would rather form neural pathways each time I talked about my life that would lead to the life I want—to the movie I want to star in—instead of reconfirming an old story.

Creating a new story doesn't mean we have to deny reality. We can look at the wide range of experiences and circumstances in our lives and choose what to hone in on. We can amplify the things that are happening that we like, we can feel excited about what's coming next, and we can do this no matter what else is going on. We can be selective with our focus, just like we're selective with what we eat. If something is displeasing to us, we don't have to put it in our mouths. If there's a condition in our lives that doesn't feel good, we don't have to give it our valuable attention or pass along the story about it to others so they give it their valuable attention too.

Telling a new story can feel awkward at first, but just like everything else in the Joy Plan, it's simply a practice that gets easier over time. The hardest part is realizing the massive power that our thoughts and words have and training ourselves to choose them wisely.

As the proverb goes, "Watch your thoughts for they become words. Watch your words for they become actions. Watch your actions for they become habits. Watch your habits for they become your character. Watch your character for it becomes your destiny."

I needed to practice telling the epic adventure side of my story to other people when I talked about my life and leave out the parts that weren't worth more than a minor film credit. If I told my story proudly and often, perhaps it would become reality right before my eyes.

I already had tremendous prosperity—loving relationships, consistent joy, and writing that I felt passionate about. But I was ready to have financial prosperity too. And I wanted to create that financial prosperity myself and take the burden off Dan so that he could choose his work based on what fills him up rather than on what would fill our bank account the most.

In the spirit of financial prosperity, I decided to spruce up my LinkedIn profile. And while I was looking at my profile, a "job recommended for you" notice popped up randomly on the screen. It was a job for a senior writer, and I recognized the name of the company as the place where my friend Grace worked with the millionaire brothers.

Something changed for me in that moment. In a flash, I could see myself commuting to Silicon Valley; and that two-hour train ride or drive with Grace no longer felt oppressive; it felt fun. I remembered how Grace had told me that they sometimes start their business meetings with a meditation and how their foundation was supporting mindfulness education in schools. I saw a future unfolding where I became the primary breadwinner for our family, working at a company where my ideas were valued and I was paid well. In my vision, I only commuted two days a week; I taught my mindfulness class at the kids' school one half day a week, and I worked from home the rest of the time.

I suddenly saw myself writing a book called *The Mindful Business*—a how-to guide for businesses to bring mindfulness into the workplace, based on my experience teaching mindfulness to elementary school children while also working in a Silicon Valley tech company. I imagined brainstorming with Grace during our commute, discussing how to spend the foundation's millions on initiatives that would make a huge difference for the planet. I liked this new story.

I looked further into the future and saw the possibility of being hired as a mindfulness teacher at various international schools, where Dan could work in admissions and as a volleyball coach, just as he had at the school where we'd worked in Bali. We could tap into our network of teachers we'd worked with in Bali, who were now scattered at international schools all over the globe.

Next, I dreamily envisioned myself as a freelance writer and author, with remote work that enabled our family to live anywhere in the world. I saw Dan enjoying an international job where he could use the five languages he speaks, and I saw him feeling passionate and excited about his work. I saw these multiple possibilities and surprised myself that I was happy considering all of them.

I no longer felt like the only way I could be in a state of joy was to follow the formula I'd created for my life in Santa Cruz: working part-time, going to the gym every day, taking baths, spending my afternoons with the kids. It was no longer an external condition that I needed to maintain; it was an internal one. I could imagine a new story in which Dan's work schedule allowed him to spend more time with the kids or in which we had a fabulous babysitter that Kira and Nava adored. These ideas—inaccessible to me before my Joy Plan—suddenly seemed not only possible but easy, and I suspected this was yet another positive effect of the Joy Plan: I now had the ability to look beyond my current situation and see other possibilities.

The next morning while I was at the gym, Erin from my women's circle called to ask if I might be up for some writing work as a contractor. She could use my help on the team where she worked at Google, she told me. I felt a world of possibilities opening up to me as my new story was being written right before my eyes.

Later that afternoon, I was driving to pick up the kids from play practice and needed to be at the theater in five minutes. I had a strong craving for my favorite chocolate chip cookie from the nearby cookie shop. The Pacific Cookie Company is located on Santa Cruz's busiest downtown street, where it's nearly impossible to find a parking space, and I didn't have Nava with me to give me parking magic. I decided I would only allow myself to have a sugary treat if I could park right in front of the shop. And what do you know? Just as I pulled up, a car pulled out of the prime parking spot directly in front. I got my cookie, fresh and warm from the oven.

As good as that cookie was, I took something away from that experience that was far better. It occurred to me, what if everything in my life was as easy as getting that cookie? Who says that wealth, health, love, possessions, or any other experience I could desire has to be any harder to achieve than that? I had craved that delicious cookie, and a parking space opened up and made it possible for me to get it. I followed my joy, and the universe revealed the path to me. What if I looked at everything in my life as a cookie and salivated over the thought of enjoying it, while trusting that I'm on my way and everything will work out if I'm meant to have it? Faith is a critical component to this cookie theory.

I love Jim Carrey's quote about faith from his commencement address to Maharishi University of Management's Class of 2014: "Why not take a chance on faith? Not religion, but faith. Not hope, but faith. I don't believe in hope. Hope is a beggar. Hope walks through the fire and faith leaps over it."

Carrey may be a comedian, but I think he summed it up better than the most serious philosopher when he said, "As far as I can tell, it's just about letting the universe know what you want and working toward it while letting go of how it might come to pass."

I knew I wanted the cookie, and I trusted the universe to make it easy for me. I knew I wanted success and prosperity, and I trusted the universe would make that easy too. I didn't have to know how.

I was doing my best to dream up a new story. Scientists and psychologists have conducted numerous studies that demonstrate a correlation between visualizing a successful outcome and actually achieving it. Daydreaming has been shown to activate regions in the brain that stimulate creativity and the realization of creative solutions.[2] I had been talking with my mindfulness students about the power of visualization and I'd shared a basketball story with them that they loved.

In a now famous experiment from the 1960s, three groups were chosen at random to practice making basketball free throws for twenty days.[3] Group One practiced free throws for twenty minutes every day. Group Two only practiced making free throws for twenty minutes on day one and day twenty and otherwise did not practice basketball at all. Group Three had the same amount of physical practice as Group Two but, instead of daily physical practice for the remainder of the twenty days, visualized themselves making baskets for twenty minutes every day. After twenty days, Group One improved their performance by 24 percent, Group Two showed no performance improvement, and Group Three improved their performance by 23 percent, demonstrating that mental practice was nearly as effective as physical practice.

In a sense, daydreaming and visualization are the opposite of mindfulness. While mindfulness is a practice of bringing awareness to the present moment, daydreaming and visualization enter another mental world, allowing images and thoughts to take us on a journey that is far from the here and now. Both practices can be advantageous, however, especially if the contents of our vision or dream are pleasant. The challenge is to maintain a level of meta-awareness while our minds wander. That way, we can remember the flashes of brilliance that may come to us while our brains are in a creative state.

I wanted to help my own visualization and daydream process, so I cut up some magazines, flyers, and brochures we had lying around and created a "vision board" with images of what I wanted my life to look like. I felt drawn to a large picture of a pod of dolphins I found in a magazine, so I cut it out and pasted it as a background image to the other pictures on my vision board. I didn't give the dolphins much thought.

Dan didn't see this vision board, but in the week after I made it—unbeknownst to me—he booked a surprise trip for our family on a whale-watching tour boat. Ten minutes into the boat ride, our ship was surrounded by hundreds of dolphins, leaping through the boat's wake and swimming along with us for twenty minutes. They jumped so close that I heard their dolphin squeals and was sprayed by their splashes. I didn't notice or remember the dolphin pod image on my vision board until a few days later, and when I saw it, I smiled and realized the vision board was already working its magic.

JOY PLAN TIP #14

What same old story have you been telling—and how could you revise it? Creating a new story doesn't mean you have to deny reality. You can look at the wide range of experiences and circumstances in your life and choose what to hone in on. You can amplify the things that are happening that you like, you can feel excited about what's coming next, and you can do this no matter what else is going on.

CHAPTER 15

EXERCISING THE JOY MUSCLE

"Joy does not simply happen to us. We have to
choose joy and keep choosing it every day."
—HENRI J. M. NOUWEN

It had been nearly six months since I created the Joy Plan, and what was intended to be a thirty-day experiment had turned into something much more, as that first month had laid the groundwork for my continued joy. Up until this point, I'd been working only part-time with a few consulting clients, writing when I had time, and engaging in motherhood and household activities. I was starting every day with fifteen minutes of gratitude and focusing on my breath. Most days, I was making it to the gym, taking at least a short walk outside, having a papaya and kale smoothie for breakfast, listening to my Allison Krauss Pandora station, and finding reasons to smile and laugh. Being on the Joy Plan had become more of a lifestyle than an experiment, but I still had to be intentional about keeping up the practice.

Grace connected me with the marketing director at the company where she worked, and we had a great talk. While they were excited for the strategy and ideas I could provide based on my background in marketing and public relations, the position they were hiring for was a full-time writer, which suited me well. The content I'd be writing about was interesting to me, they would be willing to let me work mostly from home, and I could still teach my mindfulness class once a week. It was a promising first meeting. I also entered into discussions with Erin's team at Google about an ongoing writing role for their division.

Now that I was inspired to pursue full-time work, I wanted to condense the Joy Plan into simple steps I could easily remember no matter how busy I got. Just like the muscles I'd developed from Pilates class, I didn't want my joy to atrophy if I was no longer making it my primary focus. I needed a daily exercise regimen for my joy muscle that would reinforce the new healthy habits I'd developed and the new neural networks I'd formed in my brain.

Even if I'd soon be waking up much earlier every morning to start work, I could still start my day with fifteen minutes of gratitude and breath, as well as my beloved papaya and kale. I could continue to give my attention to thoughts, images, news, conversations, and events that felt good through-out my day and turn down the volume on those that didn't. Of all the new habits I'd implemented in the last six months, the simple act of shifting my focus to things that feel good was really the crux of the Joy Plan.

In some ways, starting a new job would be a welcome challenge. My life had become quite routine. I was doing similar things each day, and although I wasn't bored, I also wasn't very challenged. Spicing things up would help keep my "joy radar" sharp. Studies have shown that people thrive when we have the right amount of stimulation.[1] Too much challenge in our lives feels like stress, which has negative implications both emotionally and physically. But too little challenge can be equally stressful. Eustress—the type of stress that feels motivating rather than daunting—is beneficial for our mental health and actually helps us achieve our goals. Perhaps a new job would bring me just the right amount of stress to stay on top of my game.

I would most likely be putting myself into a more social environment again and as such, needed to make sure I could continue to honor my introvert brain with time for solitude every day. Doing work that was primarily based on writing, rather than on the more outgoing activities of marketing and public relations that I had done previously, would help. If I commuted on a bus or train, I would cherish those hours to daydream, write for pleasure, or just zone out and mentally process my day. More social interactions could bring more potential opportunities for conflict, complaints, and challenges, but I felt excited about the opportunity to practice what I'd learned on the Joy Plan about letting go, handing it up, creating instead of complaining, and finding things to be grateful for. I was also looking forward to new friends and new experiences.

By now I was taking a variety of herbal supplements recommended by Susanna for my PMS, which had gotten much easier to manage. I was feeling more in sync and in love with Dan than I had in a long time, and I was excited about the possibilities that would open up for him once I was making more money. I marveled at how, only a few months previously, I would have considered taking a job in Silicon Valley (with its three- to four-hour round-trip commute) only as a last resort and certainly not as the path to my joy. But now I could see the path lighting up before me, and it pointed in the direction of least resistance. My attitude had changed, and the universe was responding with opportunities. Or perhaps the opportunities had been there all along, but I couldn't access them until my attitude shifted.

I also knew that this change might be really hard at times, and just like other life transitions I'd been through, my friends would have my back to help me through it. No matter how busy I got, I would gain strength from the monthly support haven of my women's circle. I thought about the benefits my kids would reap from spending more time with other positive adult influences—either Dan or a Mary Poppins clone that we would find for them once I was working more. It might take some adjusting, but they would be fine. And maybe it was time now for our family to get a new dog.

In an attempt to create something I could refer back to regularly to help keep me on track with the Joy Plan when I got busy, I wrote myself this list to hang next to my desk:

REMEMBER THESE THINGS

1. You are responsible for your own experience.
2. Start each day with gratitude.
3. Whenever possible, avoid or ignore anything that makes you feel bad.
4. Keep a mental portfolio of happy thoughts you can refer back to regularly.
5. Exercise until you sweat at least three times a week.
6. Look for opportunities to smile and laugh.
7. Walk outside, look around, and marvel at what a miracle it all is.
8. Indulge your five senses in some form of pleasure every day.
9. When in doubt, drink more water and eat more vegetables.
10. If you're having relationship troubles with Dan, have sex. Most of the time that will fix it.
11. Nothing is ever as big of a deal as you think it is.
12. Complaining about something is telling the universe you'd like a second helping, please.
13. You don't have to be defined or defeated by your hardships.
14. There's no such thing as failure, only research and plot twists.
15. When things are hard, remember you're on the verge of a breakthrough.

16. The key to success isn't intelligence or money; it's faith.

17. Parking spots and cookies are just as easy to manifest as dream jobs and financial abundance.

18. The universe has a creative way to fulfill all your desires beyond what you can imagine. Your fear and worry only get in the way.

19. Look for ways to say yes instead of no.

20. Always come back to gratitude.

The key to keeping my Joy Plan going as a lifestyle rather than as a project was to repeat these actions and thoughts every day until the habits were so ingrained that they became who I am. A habit is a behavior that's become automatic; this happens in the brain. It's possible to turn new behaviors into habits—but it takes time and repetition. In a study at University College London, researchers determined that, on average, a new behavior becomes automatic after repetition over the course of 66 days, although depending on the specific habit, person, and circumstances, it can range anywhere from 18 to 254 days.[2] I had been at it for about 180 days.

I would be turning forty soon, and that felt like a big deal. I saw this funny post on Facebook that totally resonated with me: "I'm almost forty but I still feel like I'm twenty…until I hang out with twenty-year-olds. Then I'm like, *No, nevermind, I'm forty.*" Some may interpret this to mean I don't have the energy or the body I did when I was twenty, but to me, this meant something else. I may not feel like a real grown-up yet, but I don't have the mind I had when I was twenty—thank goodness! I don't worry so much about what others are thinking about me because I realize they most likely aren't thinking about me at all. I don't worry so much about what I look like because I feel good in my skin. I've finally figured out which thoughts, activities, and people are worth giving my energy to and how to turn down the volume on everything else.

Only time would have gotten me here. Time and experience. As difficult as my hard times have been over the years, they have been my teachers and my triumphs, the stripes of honor I wear like the stretch marks from my pregnancies.

In a sense, the Joy Plan was keeping me young. I was making healthier choices for my body—including more exercise, vegetables, and sleep—and my stress level was much lower, which meant I also had lower levels of cortisol. I looked and felt younger and more energetic. But in another sense, the Joy Plan was helping me grow up. I was taking responsibility for my own thoughts, feelings, and experiences, and I was finally creating my own life rather than feeling like a victim to it.

Even though I had embarked on the Joy Plan at a crossroads in my life, I knew I was approaching it from a place of relative comfort and stability: I was in a loving relationship, and as much as he didn't like it, my husband did have a steady job. However, I wanted to be able to sustain the Joy Plan at all times, even under truly dire circumstances, should they ever arise. And I hoped to inspire others to do the same. I received a particularly moving letter from one of my blog readers and wondered if I could help her find her joy muscle, which was clearly weak at the moment:

Hi Kaia,

I always love reading your blog posts on mindbodygreen and really appreciate your insights. I know I'm emailing you out of the blue, but I'm wondering if you could give me some advice, because I'm really struggling in my life right now. You probably get emails like this all the time, but I'd be so grateful if you took the time to answer mine.

I'm thirty-six, married, and I'm a teacher in Sacramento. I have a good relationship with my family, great friends, and a nice home. On the outside, I look like everything is fine, but on the inside, I'm miserable. My husband and I have been trying to get pregnant for four years and have been through three rounds of unsuccessful fertility treatments. Recently, I've put on a lot of weight, and now the clinic won't do another round of treatment until I lose weight.

I feel like my thoughts are suffocating me. It's hard to explain all of the things that make me feel so bad, so I've been writing my negative thoughts down lately to try and get to the bottom of it. I used to be such a positive person. I was filled with hope for my future. I had dreams and goals, but now I don't. I've lost my hope and my sparkle, because I feel like I'm too old now to make any changes in my life. I compare myself to people younger than me who already have children, and I wish I hadn't wasted so much time. I'm overwhelmed with sadness and fear. There's this voice in my head that's full of regret and never lets me relax. It tells me I'm too old to have plans and dreams because I waited too long and now it's too late.

I want to stop feeling like this, but I don't know how. It's like I'm frozen. I start feeling a little bit better and having positive thoughts, but they just fizzle out. It's not just the infertility that's got me down, it's my whole life. Do you have any suggestions? Your thoughts and advice would really mean a lot to me.

Thank you,
Lauren

Oh, sweet Lauren. I knew how she felt. She was trapped in the quagmire of doubt, pulling her down like quicksand. Doubt is an insidious mental process, strengthened every time it's entertained. And there are so very many things to doubt. Your abilities. Your health. The future. Your spouse. Doctors. The government. Just to name a few. When you want something and then doubt you can have it, your brain is confused. Should it focus on a solution or a problem? If the attention to doubt is stronger than the attention to the solution, your brain will go there, and that thought pathway will be strengthened.

When we want things so badly that the lack of having them is felt more strongly than the joy they will bring, our focus on lack prevents what we want from coming to us. We want that dream job, true love, healthy body, 2.5 children, beautiful home, book publishing deal, and we wait for the phone to ring with the news that our dreams have come true. But our doubt and fear block the signal and stop the phone from ringing. The thoughts of doubt we play on repeat keep our brains stuck in the same pattern, feeling the same feelings, and experiencing the same things in life.

I could tell that Lauren was stuck in doubt, and I hoped I could offer her a buoy to grab onto and pull herself out.

Dear Lauren,

I want to thank you for reaching out to me. That took courage, and I'm honored that you trust me with your story. I'd love to support you to turn this situation around, and I believe it could be really easy. If you think about it, the only things making you miserable are your own thoughts—and your thoughts are something you can change! You may not be able to change your weight or your pregnancy status immediately, but I would bet anything that if you start with changing your thoughts, the other things will follow suit.

Let's start with the inventory you took—jotting down your

negative thoughts to get to the bottom of your sadness and regret. Now that you've taken that inventory, it's time to stop. You'll probably find that there is no bottom, and bringing your attention to those thoughts will just perpetuate them and amplify the feelings you want to leave behind. So it's time to create some new thoughts. I suggest you take that list and burn it, and then start a new inventory. This new list is of all the things you enjoy and are grateful for, that make you smile, that bring you even brief moments of joy. Get a notebook to write these things in, and carry it around with you and write in it often. Make yourself do this. You can send me the list, if that will help you be accountable.

Next I would like to personally invite the bitch in your head to get out of town. She is not welcome anymore, and if I was there I would tell her this every time she sends you a thought of regret. Regret is a mental trap, because you can't go back in time and change the past. But what you can do is notice those thoughts of regret whenever they come and find a thought that feels better each time. This can be a thought about anything—a funny video, a beautiful painting, a soft, furry friend. Please do this, Lauren, because I'm not there to kick her ass, so you have to. The more frequently you find better-feeling thoughts, the quicker your brain will release its repetitive loop of regret and gravitate toward new thoughts.

Next, how about an art project, with glitter, to bring in some sparkle? Cut out pictures of all the things you want to manifest in your life and make a vision board—and sprinkle some glitter on it and on you. Look at it every day and find a way to believe that those things are coming to you! Pray, breathe, chant, sing, dance, sweat—and keep telling that bitch to shut up when she tells you that you are crazy. You must feel the joy of the things that you want in your life even before they come into your reality. You must have faith that they are on their way.

Another thing—no more of this "I'm too old" stuff. I saw a TEDx talk last week in Santa Cruz by an eighty-year-old man who was homeless and addicted to heroin most of his life. He started his music career at seventy and is now topping the blues charts. I've known women who've gotten pregnant at forty, fifty, and I even once met a woman who got pregnant at sixty! You are as old as you feel, and in my opinion thirty-six is just about perfect. You know by now what doesn't work for you, so you're at a perfect point in your life to focus on what does.

Please keep in touch, reach out anytime, and let me know how you're doing.

Love,

Kaia

I know joy can seem far-fetched and desperately out of reach when you're depressed, when it seems like you've made too many wrong choices to turn things around, and when you feel impossibly stuck. I've been there. But often we're too focused on our problems to realize the solution. And the energy of a problem is very different than the energy of a solution: one is fearful, while the other is hopeful. Taking the first step to turn this around is often the hardest part.

When I started the Joy Plan, my joy muscle was loose and flabby. I'd spent so much time feeling overwhelmed and stressed that I'd almost forgotten how to be any other way. And just like hitting the gym and working any muscle group, when I started the process, it hurt at first. It was confronting, awkward, and even boring at times. But eventually, through repetition and over time, my joy muscle got stronger, and it started to feel good—*really good*.

So how do you reach a goal in life, if you don't have it yet, without focusing on lack? You have to step into the uncomfortable feeling of change. Dr. Joe Dispenza, author of *You Are the Placebo*, says that change is physically uncomfortable for the brain, but we must move through that discomfort to reach the other side. He writes:

> The hardest part about choices is not making the same choices we made the day before... This new state of being is unfamiliar; it's unknown. It doesn't feel "normal." We don't feel like ourselves anymore—because we're not ourselves... As uncomfortable as that may be at first, that's the moment we know we've stepped into the river of change... Once we understand that crossing the river of change and feeling that discomfort is actually the biological, neurological, chemical, and even genetic death of the old self, we have power over change and can set our sights on the other side of the river.[3]

As uncomfortable as pain, sadness, anger, or fear are, they are powerful catalysts for change. The Chinese character for "crisis" is made up of two symbols, one that means "hidden danger" and another that means "hidden opportunity." Times of crisis open us up for new realizations. At these times, due to more pressing concerns that require our attention, our normal thought processes are interrupted, and we're able to have new insights more easily. That's why a breakthrough is often waiting on the other side of a breakdown.

Perhaps we have to get lost before we can find ourselves—or perhaps, as George Bernard Shaw is often quoted as saying, "Life isn't about finding yourself. Life is about creating yourself."

JOY PLAN TIP #15

The key to embracing the Joy Plan as a lifestyle rather than a temporary project is to have a daily regimen—just as you would to keep your muscles fit—that reinforces the healthy habits and neural networks you've formed. When things are hard, remember to reach for small moments of grace and beauty. The energy of a problem is fearful, while the energy of a solution is hopeful.

CHAPTER 16

JOY IS CONTAGIOUS

"The most powerful weapon on earth
is the human soul on fire."
—FERDINAND FOCH

Over the course of the past six months, I'd noticed that my Joy Plan was having an effect on others. And it wasn't always a positive effect.

I had gotten into the habit of wearing this fabulous trucker hat with a unicorn flying over a rainbow whenever I was feeling less buoyant than I wanted to. I also often sprinkled myself with glitter and wore extra-bright pink lipstick that I borrowed from my daughters in an attempt to make my insides match my outsides. I thought of these things as my counterbalance, like the process of what's known in physics as "harmonic motion." It was my attempt at using proportional force to push an object in motion (me) in the opposite direction.

Did this work? Yes, sometimes. Sort of. Look, I'm not a physicist. But it was worth a try. So was exercise and laughter and getting more sleep and eating more vegetables and having more sex and volunteering and lots of other things with a scientific basis for why they help create the conditions for joy. And I continued to try all of them. Because I am stubbornly persistent and I think joy is worth persisting for.

But I realized that many people—people who of course didn't know about my Joy Plan—saw me in my rainbow unicorn hat and glitter and just wanted to vomit from my apparent overabundance of happiness.

I'd been quietly making joy my top priority for a while, mostly keeping it to myself. But over time, I started to mention it more often in conversation with people beyond my close friends and family. And I was frequently perplexed by the reactions I got when I told people I was making a concerted effort to feel more joy. They usually responded in one of two ways: either pensively, like, "Yeah, I need to do something like that too, but I never have the time," or with clear discomfort in which they looked away and quickly changed the subject.

The second reaction was so puzzling to me that I asked Niko about it. "Is my joy offensive?" I asked. "Or do they think I'm crazy?"

"No," she said. "They're envious of you."

That took me completely by surprise. "Why would anyone be envious of me?" I asked her.

"Um, because you've got a great marriage, two beautiful kids, you live in a beach town, and you're gorgeous? Oh, and now you're going on about joy," she said. "It's kind of ridiculous. If I didn't love you so much, I'd be envious of you too."

Oh, I realized. They're thinking, *She's so happy she has to brag about it and wear a frickin' unicorn on her head.*

"But no one should envy me!" I protested. "My marriage is great now, but we've gone through some really hard times. My kids are beautiful, but they're completely exhausting. The beach town I live in is so expensive that we struggle financially. And underneath my clothes and makeup, I'm often having a psoriasis flare up," I told her. "My journey to joy has not been easy!

I grew up in poverty, I've suffered from anxiety and depression, and I still have lots of physical problems. Believe me, if people really knew me, they would not be envious of me."

I do get it. I used to be annoyed by really happy people too. Their sticky-sweet joy highlighted all the ways I was falling short. But when someone is envious of us, they're really giving us a compliment. As irritating as it can be to be around someone who is in a state of joy, it can also help us realize qualities we'd like to embrace in ourselves. I didn't want to hold back my expression of joy in order to prevent envy from others; I wanted to pull them into joy with me.

Thankfully, my joy wasn't annoying to everyone. Many times I could tell that my interactions with people were leaving them just a little bit happier than they'd been before. I was smiling more at strangers and cracking jokes more often. I was giving compliments frequently. Since I'd mostly stopped complaining, my conversations with clients, parents and teachers at school, and people at grocery store checkout counters were often pleasant. And those who were closest to me—my kids, my husband, my family, and my friends—were definitely catching the buzz from my joy.

The Institute of HeartMath has conducted research to measure the effect of people's emotional states on the heartbeat rhythms of those around them.[1] Studies show that our hearts emit an electromagnetic field that extends out several feet, encompassing other people when we interact with them in close proximity. And when this happens, our heartbeat patterns actually synchronize. Other people's bodies are literally enveloped by our emotions. Our behavior also gets inside their brains.[2] Thanks to mirror neurons and our natural tendency to imitate any movement that we see, when we register emotion in another person and mirror the subtle movements of his or her face, we perceive and then feel the same way that person is feeling.[3] We do this involuntarily.

As psychologist Chris Frith explains in his book *Making Up the Mind*, "When we interact with someone, we imitate them. We become more like them… Other people are very contagious, even if you just think about them. Your prejudices and your observations of their behavior automatically make you become, for a moment, more like the person you are interacting with."

Joy isn't only contagious for others but for our own selves as well. Once again, thanks to neuroplasticity, our brains actually change and grow in response to our thoughts and experiences. And since our brains are physiologically wired to bring us back to predisposed neural pathways, such as those formed by frequent happy thoughts and the emotion of joy, whenever we feel joy, we become primed for more.[4]

This whole thing had started with Niko giving me the idea to focus on my own joy for thirty days—and she had been watching in amazement as I actually did it, and kept doing it, for the next six months. My Joy Plan inspired her, and she had been taking a long, deep look inside for her own joy as well. She and her husband had been running a career college for the past five years; they'd helped hundreds of people turn their lives around, and it had been a fulfilling venture in many ways. But keeping the school afloat financially was incredibly stressful for both of them. They had moved to Southern California for the business, and Niko longed to be back in the San Francisco Bay Area. Although it was scary and she had no idea how it could happen, what Niko really wanted was to sell the school and do something completely different.

Niko had an idea that had been percolating in the back of her mind— an idea that she tried to suppress whenever it popped up, because it seemed unrealistic and even frivolous to her. But as she allowed her joy to come to the surface, Niko shared with me that what she secretly wanted was to become a fitness instructor. Not just any fitness instructor, but a motivational speaker who combined exercise with an inspirational message.

Niko's TEDx talk, "Meet Yourself: A User's Guide to Building Self-Esteem," is one of the best I've ever seen.[5] She's an incredibly uplifting and inspiring public speaker who's been hired to give keynote addresses from Silicon Valley to Tajikistan. She loved the spiritual spin classes that she'd attended, but thought it was a shame that the cost of thirty dollars per class made it prohibitive for most people to have easy access to them. Niko's vision was to combine heart-pumping exercise with a heart-opening, spirit-lifting message and to make it affordable and available to the masses.

Knowing that thoughts and experiences are strengthened when they're shared, Niko and I decided to schedule a weekly daydream session.[6] This was different from the planning sessions I would have held in the past, during which I would have obsessed over details and specifics in order to determine who, what, when, where, why, and how. But now I was undergoing a transition from planner to creator, and my focus as a creator was on only two of those components: what and why.

Sometimes the secret to success is actually thinking less. By busying my head so many times in the past with details and specifics, I had often lost sight of the reason for my plans in the first place: a positive outcome. So instead, in these daydream sessions with Niko, we just skipped straight to the outcome. What were our goals? What were our objectives? What were our dreams? We could be specific, as long we didn't veer off into ancillary questions that we couldn't answer. Thinking about "what" should feel dreamy, creative, full of possibility, and unencumbered by logistics. And thinking about "why" should feel exciting, inspiring, and meaningful.

On our weekly calls, each of us spent about ten minutes daydreaming out loud. We would basically jabber away about whatever we were dreaming up, with no boundaries or exclusions and no reality check or fear of judgment. We'd talk about our visions for the future, focusing only on the fun and exciting parts. Conversations that create a feeling of bonding release endorphins from the pleasure centers in the brain—and Niko and I would talk ourselves into a literal high.[7] It was totally okay for these daydream sessions to enter the realm of fantasy but not to enter the realm of problem solving. This was not the time to figure out "how" our visions would come to be, only to feel the excitement of them and to marinate in our own joy soup.

We described our daydreams until they were so real we felt like we could touch and smell and taste them. We created a positive emotional charge around our visions, which is felt more strongly in the brain than merely intellectual thoughts.[8] Positive emotional mental imagery—in this case, infused with excited anticipation—triggers our brains to release serotonin. And since Niko and I were testing the philosophy that our thoughts create our reality—and more specifically that our feelings about those thoughts create our reality—we used our daydream sessions to create happy thoughts that inspired joyful feelings and, we hoped, a joyful life.

Niko talked at length about her inspirational-fitness business idea. It was the culmination of her business acumen and her background in education design and empowering young women, combined with her obsession with fabulous dance music and her love of working out. By exposing people to a cocktail of exhilarating music, elevated heart rates, and short inspirational "sermons," Niko believed she could help people connect to their intuition, their passion, and their ability to go beyond their previously imagined limitations. When she talked about it, she lit up with electric excitement and energy unlike anything I'd seen in her before. This idea ignited her joy like a blazing fire. She also described the perfect buyer for their college: she envisioned a buyer who would care for the students and staff while making the transition easy on everyone. And when Niko envisioned this, she felt ease, comfort, and relief.

I spoke about my vision of being a writer and making an abundant living from doing work that I loved. I saw myself mainly living and working in Santa Cruz, but also having the financial prosperity and flexibility to allow our family to spend months at a time in other countries if we wanted to. I saw myself sitting at a comfortable desk in a beautiful place, with words flying through me onto the screen—and those words taking shape in ways that became an inspiration to others. This vision felt so good that I wanted to roll around in it, inhale it, swallow it, and shoot it into my veins.

Niko and I both lead busy lives, so when we couldn't talk, we would leave each other voice mails to cheer each other on. In my messages to her, I encouraged her to keep imagining the process of selling the college and starting her new business to be easy, fun, and financially abundant. In Niko's messages to me, she spoke to me as if I were already a published author, wildly successful and reaping the financial benefits of my work. And after listening to her inspiring messages, I felt so good that I no longer cared if I would ever be an author or not.

I tried recording myself daydreaming out loud so I could play it back whenever I needed a boost, but it wasn't quite the same. There was something intangibly powerful about sharing my vision with Niko and also being privy to hers.

All this daydreaming reminded me of a long-past memory of being perched high in a tree as a little girl, giggling with my neighbor Dulcie about the lives we would live when we were grown-ups. Dulcie and I spent countless afternoons playing in the magnificent oak tree in her backyard and pretending it was our New York City penthouse apartment. We were twin-sister model-actresses named Tammy and Sammy, who married twin brothers who were firefighters and also models. We got very specific with the details in our imaginary game—describing the outfits we would wear, the pets we would have, the cars we would drive, and the food we would eat. This game was pure imagination and joy, and it provided hours of fun.

These memories made me think about the power of daydreams. Who says we have to stop daydreaming and live in the "real world"? What if our daydreams can actually *create* the world we're living in? Albert Einstein called imagination "the preview of life's coming attractions."

Dulcie and I never did live in New York City, but we did both marry gorgeous men who—although they aren't twins or firefighters—are quite similar and quite capable of putting out a fire, should the need arise. And we did briefly model for my mom's local clothing and jewelry line when we were teenagers. We also did eventually live together in a penthouse of sorts: a multistory home in Bali that we shared for a time when Dulcie and her family joined our family for a semester at the school where Dan and I worked.

Who can say what power our daydreams might wield? Those afternoons in that tree are some of the happiest memories of my childhood— and probably the last time I daydreamed out loud with a friend until these sessions with Niko, more than thirty years later.

Although it seems counterintuitive, daydreaming has a surprising effect on focus, actually contributing to our ability to complete tasks. Scientists have found that daydreams, defined as "spontaneous, self-directed thoughts and associations," activate many areas of the brain at once while stimulating increased creativity, cognitive capacity, and improved mood.[9] Research shows that daydreaming ultimately boosts success in goal-oriented tasks by encouraging the brain to solve problems in new and creative ways.[10] Essentially, as the mind wanders, the brain is trained to stay on task by increasing, rather than decreasing, attention.[11] Yes, daydreaming can help your brain multitask.

Just to dip a toe into her fitness instructor fantasy, Niko answered an ad for a spin instructor at a local studio. They responded to her email right away, and after teaching one test class, Niko was offered the opportunity to teach as many classes as she could fit into her schedule. She now had the perfect test ground to conduct market research for her concept. All it took was one email. I told Niko she was the poster child for manifestation. "This shit works," she replied. Feel good, and good things will happen.

When you find joy where you are in your life, your life changes to match your joy. Sounds simple, right? But what about when you feel good, and yet good things aren't happening or—even worse—bad things happen? Well, therein lies the rub. When you truly tap into joy, your perception changes. When you become so practiced at feeling good, thinking positive thoughts, choosing an optimistic perspective, and seeing the silver lining, even your experience of "bad things" changes. You find the good within the bad. You change the conversation in your head. Solutions come to you more easily. *This shit really does work.*

But don't take my word for it! Try it for thirty days and see for yourself. In fact, what if more and more people starting doing this? What if we started a full-on joy movement?

There was a time when vegetarians were a strange phenomenon, treated like aliens every time we ate out (trust me, I grew up vegetarian in the Deep South during that time). But now it's not only commonplace, but often cool, to go veg.

What if it could be the same with joy? What if being on the Joy Plan became the new, cool healthy lifestyle? What if more of us chose thoughts and words that felt good, spent time outside, made love, and daydreamed more often? Could we start a movement in which people start their days with gratitude, create instead of complain, and laugh instead of fight? Could our joy spread across the planet and awaken something in people that they've forgotten? Something that they're ready to remember? Could we transform the world? Could we tip the balance from doomsday to inspired possibility and create new innovations born out of people's hope and positivity? Could we shift the planet into a new era of peace? I know it sounds grandiose, but this is a daydream I want to marinate in forever.

JOY PLAN TIP #16

Numerous studies demonstrate a correlation between visualizing a successful outcome and actually achieving it. Daydreaming activates regions in the brain that stimulate the realization of creative solutions. You don't need to figure out "how" your visions will come to be; simply feel the excitement of them, and marinate in your own joy soup. What innovations and discoveries could you conjure from the creative recesses of your mind? Give yourself permission to daydream each day, and you may be pleasantly surprised to find out.

CHAPTER 17

THE JOURNEY
THAT COUNTS

"The journey is the reward."

—*TAO TE CHING*

As impassioned as I was about the Joy Plan as a movement, when I first thought about promoting this idea, I panicked. Change your life through joy? What a cliché, a subject that has been covered by so many authorities, who are much more brilliant and eloquent than I am.

As I was fighting this barrage of self-doubt, a quote popped up on my Facebook feed right when I needed it most—ironically by a talented author that I had been denigrating myself by comparing my writing to hers: "The point is not for you to do something that's never been done before. The point is for you to do something you've never done before." Thank you, Elizabeth Gilbert.

Even after six months on the Joy Plan, when I should have known better, I still doubted myself. But the Joy Plan isn't about forgetting and denying all negative thoughts, pain, anger, and aspects of myself that are less than joyful—those are real and can't be denied. I'll never reach a point where I have positive thoughts 100 percent of the time. What I'd learned on the Joy Plan was to embrace all that I've experienced, and all that I am—my darkness and my light—and to make a choice.

My true self, when it isn't clouded by the mask of my persona, is the light. And although I will forget this and doubt it and get lost in my own stories about personal tragedies and failures, although I will lose sight of my true self over and over, I will do my best to remember again—and to choose joy. Pain will happen—it's part of being human—but joy is always an option. Our hard times don't have to defeat us or define us by playing out time and time again in the form of recurrent problems in our lives. Instead, they can be the springboards to our growth, our opportunities to bless our imperfections for all that they've taught us—and then to move on, ever forward, ever upward, and ever inward.

I could escape into an introvert's paradise—quiet, peaceful, alone—and write all day long. But what would I write about after a while? Life brings me experiences, and with those experiences come challenges, and together those experiences and challenges become my story.

Why do even the most enlightened people we know still have problems? I often see successful people whom I admire greatly deal with blockages in one area or another of their lives. Do our struggles serve a purpose? Dr. Garoli, author of *The Evolutionary Glitch*, once told me that the word "boredom" should be "bore*doom*," because a lot of the destruction people create in their own lives—without recognizing it—is simply done out of boredom. Coasting along challenge free, with everything handed to us on a silver platter, is boring. Some people even turn to dangerous behavior in order to find the challenges and extreme experiences they aren't finding in their regular lives. But I believe it's possible to strike a balance between strife and boredom. Within that balance, the pursuit of new goals, dreams, and plans resides.

Our greatest gift in this world is choice. If you ever saw the film *Life Is Beautiful* or read Viktor Frankl's remarkable book *Man's Search for Meaning*, you know that it's possible, even in the most horrific conditions, to choose a positive attitude.[1] It may not be easy at first, but the more frequently we choose joy, the easier it becomes. It's often as simple as noticing when we have a negative thought and finding another, more positive thought to replace it with.

I'd developed quite a stockpile of happy thoughts to refer to as needed: funny memories, sexy images, things I'm excited about. We can also choose to notice something lovely in our surroundings. No matter where we are, there's bound to be something extraordinary in our environment that we can focus on. Even the miraculous electricity and complex wiring of a fluorescent light is beautiful, if we look at it from that perspective. Another option that's always available to us is to hone in on a sensation in our bodies, such as our breath, our skin, our muscles, or our heartbeats. In doing this, we can take our attention off whatever is unpleasant and find either a neutral or a positive feeling instead. This is possible for all of us in every moment.

Just like Newton's third law of motion, whatever you push against pushes back against you; what you resist persists. The more you curse something, the stronger it becomes. And the more you praise something, the stronger it becomes as well. This is the Law of Attraction: what you think, you become. However, often what we're thinking isn't what we'd like to become at all.

Our brains have developed programming designed to keep us safe from rejection and emotional pain, and yet that persona often governs much of our thoughts, words, and actions, even when there is no actual threat present in our lives. But when we recognize this mental trap for what it is—a defense mechanism that's not who we really are—we can reprogram our inner commentary and calm our reactionary brain response. We can choose to accept our unwanted experiences and see them from a new perspective; that's when transformation takes place.

When we find joy in spite of the conditions we're currently experiencing, those conditions morph to match our joy. By intentionally practicing thinking new thoughts, we can create new patterns in our brains, which ultimately translate into a new experience of life.

Albert Einstein said, "The world as we have created it is a process of our thinking. It cannot be changed without changing our thinking." He also explained, when describing his famous equation $E=mc^2$, that "Mass and energy are both but different manifestations of the same thing—a somewhat unfamiliar conception for the average mind." So if thoughts create our world and energy is just as real as mass, we can utilize the energy of our thoughts to create tangible results in life. This is not just philosophy; this is physics.

Quantum physics has proven that, at the subatomic level, all matter is made of energy and our thoughts influence the behavior of that energy.[2] Scientists have found in study after study that our observations of reality alter the reality we observe. In fact, quantum physicists claim it is the very act of observing reality that creates it in the first place.[3] Essentially, our thoughts shift subatomic particles and create our physical world.

Don't you love knowing this? We can use the practicality of physics to create joy that is ridiculous, joy that isn't reliant on external situations but that influences those external situations to match it. "That's not how things work in the *real world*," I hear my critics say. But how do you know? Just because we've been told we're victims of circumstance doesn't mean it's true. I believe our expectation and desire create the reality we experience—the real world as we know it. And I have tested this hypothesis and proven it in my own life.

If I can do it, I believe anyone can do it—and not because I was destitute or worse off than others. We can be in a state of acute stress even when we aren't in immediate danger, and not long ago, I had been in such a state of acute stress that I couldn't see beyond my failure to any new possibilities for my future. I could barely get out of bed. By taking small steps to change my very negative state of mind, I created a radical shift in my emotional experience and—very quickly—a significant change in my reality. This happened within thirty days, and the positive effects continued to build for the next several months.

Just like any repetitive action, our emotional state becomes a habit. Mine had become fear—perhaps its milder version, worry or anxiety—but essentially it was fear. And I was so practiced at it, I lived in it almost all the time. However, I wanted to change my emotional habit to joy. If joy became my default condition, my brain would be predisposed to go back to joy-related neural patterns, my limbic system would be primed for a joyful emotional state, and I'd return there more easily and frequently, even when times were tough in my life.

Was this just a matter of anatomy? Was the Joy Plan tapping into a purely physical mechanism, hacking into my own emotional system? (Is *joy hacking* a thing?) By activating my parasympathetic nervous system and reducing my stress, my amygdala was calm and my prefrontal cortex was open and available to do my best thinking, my best problem solving, and my best creating.

But how does that explain the seemingly miraculous coincidences that were happening in my life, like running into my old boss in the grocery store and having him offer me a consulting job? Perhaps coincidences like that were happening all the time and I just didn't notice them because I was too jacked up on stress and cortisol. As the ancient saying goes, "We don't see things as they are; we see them as we are." Had I simply dissipated my negativity enough so that I could see a natural shift take place that would have happened anyway? Or by accessing my joy, was I indeed tapping into a higher power? I mean, who created me with this cool brain anyway? Maybe I only needed to remove my magic-blocking fear and let the Universe/God/Source/Great Spirit do its thing.

The truth is, I don't know why this stuff works. But I can tell you unequivocally that it does. Because it's counterintuitive to how so many of us live our lives, it can seem like magic. But maybe it's not magic at all; maybe it's just chemistry. In the end, how it worked in my case didn't matter. It did work, and I was eternally grateful.

That said, the Joy Plan wasn't a quick fix that was complete after thirty days. I had to keep it up as a lifestyle if I didn't want to fall back into old habits.

In early May, Niko came to spend a weekend with me in Santa Cruz. I took her to a guided meditation at one of my favorite places on the planet, the Land of the Medicine Buddha, a Buddhist retreat center nestled among hundreds of acres of redwood forest and hiking trails. There, in the middle of the forest, an ornate temple houses a gigantic golden Buddha. Guided meditations are offered multiple times a week in this aptly named sanctuary, the Wish Fulfilling Temple.

The hiking trails at the Land of the Medicine Buddha are free and open to the public, as long as hikers respect the retreat center's guidelines. Signs posted at the trailheads read: Be Kind to Others, No Killing (even insects), No Stealing, No Lying, No Sexual Misconduct, and No Use of Intoxicants. As we got situated in our seats and prepared for the meditation, there were several mosquitoes buzzing around us inside the temple. When I raised my hand to swat at them, Niko gently touched my shoulder and reminded me of the rules: "Not even insects," she whispered.

As we sat in silence, I closed my eyes and focused on my breath, using the mindfulness exercises I taught at my daughters' school. I put my hand on my heart and felt its slow, steady beat. I turned my thoughts into bubbles as they rushed into my mind and imagined them floating away. Fewer and fewer thoughts came. I heard my breath—deep, slow, reassuring. I knew that in this moment I was alive. *I am alive.* The mantra came to me and I repeated it with each breath.

I am alive. I am alive. I am alive. There's nothing that I have to do in this moment. My body breathes on its own. My heart doesn't need a reminder to beat. It is truly a miracle. I am alive! I get to be here, in this body, on this playground planet, with all these other people who are living miracles too. I am alive. What a blessing. What a gift.

I felt the presence of my spirit, temporarily visiting this body and yet so much bigger than its confines. I felt such peace, such stillness, and such calm that I even felt love and compassion for the mosquitoes buzzing around me in the temple.

A vivid vision came to me of a fast-moving river of colorful energy, and when I looked into it, I could see that it contained everything I had ever wanted. I saw myself standing on the outside of the river of energy gazing in, wondering how I could ever get what I wanted out. Suddenly, I realized that all I had to do was jump in, and the river would carry me right where I wanted to go. But I had to take a leap of faith.

Okay, Universe/God/Source/Great Spirit, I thought, *you've really got this?*

And I heard a voice answer me: *Don't worry about how you will get there, Kaia. Don't obsess about the money or how any of the details will work out—just focus on your inspiration. There is incredible momentum waiting to carry you to all your wildest dreams, whenever you're ready. This river is always flowing and available to you, all you have to do is jump in and let go, trusting that I've got your back. Trusting that all will unfold perfectly for you and I will always catch you. You don't have to plan it all out, you just have to feel good and have faith.*

As I came out of this meditation, I was left with the thought that every future I could possibly dream up already exists, because my desire has created it. And the river of energy I saw in my vision is always flowing toward my own dreams for the future, ready and available to take me there. But the future is never actually reached. There's no need to wait for a happy ending, because each moment is an ending and an opportunity to choose joy.

I was twenty-five years old when a fellow traveler handed me a copy of *The Power of Now* by Eckhart Tolle on a train somewhere in Europe, but I wasn't yet ready for its message.[4] I read some of it and then passed it on to another traveler, not really seeing what all the buzz was about. It seemed to me, at the time, to be a book about nothing. But I missed the point. That nothingness is everything. I'm only now, fifteen years later, starting to understand the power of the present moment.

Like many people, I've spent most of my life either thinking about (or usually worrying about) the future or remembering things from the past. The present seemed irrelevant, fleeting, not nearly as important as the future I was heading toward. But I'm finally getting it: THERE IS NO FUTURE. All that ever exists is this present moment, and each one of those moments creates my life. What would happen if instead of worrying about the future, I cared only about making the most of my current moment? Would each moment then unfold to be more glorious than the last? What if I viewed the present as a *present*—to be cherished, relished, and appreciated, rather than barely noticed while my thoughts are elsewhere? I could have a happy ending now. And now. And now. And every single moment. Because each moment ends. And those moments become our lives. We might as well enjoy them.

The Joy Plan is my life story as it unfolded over six months—a fantastic and epic adventure, although I didn't travel to an exotic country or even interact with that many people. Most of the story transpired in my mind. In my adventure, I was on a quest, a quest to find joy—something I thought I had lost, or perhaps never had. It was like a pilgrimage to find my home. But in the end, I realized that I had been home all along. Joy was always inside me, because joy is my natural state of being—when I remember to look within for it. My story was never about reaching my destination, because I never left in the first place. Joy—and love—is who I am. It's who we all are at our core.

We often see our hard times as blessings only in hindsight. I have been miserable, self-loathing, and hopeless, but I know it's possible to go from a low place to a high place, if I can only remember how. And I know I'll need to remember often, because life rarely sails along calmly and smoothly for very long. Experiencing and overcoming challenges is an essential part of the human experience; many spiritual teachers say that's why we are here. Through challenges, we become clearer about the lives we want and learn how to create them. Hard times help us grow up, grow in, and become who we came here to be. As painful as this process is at times, it's like birth: there's a sweet reward at the end. We are, in a sense, giving birth to ourselves.

So when life rocks my boat again, I'll do my best to return to the simple steps that I know can bring me back to joy. I'll reach for small moments of grace and beauty—a lovely sunset, my favorite music, a hot bath, a nourishing meal, a funny joke with a friend—and reconnect with my true self, which is pure, unconditional love. *Unconditional love* means love and joy despite any external conditions I'm currently experiencing. This is my life's work, and if I never had hard times, I wouldn't have an opportunity to practice it.

Living happily ever after is not how my story ends. In the end, the point is not to be happy all the time but to always be able to tap into the well of joy within. Ups and downs are the juice of life. Without the lows, we'd never appreciate the highs. Even though I'd heard it plenty of times before, I finally understand it: it's the journey that counts, not the destination. If we never feel sadness, anger, fear, worry, or any host of other negative emotions, we won't recognize joy when we feel it. The juiciest pleasure comes from making the turnaround—standing at the edge of despair or rage or dread, stopping yourself in your tracks, and choosing another path.

Everyone who has climbed a mountain, run a marathon, given birth, gone through a painful breakup, suffered an injury, fought illness, or experienced a loss knows the exhilaration that comes from surviving a massive challenge—either physically or emotionally. Survival in the face of adversity has been the inspiration for countless works of art, songs, and stories of empowerment; going into and through my own pain and coming out the other side a survivor was the same for me. I know this can be difficult to believe when you're in the midst of a crisis. Trust me, I've been there. But from my current vantage point, in a moment of grace, I see all that I've survived—whether it was divinely ordained or self-inflicted—as rich, fertile experience that has created who I am now. And I wouldn't change a thing.

Transformation doesn't come from the light; it comes from moving through the darkness.

JOY PLAN TIP #17

The more you practice showing up in joy, the easier it becomes. It's often as simple as noticing when you have a negative thought and switching to another, more positive thought or honing in on a sensation in your body. In doing this, you can shift your attention from whatever was unpleasant to either a neutral or positive feeling instead. When you find joy in spite of the conditions you are currently experiencing, those conditions will morph to match your joy.

AFTERWORD

When this story started, I was in a very low place. I measured my self-worth by dollar signs and outward recognition, and when I saw neither, I deemed myself a failure. I was miserable pretty much all the time.

Fast forward to now, and my life has changed completely. I wrote this book and started a blog about joy, immersing myself in a subject that's very close to my heart, a subject I would venture to say is very close to the heart of all of humanity. I let go of planning what would happen next in my life (that wasn't working out so well anyway) and simply focused on feeling good. Was I impatient to move on? Absolutely. But I allowed my impatience to take a backseat to my enjoyment of the moment, a shift I'd never been able to make before. And the results were better than anything I could have planned.

Today, I'm a mindfulness teacher to elementary school students, a privilege that opens my heart and expands my faith in the future every day. I also get paid to write, something I'd done for pleasure since I was five years old but never realized could be my livelihood. Not every opportunity that presented itself since I started the Joy Plan ended up panning out, but I've learned to enjoy the process, not just the grand finale. Most importantly, I've learned how to quiet the incessant nagging of the bitch in my head. I'm not going to lie, this still doesn't always come easily for me. But the more I practice, the more I'm training my brain to chill out.

When I get impatient, I want what I want and I want it NOW. When my bank account balance isn't as high as I want it to be, I want more money *immediately*. When I'm sick, I *desperately* want to be healthy. When I'm confused about what to do next, I *achingly* long for clarity. When I'm in the midst of any struggle, I just want it OVER so I can move on. But I'm doing my best to think of my impatience as that annoying person who talks loudly in the movie theater while I'm trying to enjoy the show. When it pipes up, I tell it, "Hey, I'm experiencing my life unfolding magically right now. Do you mind keeping it down?"

When I look back at my journey, as hard as it's been at times, I'm grateful for all of it. If I'd snapped my fingers and jumped forward in time to where I am now, I would have missed out on important lessons and growth along the way. Life isn't a race to get through as fast as possible, it's a journey to be experienced fully and languidly—with all its ups, downs, messiness, and downright scary shit. All of it is valuable. All of it makes us who we are. Experiencing what we don't want helps us become even clearer about what we do want.

Even though I'm no longer clueless about all this, I'm not yet wise. As easy as it may be for me to say "just stay in joy," it's not always easy to do. Several months after I started my Joy Plan, my husband Dan launched a Joy Plan of his own, with the goal of making a transition into a new career that he could feel excited about. He exercised more, cleaned up his diet, kept a gratitude journal, and made a concerted effort to change his thought processes. He even tried meditation.

One day, Dan came home from work with an ecstatic look on his face. "I have great news!" he exclaimed. "The whole department is being shut down, and we've all been laid off!" *Gulp. This was great news?* My fear about money kicked in almost immediately.

But for Dan, this was a dream scenario: his layoff came with five months of severance pay. Suddenly, Dan was a free man. He filled his days with volleyball and surfing, grew a beard, and lost fifteen pounds. He looked ten years younger and was happier than he'd been in years. Amazing, right?

Well, it was amazing until I started worrying that Dan might never work again. I mean, he was really enjoying "funemployment" and showed no signs of looking for new work. And as much as I know better, I had moments of panic. What if Dan's Joy Plan kept him in this life of leisure forever? How would we pay our bills once his severance package ended?

However, I did have some reassurance from the universe. In the very same week that Dan got laid off, I landed a huge freelance writing gig. While Dan became more and more joyful as each month of his unemployment went by, I made my highest earnings ever, month after month. I worked more, and Dan had more free time to spend with the kids. We both liked this new arrangement. I wanted to let go of all my fear and just believe that this would continue, but I still had doubt. My anxiety was back and kicking my ass again.

During this time, Niko told me a story about a day she was sitting on an empty beach writing in her journal. An old woman approached her out of the blue and said, "You have to hand your worries over to God. If you let God hold you and your troubles, he will take care of everything. But you have to believe." Niko looked down at the words she had just written in her journal, stunned: *Source, I will let you hold this and I will let it go.* Had she just been visited by an angel?

Shortly after Niko told me this story, I called her in a state of anxious worry one night. "I don't know if Dan is ever going to work again," I said, "How can I let go of my fear about this? I just need an angel to come visit me on the beach and tell me to hand it all over to God." I slept fitfully that night and got up at dawn to quietly slip away and watch the sunrise. I drove to my favorite beach in Santa Cruz, and as soon as I got out of my car, I saw the most miraculous sign from God I had ever seen.

Three gigantic gray whales were feeding in the breaking waves, only forty feet from the shore. They were about twenty feet long each, and I waded into the ocean to be closer to them. I could feel their spray on my face as the majestic whales dove, splashed, and fed right next to me for forty-five minutes. Each time a wave crashed over their backs, the sunlight filtered through the ocean spray and formed a rainbow over the whales. The message could not have been any clearer. The angel I asked for had showed up in style.

I took the sign to heart. Dan was joyful, I was doing work that I loved and could do from anywhere, and we had a tremendous list of things to be grateful for. I let go of worry and focused on enjoying the life we had.

Just like each of us experiences joy in a different way, each person's Joy Plan will unfold differently. And if there's a larger force at work—a greater power that knows the bigger picture even when we don't—we may not understand the timing of things. Dan's Joy Plan didn't lead him in a beeline to a new career in thirty days. But he's making decisions based on what feels good, he's forging a new path that inspires him in a way I've never seen before, and doors are opening for him. While he creates his next chapter, his joy is palpable.

Our story didn't get tied up in a neat little bow and stamped with *happily ever after*, but that's not the point. The goal of the Joy Plan isn't to arrive at an ending—it's to constantly welcome a new beginning. And if we can keep the faith, *this shit works*.

Many people subscribe to the idea that we have to work hard to achieve our goals. I used to think so too. But I see "hard work" differently now; it all depends on how it feels to you. For example, let's say you're launching a new business and you want to attract customers. If in-person networking—doing things like having frequent professional coffee dates and attending conferences—is fun for you, then by all means, go for it, and it will most certainly drum up new business. But if you feel like you're forcing yourself to do those activities and you're wishing you were curled up in bed with a good book the whole time you're out networking, then you might as well stay home and curl up with a good book—as long as you're doing that with joy (rather than feeling guilty for not pounding the pavement). While you're curled up in bed, you'll probably read something that provides a new insight for your business that you wouldn't have come across otherwise. And that insight will most likely lead you to the right people in ways that do feel joyful to you.

Of course, action is always required to turn concepts into reality, but action doesn't have to feel like hard work. In fact, if you're following bursts of inspiration and taking quick, deliberate action when those bursts come, even though you're exerting effort, it can almost feel effortless.

So if you're thinking about starting a Joy Plan of your own, be patient with yourself. Take a deep breath. Slow down. Sometimes you will feel lost, stuck, or worse, and you really won't know what to do. In those times, it's best just to do something that feels good. Take a bath, go for a run, pet a furry friend, put on some uplifting music and dance around in your underwear. Whatever it takes. At other times, there are logical steps you can take to help alleviate the situation you're in. Take them, and pat yourself on the back for moving forward.

When you let go of control—even a bit—and let your life reveal the plan to you, signs will start to appear. They might be subtle, like running into an old friend, seeing a quote that catches your eye on Facebook, or having an idea pop into your head—these are life sending you clues. And like a detective, your job is to follow those clues and see where they lead. A chance conversation could result in a dream job offer. A craving for coffee could lead you to meet your future husband in the coffee shop. You get the idea. Pay attention and follow the signs, with faith that they won't steer you in the wrong direction.

When you have a sudden burst of inspiration to take some specific action, listen to it. It will feel compelling, even if it doesn't always make sense. When that flash comes to you, don't wait, don't second guess yourself. Take the impulse and run with it—and trust that it's leading you somewhere exciting. And lastly, dear readers, please play this on repeat in your head until you believe it: *Everything is unfolding perfectly for me. I trust that life has my back.*

You've got this.

With immense gratitude and **JOY**,

APPENDIX:
CREATE YOUR
OWN JOY PLAN

I took on the Joy Plan as a one-month experiment but quickly realized it was so much more than that. The Joy Plan wasn't going to change my life after thirty days if I simply slipped back into my old habits of negative thoughts, complaining, and rampant self-doubt. However, those thirty days did provide the foundation I needed to continue building joy. The Joy Plan is a lifestyle, and the key to living life on the Joy Plan is consistency. It takes practice and repetition; that repetition becomes new habits of thought, feelings, behavior, and ultimately—our experience of life.

The Joy Plan is my personal story—my book-length sticky note to refer back to when I face hard times again, which I undoubtedly will. But I didn't just write this book for myself. I faced being exposed and vulnerable in order to share my story with you because I hope it will inspire you to create your own Joy Plan too. The quest for joy is universal. Experiencing joy—lasting contentment that permeates your being regardless of the conditions that surround you—is universally possible, even if it seems elusive at times. It just takes dedication and practice. These exercises are designed to help you accomplish that goal.

You can perform these exercises by yourself or in a group. In a group setting, work one-on-one with a partner when appropriate, then come back into the larger group and share your experiences.

EXERCISE #1

FIND YOUR RESONANT WAVE

In chapter 2, I mention eight resonant wave patterns from Dr. Albert Garoli's book, *The Evolutionary Glitch*. According to Dr. Garoli's brain research, there are eight distinct resonant wave patterns, and each person has one that is primary. Finding your resonant wave could help you choose activities that are more likely to bring you joy. Your body emits physical vibrations, called thermal noise, which help point to your natural resonances.[1]

Read through the following resonant wave pattern descriptions and see if you have an "aha moment," indicating that you've found your match:

1. **The Soothing Wave**

    This resonates with you if you love to help others relax, recover, and recuperate, or if you feel fulfilled when you can nurture, look after, comfort, and care for others.

2. **The Impacting Wave**

    This resonates with you if you are happy and energized by being physically active and helping to motivate others by pushing them to be stronger, fitter, and to overcome their problems.

3. **The Synchronizing Wave**

    This resonates with you if you feel invigorated by helping others find solutions, serenity, and peace by using your intuition and insight.

4. **The Standing Wave**

    This resonates with you if you feel satisfied when you are maintaining structures or assets, providing funding or resources for good projects, and if you enjoy helping to create stability for others.

5. **The Rising Wave**

This resonates with you if you find joy in helping others through education, self-improvement, discipline, organization, and achievement.

6. **The Expanding Wave**

This resonates with you if you thrive in social environments and love to bring people together, publicize information, organize meetings or gatherings, and get satisfaction from other people's pleasure.

7. **The Yielding Wave**

This resonates with you if find gratification in knowledge acquisition, multitasking, research, developing a deeper understanding of life, and using your problem-solving skills to find resolution and balance for others.

8. **The Intensifying Wave**

This resonates with you if you are driven to construct, invent, and create new innovations and discoveries, or if you enjoy leading others in an inspiring push forward.

You've probably heard "follow your passion" or "follow your bliss" a million times, but finding your resonant wave may not feel like a burning passion or ecstatic bliss. It may simply feel like noticing what you naturally gravitate toward. The key to figuring out which wave you resonate with (without complex brain-measuring equipment) is to notice when you feel comfortable, excited, or at ease. That means you're in the right place at the right time with the right people. Pay attention to your feelings, reactions, and preferences when different events and circumstances occur in your life, and tune into the wave that excites and inspires you.

EXERCISE #2

START (AND STICK WITH!) A GRATITUDE PRACTICE

My regular gratitude practice is an essential component in my ongoing Joy Plan. But it took dedication to get started and even more dedication to stick with it. Take these steps and you'll be cultivating an attitude of gratitude daily before you know it.

1. **Commit.**

   Promise yourself that you'll take on a gratitude practice for one full month. If you don't see the benefits of this exercise after thirty days, you can stop. But give the practice a full month to work its magic. I believe you'll see more benefits in your life than you can currently imagine, but first you have to COMMIT.

2. **Designate a notebook.**

   Are you the type of person who is more likely to write in a gratitude notebook if it's fancy and pretty, or would a fancy notebook inhibit you because you don't want to mess it up? Would you rather use a notebook from the dollar store? Decide which type of notebook suits you best, buy it, and carry it with you at all times.

3. **Write it down.**

   Every time you think of something you're grateful for, write it down. You will likely find yourself writing the same things over and over again. That's fine. Write about your loved ones, your surroundings, your body, your work, and your passions. And whenever you're frustrated, sad, fearful, or angry about something or someone, write about that too. But only list the aspects you're grateful for: the lessons you're learning, the strength you're gaining, the opportunities you trust are right around the corner. Write in list form, write in story form, write in shorthand, or even draw pictures. No one else will see this notebook but you, so you don't have to worry about impressing anyone. But you do have to write in it. A lot.

4. **Use technology to back you up.**

If you'd rather type than write in a notebook, there are various gratitude apps available that you may want to investigate. You can also keep a virtual notebook on your phone, tablet, or computer, if you'd prefer to go paperless.

5. **Set aside time every day.**

Sometimes writing in a notebook throughout the day just isn't possible. If this is the case for you, set aside five to fifteen minutes at the same time every day, such as first thing in the morning or right before bed, for your gratitude writing. Put this time on your calendar if you need to, and covet it as sacred. Don't let anything stop you from having your gratitude time.

6. **Repeat, repeat, repeat.**

Feelings of gratitude have been shown to release dopamine, a neurotransmitter in the brain that induces feelings of reward and satisfaction. This happens because when you think of what you're grateful for, the brain registers it as something you've earned and sends you a hit of dopamine for doing a good job. Each time you write in your gratitude notebook and focus on the things you're grateful for, your brain will activate the neural networks associated with the subjects you're focusing on and strengthen the neural pathways that predispose your thought process toward positive and grateful thoughts. You will literally be rewiring your brain.[2]

After one month of this, I predict that you will feel lighter, more optimistic, and generally more joyful. You'll start seeing your world through the eyes of gratitude, and you'll be surprised at how this new perspective will change your life in delightful and unexpected ways. You may find that you're so grateful for your gratitude practice that you even write about it in your gratitude notebook!

EXERCISE #3

EXPERIENCE JOY WITH ALL FIVE SENSES

When I made joy my top priority, I knew I needed to surround myself with joyful experiences as much as possible. I decided to engage my five senses—taste, smell, sound, sight, and touch—and find ways to experience pleasure through each of them every day. You can use this list to brainstorm ideas and prompt yourself to immerse each of your five senses in at least one pleasurable experience every day.

Today I will find joy in:

Taste _____

_____

_____

Smell _____

_____

_____

Sound _____

_____

_____

Sight _____

_____

_____

Touch _____

_____

_____

EXERCISE #4

TURN A COMPLAINT INTO A CREATION

When I stopped and paid attention to my thought patterns, I realized I was frequently complaining. It had become such an ingrained habit that I often started conversations with a complaint without even noticing. But once I made an effort to stop complaining, I did my best to see experiences I would have formerly complained about as opportunities for learning or growth. I shifted my focus from what I *don't* want to what I *do* want, and you can too. You can use this process to reframe your complaints into creations. Just fill in the blanks whenever there is something or someone you feel like complaining about.

What happened _____

_____

_____

How I felt _____

_____

_____

What I learned/how I grew _____

_____

_____

How I feel now _____

_____

_____

What I want now _____

_____

_____

EXERCISE #5

WRITE THE LETTER YOU WANT TO RECEIVE

When I received a letter from one of my blog readers that was less than glowing, I decided to write myself a letter from a make-believe reader that I would have preferred to receive instead. The very next day, I received a similar letter to the one I had written! And on the next day and in the following days, I continued to receive letters from readers that were supportive and heartwarming. That simple exercise was so effective at creating a tangible result in my life that I've continued to write letters to myself.

Even though I know logically that I'm the one who's written the letters, my brain still processes the words when I read them and has a positive response. I've written myself apology letters, job offer letters, love letters, and thank-you letters. I don't always receive a similar letter from a real live person the very next day, but I do always feel better when I read them. I encourage you to try it.

Is there a relationship in which you'd like closure or healing? Would you like to hear praise from your boss or coworkers? Perhaps you miss someone who has passed away. Maybe you'd love to get a letter from a fan or a secret admirer. Have fun with this! All you have to do to get started is begin writing.

Dear (Your Name) _____

_____

_____

_____

_____

_____

_____

EXERCISE #6

MAKE A VISION BOARD

A vision board is a visual representation of what you want to create in your life. Making one is a creative art project that's fun to do either by yourself or with others. Vision boards are also fantastic to make with kids. If you can, set aside at least a couple of hours for this project so you don't feel pressed for time while you're in the creative process. Here's how to proceed.

1. **Collect your supplies.**

   Gather a collection of magazines, newspaper clippings, brochures, art snippets, and any other images you find inspiring. You will also need a piece of poster board (the size is up to you—I usually make mine the size of a regular piece of paper so it fits easily above my desk), scissors, glue, and optional craft materials such as markers, paint, glitter, and any other decorative items.

2. **Plan it out or let it flow.**

   Decide if you'd like to plan your vision board out in advance or just let it unfold as you create it. You may want it to contain words and images to inspire every aspect of your life—personal, professional, romantic, spiritual, etc.—or you may want it to be focused on only one area of your life. Once you know what you want to create, choose a comfortable workspace, put on some uplifting music, and get started.

3. **Let your intuition guide you.**

   Whether your theme is preconceived or emerging as you go, start cutting out the words and images that you gravitate toward. Allow your creativity to flow, without stopping to question your choices too much. I often find I slip into an almost altered state of consciousness when I'm making a vision board, letting my intuition guide the process rather than my logical mind.

4. **Cut, glue, create, repeat!**

   Feel free to cut in asymmetrical shapes, layer your images, write words in marker, paint a border, or add a sprinkle of glitter over the top of the whole thing if you'd like. You're welcome to use pictures that might not make sense to anyone else besides you. This vision board is just for you, and ultimately the specific images and words you use aren't even what matters in the finished product as much as how it makes you feel when you look at it.

5. **Hang it in a place of honor.**

   Display your vision board somewhere where you can look at it every day. When you look at it, be sure to take a few moments to internalize the images and words and welcome them into your life. Allow yourself to drift into a daydream when you stare at your vision board, merging into the vision you are manifesting for yourself. You may be surprised when images from your vision board show up in your real life and how quickly the vision you created becomes a reality. When that happens, you'll know it's time to make a new vision board.

EXERCISE #7

DAYDREAM IT INTO REALITY

Planners like me can often become so busy with the details that we lose sight of the reason for our plans in the first place—a positive outcome. We obsess about who, what, when, where, and why, and feel stressed when we don't have clear answers. But when we daydream, we can just skip straight to the happy ending. In this case, it's helpful to focus on only two questions: what and why.

1. **Speak or write your dreams.**

   This can be either a spoken or a written exercise. If you're going to speak your daydream out loud, you can do it with a partner, in a group, or by yourself (and record yourself so you can listen to it later)—or try it all three ways! Visualizations such as this daydreaming exercise have been shown to produce real outcomes in multiple scientific studies.[3] So if it feels strange to talk or write about things that don't exist yet, just remind yourself that it's a scientifically valid practice, and let your thoughts and words run wild.

   Start by picking a topic. It can be something you're longing for in your life, a goal you'd like to accomplish, or a vision you'd like to see become a reality.

2. **Hone in on the what.**

   Describe your goals. What are your objectives? What are your dreams? Be specific, but don't veer off into ancillary questions you can't answer. Thinking about "what" should feel dreamy, creative, full of possibility, and unencumbered by logistics. Talk or write about your "what" until it feels so real that you can touch and smell and taste it.

3. **Delve into the why.**

Describe your inspiration. Why are you moved by this vision? Why do you want it to come true? Tap into the excitement and passion this elicits in you, but steer clear of any uncertainties if they come up. Thinking about "why" should feel exciting, inspiring, and meaningful. Talk or write about your "why" until you feel so inspired that you could light up the sky with the fire it has ignited in you!

4. **Daydream often.**

Spend about ten minutes daydreaming out loud or on paper as often as you like. You can schedule a regular daydream session with a partner. Set a weekly time on your calendars when you can meet up or speak on the phone for a half an hour or so. Each of you can take turns jabbering away about whatever you're dreaming up that week. Talk about your visions for the future, focusing only on the fun and exciting parts, with no boundaries or exclusions and no reality check or fear of judgment.

These daydream sessions can enter the realm of fantasy—but not the realm of problem solving. This is not the time to figure out "how" your visions will come to be, only to feel the excitement of them and to marinate in your own joy soup.

Scientists have found that daydreams activate many areas of the brain at once while stimulating increased creativity, cognitive capacity, and improved mood.[4] Research shows that daydreaming ultimately boosts success in goal-oriented tasks by encouraging the brain to solve problems in new and creative ways.[5]

EXERCISE #8

TRAIN YOUR BRAIN FOR OPTIMISM

Our brains really are remarkable. Thanks to the phenomenon known as neuroplasticity, they continuously grow and change shape, forming new neuron connections through our repeated thoughts and experiences. Existing neuron connections become strengthened through repetition, which means whatever we do frequently will become our brain's preferred neural pathway. Eventually, thoughts and actions become an automatic process. This is how habits are formed—it all starts in the brain.

Optimism is a habit that can be learned. By repeating positive thoughts and actions in the face of difficult or stressful situations, the brain is trained to choose optimism when challenged. Positive self-talk creates an optimistic state of mind, which is observable in brain scans.[6]

While—for most people anyway—feeling positive emotions and thinking happy thoughts is clearly preferable to feeling negative emotions and thinking pessimistic thoughts, it's easier said than done. How can we train ourselves to choose optimism even under stress or during hard times? This is a question that has been pondered for millennia and a challenge people undertake every day through mindfulness and other practices such as meditation, deep breathing, yoga, prayer, affirmations, mantras, and more. What works for one person may not work for you. The trick is to discover your own "secret sauce," the optimism trigger that your brain responds to and that you can do consistently. Here are some ideas.

1. **Start your day with gratitude.**

   How you start your day sets the tone for your day, so you may as well start with appreciation. First thing in the morning, write a list of things you're thankful for in your life or simply recite the list in your head. Thoughts of gratitude trigger the parasympathetic nervous system, which calms and relaxes our bodies and induces feelings of optimism, creating a sense of contentment.

2. **When you feel stress taking hold, pause and breathe deeply.** Stress happens—it's part of life. But you don't have to let it take hold and take over. When you notice stressful thoughts and feel corresponding physical responses—such as a faster heartbeat, sweaty palms, or shallower breath—pause, notice your reaction, and take a countermeasure. Ten deep, slow breaths will flood your brain with oxygen, triggering your amygdala to turn off the internal alarm, which will then help you to calm down.

3. **Focus on the pleasure of your senses.** Sight, smell, taste, touch, and hearing are your sensory feedback portals to the brain. You use your senses every day, but how often do you truly notice the pleasure they give you? Simply bringing more awareness to the delicious sensations you experience throughout the day will draw your attention to gratitude and positivity. How flavorful is your morning coffee? How sweet is the fragrance of the flowers in your yard? How invigorating does the wind feel against your skin? How vibrant are the colors of the sunset? How lovely is the sound of your child's voice? Consciously notice these things more often, and train your brain to tune in to pleasure.

4. **Take cues to think positive thoughts.** Choose an activity you do multiple times a day, such as brushing your teeth, getting in your car, or going to the bathroom. And then every time you do that activity, use it as a cue to focus on positive

thoughts. You might want to post reminders to yourself, such as a Post-it on the mirror that says "All is well in my world" or "Choose joy" or whatever words speak to you. You may want to set an alarm on your cell phone to go off at certain times throughout the day. Give yourself regular prompts to choose optimism so that your brain will start to go there more naturally and easily.

5. **Surround yourself with optimistic people.**

There is a popular saying that you become like the five people you spend the most time with. This is logical, really. We have a profound effect on one another. In fact, studies have shown that when you observe a friend who lives less than a mile away from you become happy, your happiness increases by 25 percent.[7] So whenever possible, surround yourself with optimistic people and catch their buzz. Encourage and support each other to be positive—your brain will thank you for it.

EXERCISE #9

PRACTICE ACTS OF KINDNESS

Practicing acts of kindness is an excellent way to generate joy. Having compassion and empathy for others can improve your mood, not only by taking your attention off your own troubles but also by creating a feeling of interconnectedness. When we perform acts of kindness, our brains reward us with a release of the feel-good neurotransmitter dopamine. Studies have shown that both givers and receivers of kindness feel more optimistic afterward, and these effects can be long lasting.[8] Here are some suggestions for incorporating kindness into your Joy Plan.

1. **Smile more.**

   Smiling may be the simplest thing you can do to both experience and spread the positive benefits of kindness. Even if you force a smile, it immediately triggers the release of endorphins in your body.[9] A Swedish study found that when people looked at others who were smiling, their facial muscles twitched into smiles involuntarily. It seems that smiling truly is contagious.[10]

2. **Give compliments.**

   A simple compliment can make someone feel like a million bucks. Literally. Researchers at the National Institute for Physiological Sciences in Japan found that the same area in the brain, the striatum, is activated when a person receives a compliment as when they are given money.[11] Generating more positive energy through the simple act of speaking kind words can be a powerful way to make a difference in the lives of those around you.

3. **Volunteer your time, talents, or treasures.**

   Volunteering has been shown to lower depression, increase one's sense of well-being, lower blood pressure, and extend life expectancy.[12] You may have more time than money on your hands, or vice versa, but there is always something that you can give and people and organizations that will welcome your contribution. Consider cleaning out your closet and taking a donation to your nearest charity thrift store. Offer your time, skills, or financial resources to an organization whose mission you wish to support. Or simply help a person in need (or an animal or the ecosystem) the next time you have the opportunity.

4. **Reach out in small ways every day.**

   Most of us are busy, but it doesn't take much time to send a short message, write a kind note, wish a happy birthday, or let someone know that you're thinking about them. Small acts of kindness performed frequently will create a regular boost in your own mood as well as improve the days of others.

5. **Think big.**

   Your acts of kindness might begin within your small community, but you may soon find yourself wanting to make a bigger contribution to the world. There are endless ways to do this, from connecting with organizations that are doing work you feel passionate about to starting a business with an altruistic aim. There is no limit to what your kindness can do. And since dopamine is released with each act of kindness, you may find it becomes a bit of an addiction.

EXERCISE #10

USE MINDFULNESS MEDITATION

Meditation is a powerful tool for soothing the stress response in the brain; deep breaths send calming oxygen to the amygdala. Mindfulness is simply the practice of bringing your attention to the present moment. The present moment can include your bodily sensations—such as your breath and heartbeat—as well as your surroundings, thoughts, actions, and feelings. Mindfulness meditation can be performed anywhere and anytime, even when your eyes are open and you're among other people. The simple practice of mindfulness has been shown to improve decision making, impulse control, learning, memory, self-confidence, and emotion regulation.[13]

While it may be a general misconception that the goal of mindfulness is to "stop" thoughts, it is true that practicing mindfulness can help us distinguish ourselves from our thoughts. Each time we sit in meditation and try to focus only on our breath, we will most likely be distracted by thoughts—probably about one every second. But if we notice those thoughts and classify them—*There's judgment, there's planning, there's worry. Oh, it's you again, fear*—especially noticing their repetitive nature, we can start to let them come and go without becoming engaged in them.

Your thoughts are not you. It's something we all know conceptually, but how often do we allow a simple (usually repetitive) thought to stress us out, make us sad or angry, or give us full-on anxiety? Our thoughts are here to stay. They're often generated by our personas. But practicing mindfulness is a way we can free ourselves from the hold they have over us when it feels like our thoughts are thinking *us* instead of the other way around. Thoughts come and go. So do breaths. And if we practice it often enough, we can train our minds to let thoughts slip in and out just like our breath, not holding us captive when we don't want them to.

Following is a meditation you can practice whenever you're able to sit quietly and close your eyes, but keep in mind that you can always modify this practice for use at other times, such as when you're waiting in line, sitting in traffic, riding the bus, or even while you're having a challenging conversation.

1. Sit comfortably and close your eyes.

2. Notice the sensations in your body. Make adjustments so that you are as comfortable as possible. If you notice any discomfort, simply acknowledge it and bring your attention to your breath.

3. Breathe deeply and slowly. Count in your mind 1-2-3-4-5 for each inhale and 1-2-3-4-5 for each exhale until you are naturally breathing in a slow, steady pace. You may also want to count to five during a pause between each inhale and exhale.

4. As thoughts come into your mind, notice them—and then imagine they are turning into bubbles and floating away.

5. If it feels comfortable, you can place your hand on your chest and feel your heart beat.

6. Instead of counting, you may want to choose a mantra to repeat in your mind, such as one of these: *I am alive. I am grateful. I am here and now. I am love. I am joy. I am calm. I am at peace. I am a miracle. Om.*

7. Continue to breathe deeply while you count or repeat your mantra for five to fifteen minutes.

For best results, repeat this or another meditation every day. Don't worry if you find you're often distracted from your breath and mantra by your thoughts. The act of noticing your own distraction and then bringing your attention back to your breath is like exercise for your brain. This frequent practice trains your brain to notice thoughts while not engaging in them and can eventually reduce stress while leading to a greater sense of inner calm and peace. Even if you only practice mindfulness meditation for one minute every day, you can experience multiple benefits from cultivating this mental habit.

Meditate Anywhere and Everywhere

The most common mindfulness method of bringing your attention to the present moment is to focus on the breath, but it doesn't only work while sitting quietly in lotus pose. You can practice mindfulness breathing at any time, under almost any circumstance. Whenever you need an infusion of calm, take a few minutes wherever you are to count the seconds as you breathe. Breathing intentionally will send oxygen to your amygdala, and the task of counting will distract your mind from its woes.

You can even practice mindfulness while doing household chores. Wash dishes mindfully by paying attention to the scent of the soap, the feeling of warm bubbles on your hands, and the texture and sensation of the dishes as you wash them. Try adding a relaxing mantra or breathing technique or listening to a recorded meditation, inspirational talk, or uplifting music while you scrub the floors or fold the laundry. Done mindfully, these tasks can become a source of stress relief rather than just annoying chores.

THE JOY PLAN DISCUSSION GUIDE

Support groups have been shown to increase the effectiveness of treatment programs (such as Alcoholics Anonymous and Weight Watchers). Similarly, starting or joining a group can help you be more effective in your Joy Plan. Scientific studies have shown that focused group intention can amplify the results of individual thought—so why not harness that power while also getting together with a group of like-minded folks for some fun and good times? A Joy Plan reading group (or any other name you give it) is a great way to make new friends, deepen existing relationships, and be inspired by others while also receiving support for your joyful endeavors.

If you have people in mind whom you'd like to form a group with, start by suggesting that they read this book, or give them a copy. You can also contact me through TheJoyPlan.com to inquire about existing groups.

GROUP AGREEMENTS

Once you've got your group together, decide on your Group Agreements. Here are some suggestions.

- We will foster joy and empowerment within our group, and spread it to our larger community.
- We will treat one another with respect and value our differences.
- We will hold each other accountable in a positive, compassionate manner.
- We will encourage conversations that inspire growth and learning.
- We will bring the principles discussed in the group into practice in our daily lives.

CHECK-IN

I suggest you start your meetings with a "check-in," a short turn for each member to speak without interruption about how they're feeling in this moment, what's happened since the last meeting, or anything else they want to share. The rest of the group simply listens with full attention and doesn't comment or ask questions during check-in.

DISCUSSION GUIDE

You may want to go through *The Joy Plan* chapter by chapter and discuss the following questions as a group. Perhaps you have stories of your own to share after reading this book. Sometimes expressing your ideas and sharing your experiences with others brings greater clarity not only to you but to those around you as well. Here are some questions to help you get the conversation started.

Chapter 1: Now What?

1. When have things not gone according to plan in your life?
2. How do you react when things don't go as planned?
3. Have you ever faced failure or heartbreak and not known what to do next?

4. What do you think about the concept of the Law of Attraction?

5. What would you do if you had a month to focus solely on your own joy?

Chapter 2: The Bitch in My Head

1. How does your persona, or ego, show up in your life?

2. What repetitive messages does it send you?

3. How do you quiet it?

4. Can you tell when your subconscious mind, or intuition, is telling you something?

5. Have you ever noticed "signs" in your life?

Chapter 3: Know Thyself

1. If you put the content of your daily thoughts into primary categories, what would those categories be?

2. What do you truly enjoy doing?

3. What are you skilled at?

4. Are you an introvert or an extrovert?

5. How often do you like to have alone time?

Chapter 4: Does This Feel Good?

1. How could you move up the Emotional Tone Scale in your life?

2. What would you give a "thumbs up" to in your life?

3. How about a "thumbs down"?

4. How can you reduce negative images and input in your life?

5. Is there a problem you've been thinking about for which you could focus on a solution instead?

Chapter 5: Reboot: From Stressed to Blessed

1. Are you a worrier?

2. Do you consider yourself to be an optimist?

3. What are five things you are grateful for?

4. How can you express appreciation on a more regular basis?

5. Would you like to have a daily gratitude practice?

Chapter 6: Mindfulness Over Matter

1. Have you ever tried meditation? If so, how is it for you?

2. What are some pleasant thoughts you could focus on whenever you need to find a thought that feels better?

3. How can you experience joy with each of your five senses every day?

4. What activities quiet your mind so that your inner voice can burst through?

5. Have you ever received a flash of intuition?

Chapter 7: Eat, Play, Love

1. How can you improve your diet?

2. How can you bring more laughter into your life?

3. How much time do you spend outside?

4. How often do you exercise?

5. In your romantic relationship, do you need to feel connected emotionally before you want to have sex, or do you need to have sex before you open emotionally?

Chapter 8: The Quest for Happy Hormones

1. How are you (or someone you love) affected by hormones?

2. How do you deal with it?

3. Have you (or someone you love) ever wanted to escape into the "red tent" for a week?

4. When you're in a bad mood, would you rather be alone or be with other people?

5. Do you usually go to bed before eleven o'clock at night?

Chapter 9: Let It Go, Let It Go

1. What letters would you like to receive?

2. When you think about what you want in your life, do any fears come up?

3. If so, can you find a way to be okay with the things you're afraid of, even for a minute?

4. How can you implement your Joy Plan at work?

5. What's on your list of things that you are "handing up"?

Chapter 10: Complaining Versus Creating

1. How often do you complain?

2. If you didn't complain, how would you react when something happened that you didn't like?

3. Would you like to try a "week without complaining" challenge?

4. How can you turn your complaints into creations?

5. Do you ever feel guilty for being happy?

Chapter 11: That's True Love

If you're not in a romantic relationship, apply these questions to any close relationship in your life.

1. What do you appreciate about your partner?

2. Are there times when you can praise your partner more?

3. Are there times when you can criticize your partner less?

4. How can you bring more fun into your relationship?

5. How do you think the Gottman ratio—the number of positive interactions compared to negative—applies in your relationship?

Chapter 12: Personal Board of Directors

1. How much time do you spend with friends?

2. Can you think of specific friends who always cheer you up?

3. How do your friends bring you joy?

4. How do you bring joy to your friends?

5. Would you be interested in being part of a women's circle (or men's circle or coed circle)?

Chapter 13: Kids and Other Spiritual Teachers

1. If there are children in your life, what lessons can they teach you?

2. Can you think of an example of wisdom you've heard from a child?

3. How does your mood affect the children you interact with?

4. Can you see any ways that your children copy your behavior?

5. How can you teach your children about their ability to create their reality?

Chapter 14: Writing a New Story

1. Is there a story you've been telling repeatedly that you'd like to tell in a new way?

2. Has there been a reoccurring theme in your life that you'd like to change?

3. What genre of movie would you star in as the story of your life?

4. How would you describe yourself if you were describing the hero of your life story?

5.   What would you like the universe to provide for you as easily as finding a good parking space?

Chapter 15: Exercising the Joy Muscle

1.   What actions can you repeat every day to keep you on track with your Joy Plan?
2.   Do you have any habits you'd like to change?
3.   Do you have any habits that are serving you well?
4.   Do you have any repetitive thoughts you'd like to change?
5.   Is there anything you've been wanting but doubting?

Chapter 16: Joy Is Contagious

1.   Is there anything you'd like to daydream into reality?
2.   Is there a friend you can have a daydream session with?
3.   Do you usually talk more about what you don't want or what you do want?
4.   How do others, even people you don't know well, spread their joy to you?
5.   How can you spread joy to others more often?

Chapter 17: The Journey That Counts

1.   Do you think problems and hard times serve a purpose in your life?
2.   Is there anything you've been resisting that's been persisting in your life?
3.   What would happen if you only cared about making the most of the present moment?
4.   Have you had any difficulties you can see as a blessing in hindsight?
5.   Do you have faith that everything is working out for you?

ENDNOTES

CHAPTER 1

1   Dario Nardi, *Neuroscience of Personality: Brain Savvy Insights for All Types of People* (Los Angeles: Radiance House, 2011).

2   Esther and Jerry Hicks, *The Law of Attraction: The Basics of the Teachings of Abraham* (Carlsbad, CA: Hay House, 2006).

3   Robert Fritz, *The Path of Least Resistance: Learning to Become the Creative Force in Your Own Life* (New York: Fawcett Books, 1989).

4   Rhonda Byrne, *The Secret* (Hillsboro, OR: Beyond Words, 2006). Esther and Jerry Hicks, *Ask and It Is Given: Learning to Manifest Your Desires* (Carlsbad, CA: Hay House, 2004), Napoleon Hill, *Think and Grow Rich* (TarcherPerigee, 2005), Michael Bernard Beckwith, *Life Visioning: A Transformative Process for Activating Your Unique Gifts and Highest Potential* (Boulder, CO: Sounds True, Inc. 2012).

5   Diane Ruge, Li-Min Liou, and Damon Hoad, "Improving the Potential of Neuroplasticity," *Journal of Neuroscience* 32, no. 17 (2012): 5,705–5,706, http://www.jneurosci.org/content/32/17/5705.

6   Roy F. Baumeister et al., "Bad Is Stronger Than Good," *Review*

of General Psychology 5, no. 4 (2001): 323–370, http://assets.csom
.umn.edu/assets/71516.pdf.

7   Barbara Fredrickson and Marcial F. Losada, "Positive Affect and the
    Complex Dynamics of Human Flourishing," *American Psychologist*
    60, no. 7 (2005): 678–686, http://www.ncbi.nlm.nih.gov/pmc
    /articles/PMC3126111/.

8   Jessica Cerretani, "The Contagion of Happiness," *Harvard Medicine*,
    Summer 2011, https://hms.harvard.edu/news/harvard-medicine
    /contagion-happiness.

9   Craig Lambert, "The Science of Happiness," *Harvard Magazine*,
    January/February 2007, http://harvardmagazine.com/2007/01
    /the-science-of-happiness.html.

CHAPTER 2

1   Albert Garoli, *The Evolutionary Glitch: Rise Above the Root of Your
    Problems* (Ann Arbor: Loving Healing Press, 2010).

2   Eckhart Tolle, *A New Earth: Awakening to Your Life's Purpose* (New
    York: Plume, 2005).

3   C. G. Jung, *Two Essays on Analytical Psychology* (Princeton, NJ:
    Princeton University Press, 1972).

4   Naomi I. Eisenberger, Matthew D. Lieberman, and Kipling D.
    Williams, "Does Rejection Hurt? An FMRI Study of Social
    Exclusion," *Science* 302, no. 5643 (2003): 290–292, http://www
    .ncbi.nlm.nih.gov/pubmed/14551436.

5   Garoli, *The Evolutionary Glitch*.

6   Chris Frith, *Making Up the Mind: How the Brain Creates Our Mental
    World* (Malden, MA: Blackwell, 2007).

7   Raymond J. Corsini and Danny Wedding, *Current Psychotherapies*,
    9th ed. (Belmont, CA: Brooks/Cole, 2011).

8   C. G. Jung, *Synchronicity: An Acausal Connecting Principle* (1955; repr., East Sussex: Routledge, 2008).

CHAPTER 3

1   Amy F. T. Arnsten, "Stress Signaling Pathways That Impair Prefrontal Cortex Structure and Function," *Nature Reviews Neuroscience* 10, no. 6 (2009): 410–422, http://www.ncbi.nlm.nih .gov/pmc/articles/PMC2907136/.

2   Christine Comaford, "Got Inner Peace? 5 Ways to Get It NOW," *Forbes*, April 2012, http://www.forbes.com/sites/christinecomaford /2012/04/04/got-inner-peace-5-ways-to-get-it-now/.

3   Herbert L. Mathews and Linda W. Janusek, "Epigenetics and Psychoneuroimmunology: Mechanisms and Models," *Brain, Behavior, and Immunity* 25, no. 1 (2011): 25–39, https://www.ncbi.nlm.nih .gov/pmc/articles/PMC2991515/.

4   Bruce H. Lipton, *The Biology of Belief: Unleashing the Power of Consciousness, Matter & Miracles*, (Hay House, Inc., 2008).

5   Dawson Church, *The Genie in Your Genes: Epigenetic Medicine and the New Biology of Intention* (Santa Rosa, CA: Elite Books, 2007).

6   Will Storr, "A Better Kind of Happiness," Elements, *New Yorker*, July 7, 2016, http://www.newyorker.com/tech /elements/a-better-kind-of-happiness.

7   Inna Fishman, Rowena Ng, and Ursula Bellugi, "Do Extraverts Process Social Stimuli Differently from Introverts?" *Journal of Cognitive Neuroscience* 2, no. 2 (2011): 67–73, https://www.ncbi .nlm.nih.gov/pmc/articles/PMC3129862/.

8   "Extraversion or Introversion," the website of The Myers and Briggs Foundation, accessed October 29, 2016, http://

www.myersbriggs.org/my-mbti-personality-type/mbti-basics /extraversion-or-introversion.htm.

CHAPTER 4

1   P. D. Eastman, *Are You My Mother?* (1960; repr., New York: Random House, 1998).

2   Andy Roman, *Deep Feeling, Deep Healing: The Heart, Mind, and Soul of Getting Well* (Jupiter, FL: Spectrum Healing Press, 2011).

3   Thomas Chavez, *Body Electronics: Vital Steps for Physical Regeneration* (Berkeley: North Atlantic Books, 2005).

4   Ibid.

5   Daniel Goleman et al., *Measuring the Immeasurable: The Scientific Case for Spirituality* (Boulder, CO: Sounds True, 2008).

6   Will Storr, "A Better Kind of Happiness," *The New Yorker*, July 7, 2016, http://www.newyorker.com/tech /elements/a-better-kind-of-happiness.

7   Steven Pinker, *The Better Angels of Our Nature: Why Violence Has Declined* (New York: Viking, 2011).

8   Amrisha Vaish, Tobias Grossmann, and Amanda Woodward, "Not All Emotions Are Created Equal: The Negativity Bias in Social-Emotional Development," *Psychological Bulletin* 134, no. 3 (2008): 383–403, http://www.ncbi.nlm.nih.gov/pmc /articles/PMC3652533/.

9   Steven Pinker, "Violence Vanquished," The Saturday Essay, *Wall Street Journal,* September 24, 2011, http://www.wsj.com/news /articles/SB10001424053111904106704576583203589408180.

10   Derek M. Isaacowitz, "The Gaze of the Optimist," *Personality and Social Psychology Bulletin* 31, no.3 (2005): 407–415, https://www .ncbi.nlm.nih.gov/pubmed/15657455.

CHAPTER 5

1   Don Colbert, *Deadly Emotions: Understand the Mind-Body-Spirit Connection That Can Heal or Destroy You* (Nashville: Thomas Nelson, 2003).

2   Wolfram Schultz, "Reward Signaling by Dopamine Neurons," *Neuroscientist* 7, no.4 (2001): 293–302, https://www.ncbi.nlm.nih .gov/pubmed/11488395.

3   Sherrie Bourg Carter. "The Benefits of Adding Gratitude to Your Attitude," *Psychology Today*, November 25, 2013, https://www.psychologytoday.com/blog/high-octane-women /201311/the-benefits-adding-gratitude-your-attitude.

4   Dan Baker and Cameron Stauth, *What Happy People Know: How the New Science of Happiness Can Change Your Life for the Better* (New York: St. Martin's Griffin, 2004).

5   David Hecht, "The Neural Basis of Optimism and Pessimism," *Experimental Neurology* 22, no. 3 (2013): 173–199, http://www .ncbi.nlm.nih.gov/pmc/articles/PMC3807005/.

6   MindUP.org, the website of the Hawn Foundation, accessed October 29, 2016, https://www.mindup.org.

7   Jordan Gaines Lewis, "The Neuroscience of Optimism," *Psychology Today*, August 23, 2012, https://www.psychologytoday.com /blog/brain-babble/201208/the-neuroscience-optimism.

8   Rollin McCraty and Doc Childre, *The Appreciative Heart: The Psychophysiology of Positive Emotions and Optimal Functioning* (Boulder Creek, CA: Institute of HeartMath, 2002).

9   Sho Sugawara et al., "Social Rewards Enhance Offline Improvements in Motor Skill," *PLoS ONE* 7, no. 11 (2012), http://journals.plos.org/plosone/article?id=10.1371/journal .pone.0048174.

CHAPTER 6

1   Carolyn Gregoire, "The Habit of These Outrageously Successful People," *Third Metric* (blog), Huffington Post, July 5, 2013, http ://www.huffingtonpost.com/2013/07/05/business-meditation -executives-meditate_n_3528731.html.

2   Elisha Goldstein, *Uncovering Happiness: Overcoming Depression with Mindfulness and Self-Compassion* (New York: Atria Books, 2015).

3   Jessica Cerretani, "The Contagion of Happiness," *Harvard Medicine*, Summer 2011, https://hms.harvard.edu/news/harvard-medicine /contagion-happiness; Perla Kaliman et al., "Rapid Changes in Histone Deacetylates and Inflammatory Gene Expression in Expert Meditators," *Psychoneuroendocrinology* 40 (February 2014): 96–107, http://www.ncbi.nlm.nih.gov/pmc/articles/PMC4039194/; Linda E. Carlson et al., "Mindfulness-Based Cancer Recovery and Supportive-Expressive Therapy Maintain Telomere Length Relative to Controls in Distressed Breast Cancer Survivors," *Cancer* 121, no. 3 (2015): 476–484, http://onlinelibrary.wiley .com/doi/10.1002/cncr.29063/full.

4   Morten L. Kringelbach and Kent C. Berridge, "Towards a Functional Neuroanatomy of Pleasure and Happiness," *Trends in Cognitive Science* 13, no.11 (2009): 479–487, https://www.ncbi .nlm.nih.gov/pmc/articles/PMC2767390/.

5   Robert L. Matchock, "Pet Ownership and Physical Health," *Current Opinion in Psychiatry* 28, no. 5 (2015): 386–392, https ://www.ncbi.nlm.nih.gov/pubmed/26164613.

6   K. M. Stephan et al., "Functional Anatomy of the Mental Representation of Upper Extremity Movements in Healthy Subjects," *Journal of Neurophysiology* 73, no. 1 (1995): 373–386, http://jn.physiology.org/content/jn/73/1/373.full.pdf.

CHAPTER 7

1   Paul C. Aebersold, *Radioisotopes: New Keys to Knowledge* (Washington, DC: The Smithsonian Institute, 1953).

2   Kirsty Spalding et al., "Dynamics of Hippocampal Neurogenesis in Adult Humans," *Cell* 153, no. 6 (2013): 1,219–1,227, http ://www.cell.com/abstract/S0092-8674(13)00533-3.

3   Candace Pert, *Molecules of Emotion: The Science Behind Mind-Body Medicine* (New York: Simon and Schuster, 1999).

4   Dariush Dfarhud, Maryam Malmir, and Mohammad Khanahmadi, "Happiness and Health: The Biological Factors—Systematic Review Article," *Iran Journal of Public Health* 43, no. 11(2014): 1,468–1,477, http://www.ncbi.nlm.nih.gov/pmc/articles/PMC4449495/.

5   Drew Ramsey and Jennifer Iserloh, *Fifty Shades of Kale: 50 Fresh and Satisfying Recipes That Are Bound to Please* (New York: Harper Collins, 2015).

6   M. H. Mohajeri et al., "Chronic Treatment with a Tryptophan-Rich Protein Hydrolysate Improves Emotional Processing, Mental Energy Levels and Reaction Time in Middle-Aged Women," *British Journal of Nutrition* 113, no. 2 (2015) 350–365, https ://www.ncbi.nlm.nih.gov/pubmed/25572038.

7   R. I. M. Dunbar et al., "Social Laughter Is Correlated with an Elevated Pain Threshold," *Proceedings of the Royal Society B: Biological Sciences* 279, no. 1731 (2012): 1,161–1,167, http://rspb .royalsocietypublishing.org/content/279/1731/1161.

8   Melinda Wenner, "Smile! It Could Make You Happier," *Scientific American*, September 1, 2009, http://www.scientificamerican .com/article/smile-it-could-make-you-happier/.

9   James D. Laird and Charles Bresler, "The Process of Emotional Experience: A Self-Perception Theory," vol. 13 of *Emotion:*

Review of Personality and Social Psychology, ed. Margaret S. Clark (Newbury Park, CA: Sage, 1992), 223-34, https://www .researchgate.net/publication/232517707_The_process_of _emotional_experience_A_self-perception_theory.

10 Qing Li, "Effect of Forest Bathing Trips on Human Immune Function," *Environmental Health and Preventative Medicine* 15, no. 1 (2010): 9–17, https://www.ncbi.nlm.nih.gov/pmc/articles /PMC2793341/.

11 Peter Aspinall et al., "The Urban Brain: Analysing Outdoor Physical Activity with Mobile EEG," *British Journal of Sports Medicine* 49, no. 4 (2015): 272–276, https://www.ncbi.nlm.nih .gov/pubmed/23467965.

12 Tracy Wikander, "Want More Sexual Intimacy? This Plan Can Help," mindbodygreen, November 30, 2014, http://www .mindbodygreen.com/0-16331/want-more-sexual-intimacy-in -your-relationship-this-plan-can-help.html.

13 R. M. Nicoli and J. M. Nicoli, "Biochemistry of Eros," *Contraception, Fertilite, Sexualite* 23, no 2. (1995): 137–144, https ://www.ncbi.nlm.nih.gov/pubmed/7894546.

14 David Weeks and Jamie James, *Secrets of the Superyoung* (New York: Berkley Books, 1999).

15 Lothar Schwarz and Wilfried Kindermann, "Changes in Beta-Endorphin Levels in Response to Aerobic and Anaerobic Exercise," *Sports Medicine* 13, no. 1 (1992): 25–36, http://www .ncbi.nlm.nih.gov/pubmed/1553453.

16 Jeremy Sibold and Jennifer Mears, lecture to the 56th Annual Meeting of the American College of Sports Medicine, Seattle, WA, May 2009.

17 Lynette L. Craft and Frank M. Perna, "The Benefits of Exercise

for the Clinically Depressed," *The Primary Care Companion to the Journal of Clinical Psychiatry* 6, no. 3 (2004): 104–111, http://www.ncbi.nlm.nih.gov/pmc/articles/PMC474733/.

18 Rachel Leproult et al., "Sleep Loss Results in an Elevation of Cortisol Levels the Next Evening," *Sleep* 20, no. 10 (1999): 865–870, https://www.ncbi.nlm.nih.gov/pubmed/9415946.

19 Simon N. Archer and Henrik Oster, "How Sleep and Wakefulness Influence Circadian Rhythmicity: Effects of Insufficient and Mistimed Sleep on the Animal and Human Transcriptome," *Journal of Sleep Research* 24, no. 5 (2015): 476–493, http://onlinelibrary.wiley.com/doi/10.1111/jsr.12307/pdf.

20 Susan Scutti, "7 Health Consequences of Going to Bed Past Midnight," *Medical Daily*, June 28, 2013, http://www.medicaldaily.com/7-health-consequences-going-bed-past-midnight-247247.

21 Christopher Bergland, "How Can Daydreaming Improve Goal-Oriented Results?" *Psychology Today*, November 26, 2014, https://www.psychologytoday.com/blog/the-athletes-way/201411/how-can-daydreaming-improve-goal-oriented-results.

CHAPTER 8

1 Colette Bouchez, "Escape From Hormone Horrors—What You Can Do," WebMD, November 19, 2008, http://www.webmd.com/women/features/escape-hormone-horrors-what-you-can-do.

2 Gabrielle Lichterman, "Female Hormone Cycle," Hormone Horoscope, October 29, 2016, http://hormonehoroscope.com/the-female-hormone-cycle/.

3 Simon N. Young, "How to Increase Serotonin in the Human Brain Without Drugs," *Journal of Psychiatry and Neuroscience* 32, no.

6   (2007): 394–399, http://www.ncbi.nlm.nih.gov/pmc/articles
/PMC2077351/.

4   Alex Korb, "Boosting Your Serotonin Activity," *Psychology Today*,
November 17, 2011, https://www.psychologytoday.com/blog
/prefrontal-nudity/201111/boosting-your-serotonin-activity.

5   Michael W. Otto et al., "Exercise for Mood and Anxiety Disorders,"
The Primary Care Companion to the Journal of Clinical Psychiatry
9, no. 4 (2007): 287–294, http://www.ncbi.nlm.nih.gov/pmc
/articles/PMC2018853/; Salam Ranabir and K. Reetu, "Stress
and Hormones," *Indian Journal of Endocrinology and Metabolism* 15,
no. 1 (2011): 18–22, http://www.ncbi.nlm.nih.gov/pmc/articles
/PMC3079864/.

6   Eve Van Cauter et al., "The Impact of Sleep Deprivation on
Hormones and Metabolism," *Medscape Neurology* 7, no. 1 (2005),
http://www.medscape.org/viewarticle/502825.

CHAPTER 9

1   Kahlil Gibran, *The Prophet* (New York: Alfred A. Knopf, 1923).

2   Ezequiel Morsella, "What Is a Thought?" *Psychology Today*,
February 9, 2012, https://www.psychologytoday.com/blog
/consciousness-and-the-brain/201202/what-is-thought.

3   Stephanie Watson, "Volunteering May Be Good for Body and
Mind," *Harvard Health Blog*, June 26, 2013, http://www.health
.harvard.edu/blog/volunteering-may-be-good-for-body-and
-mind-201306266428.

4   Vadim Zeland, *Reality Transurfing 1: The Space of Variations*, trans.
Gregory Blake (Ropley, UK: O Books, 2008).

CHAPTER 10

1   James R. Krebs and Gayle A. Brazeau, "No Complaining…" *American Journal of Pharmaceutical Education* 75, no. 4 (2011): 67, http://www.ncbi.nlm.nih.gov/pmc/articles/PMC3138359/.

2   Hans Selye, "Stress and Distress," *Comprehensive Therapy Journal* 1, no. 8 (1975): 9–13, https://www.ncbi.nlm.nih.gov/pubmed/1222562.

3   Susan Krauss Whitbourne, "The Definitive Guide to Guilt," *Psychology Today*, August 11, 2012, https://www.psychologytoday .com/blog/fulfillment-any-age/201208/the-definitive-guide-guilt.

4   Tracy Wikander, "How to Communicate More Mindfully: An 8-Step Plan," mindbodygreen, June 6, 2015, http://www .mindbodygreen.com/0-20189/how-to-communicate-more -mindfully-an-8-step-plan.html.

CHAPTER 11

1   Ian J. Mitchell, Steven M. Gillespie, and Ahmad Abu-Akel, "Similar Effects of Intranasal Oxytocin Administration and Acute Alcohol Consumption on Socio-Cognitions, Emotions and Behavior: Implications for the Mechanisms of Action," *Neuroscience and Behavioral Reviews* 55 (May 2015): 98–106, https://www.ncbi .nlm.nih.gov/pubmed/25956250.

2   Chade-Meng Tan, *Search Inside Yourself: The Unexpected Path to Achieving Success, Happiness (and World Peace)* (New York: Harper One, 2012).

3   Amie M. Gordon et al., "To Have and To Hold: Gratitude Promotes Relationship Maintenance in Intimate Bonds," *Journal of Personality and Social Psychology* 103, no. 2 (2012): 257–274, http ://www.ncbi.nlm.nih.gov/pubmed/22642482.

CHAPTER 12

1   James H. Fowler and Nicholas A. Christakis, "Dynamic Spread of Happiness in a Large Social Network: Longitudinal Analysis Over 20 Years in the Framingham Heart Study," *British Medical Journal* 337, no. a2338 (2008): 1–9, http://www.bmj.com/content/337/bmj.a2338.

2   Sheldon Cohen et al., "Sociability and Susceptibility to the Common Cold," *Psychological Science* 14, no.5 (2003): 389–395, https://www.ncbi.nlm.nih.gov/pubmed/12930466.

3   Ryan E. Adams, Jonathan B. Santo, and William M. Bukowski, "The Presence of a Best Friend Buffers the Effects of Negative Experiences," *Developmental Psychology* 47, no.6 (2011): 1,786–1,791, https://www.ncbi.nlm.nih.gov/pubmed/21895364.

4   James Harter and Raksha Arora, "Social Time Crucial to Daily Emotional Wellbeing in U.S.," Gallup.com, June 5, 2008, http://www.gallup.com/poll/107692/social-time-crucial-daily-emotional-wellbeing.aspx.

5   Simone Schnall et al., "Social Support and the Perception of Geographical Slant," *Journal of Experimental Social Psychology* 44, no. 5 (2008): 1,246–1,255, https://www.ncbi.nlm.nih.gov/pmc/articles/PMC3291107/.

6   Young Women Social Entrepreneurs, http://www.ywse.org.

7   Raimo Tuomela, *The Importance of Us: A Philosophical Study of Basic Social Norms* (Redwood City, CA: Stanford University Press, 1995).

8   Office of National Drug Control Policy, *Treatment Protocol Effectiveness Study (white paper)*, (Washington, DC: Office of the National Drug Control Policy, 1996), https://www.ncjrs.gov/ondcppubs/publications/treat/trmtprot.html.

CHAPTER 13

1   Giacomo Rizzolatti and Laila Craighero, "The Mirror-Neuron System," *Annual Review of Neuroscience* 27 (2004): 169–192, https://www.ncbi.nlm.nih.gov/pubmed/15217330.

2   John A. Bargh, Mark Chen, and Lara Burrows, "Automaticity of Social Behavior: Direct Effects of Trait Construct and Stereotype-Activation on Action," *Journal of Personal Social Psychology* 71, no. 2 (1996): 230–244, https://www.psychologytoday.com/files /attachments/5089/barghchenburrows1996.pdf.

3   Ravinder Jerath et al., "Physiology of Long Pranayamic Breathing: Neural Respiratory Elements May Provide a Mechanism That Explains How Slow Deep Breathing Shifts the Autonomic Nervous System," *Medical Hypotheses* 67, no.3 (2006): 566–571, https://www.ncbi.nlm.nih.gov/pubmed/16624497.

4   Susan Reynolds, "Happy Brain, Happy Life," *Psychology Today*, August 2, 2011, https://www.psychologytoday.com/blog /prime-your-gray-cells/201108/happy-brain-happy-life.

5   MindUP.org, the website of the Hawn Foundation, accessed October 29, 2016, https://www.mindup.org.

CHAPTER 14

1   Suze Orman, *The 9 Steps to Financial Freedom: Practical and Spiritual Steps So You Can Stop Worrying*, 3rd ed. (New York: Three Rivers Press, 2000).

2   Christopher Bergland, "How Can Daydreaming Improve Goal-Oriented Results?" *Psychology Today*, November 26, 2014, https ://www.psychologytoday.com/blog/the-athletes-way/201411 /how-can-daydreaming-improve-goal-oriented-results.

3   Alan Richardson, "Mental Practice: A Review and Discussion

Part 1," *Research Quarterly* 38, no.1 (1967): 95–107, http://www
.tandfonline.com/doi/abs/10.1080/10671188.1967.10614808.

CHAPTER 15

1 Hans Selye, "Stress and Distress," *Comprehensive Therapy Journal* 1, no. 8 (1975): 9–13, https://www.ncbi.nlm.nih.gov /pubmed/1222562.

2 Phillippa Lally et al., "How Are Habits Formed: Modelling Habit Formation in the Real World." *European Journal of Social Psychology* 40, no. 6 (2010): 998–1,009, http://onlinelibrary.wiley.com /doi/10.1002/ejsp.674/abstract.

3 Joe Dispenza, *You Are the Placebo: Making Your Mind Matter* (Carlsbad, CA: Hay House, 2014), 63–64.

CHAPTER 16

1 Rollin McCraty, "The Energetic Heart: Bioelectromagnetic Interactions Within and Between People," in *Clinical Applications of Bioeletromagnetic Medicine*, ed. P. J. Rosch and M. S. Markov (New York: Marcel Dekker, 2004), 541–562, https://www.heartmath .org/research/research-library/energetics/energetic-heart-bioelectro magnetic-communication-within-and-between-people/.

2 Elaine Hatfield, John T. Cacioppo, and Richard L. Rapson, "Emotional Contagion," *Current Directions in Psychological Science* 2 (June 1993): 96–99, http://cdp.sagepub.com/content/2/3/96.citation.

3 J. S. Morris et al., "A Differential Neural Response in the Human Amygdala to Fearful and Happy Facial Expressions," *Nature* 383, no. 6603 (1996): 812–815, https://www.ncbi.nlm.nih.gov /pubmed/8893004.

4 Susan Reynolds, "Happy Brain, Happy Life," *Psychology Today*,

August 2, 2011, https://www.psychologytoday.com/blog /prime-your-gray-cells/201108/happy-brain-happy-life.

5   Niko Everett, "Meet Yourself: A User's Guide to Building Self-Esteem," TEDx video, 9:31, posted February 11, 2013, http ://tedxtalks.ted.com/video/Meet-Yourself-A-Users-Guide-to.

6   Erica J. Boothby, Margaret S. Clark, and John A. Bargh, "Shared Experiences Are Amplified," *Psychological Science* 25, no. 12 (2014): 2,209–2,216, http://pss.sagepub.com/content/25/12/2209.abstract.

7   R.I.M. Dunbar, "Gossip in Evolutionary Perspective," *Review of General Psychology* 8, no. 2 (2004): 100–110, http://allegatifac .unipv.it/ziorufus/Dunbar%20gossip.pdf.

8   Stephan Hamann, "Cognitive and Neural Mechanisms of Emotional Memory," *Trends in Cognitive Science* 5, no. 9 (2001): 394–400, https://www.ncbi.nlm.nih.gov/pubmed/11520704.

9   Joseph Stromberg, "The Benefits of Daydreaming," Smithsonian .com, April 3, 2012, http://www.smithsonianmag.com /science-nature/the-benefits-of-daydreaming-170189213/.

10   R. Nathan Spreng et al., "Goal-Congruent Default Network Activity Facilitates Cognitive Control," *Journal of Neuroscience* 34, no. 42 (2014): 14,108–14,114, http://www.jneurosci.org/content/34/42/14108.

11   Daniel B. Levinson, Jonathan Smallwood, and Richard J. Davidson, "The Persistence of Thought: Evidence for a Role of Working Memory in the Maintenance of Task-Unrelated Thinking," *Psychological Science* 23, no. 4 (2012): 375–380, https://www.ncbi .nlm.nih.gov/pmc/articles/PMC3328662/.

CHAPTER 17

1   Viktor E. Frankl, *Man's Search for Meaning,* trans. Ilse Lasch (Boston: Beacon Press, 2006).

2   Zeeya Merali, "Quantum Physics: What Is Really Real?" *Nature* 521, no. 7552 (2015): 278–280, http://www.nature.com/news /quantum-physics-what-is-really-real-1.17585.

3   Weizmann Institute of Science, "Quantum Theory Demonstrated: Observation Affects Reality," *Science Daily*, February 27, 1998, https://www.sciencedaily.com/releases/1998 /02/980227055013.htm.

4   Eckhart Tolle, *The Power of Now: A Guide to Spiritual Enlightenment* (Novato, CA: New World Library, 2004).

APPENDIX: CREATE YOUR OWN JOY PLAN

1   Albert Garoli, *The Evolutionary Glitch: Rise Above the Root of Your Problems* (Ann Arbor: Loving Healing Press, 2010).

2   Wolfram Schultz, "Reward Signaling by Dopamine Neurons," *Neuroscientist* 7, no.4 (2001): 293–302, https://www.ncbi.nlm.nih .gov/pubmed/11488395.

3   Angie LeVan, "Seeing Is Believing: The Power of Visualization," *Psychology Today*, December 3, 2009, https://www.psychologytoday .com/blog/flourish/200912/seeing-is-believing-the-power -visualization.

4   Joseph Stromberg, "The Benefits of Daydreaming," Smithsonian .com, April 3, 2012, http://www.smithsonianmag.com/science -nature/the-benefits-of-daydreaming-170189213/.

5   R. Nathan Spreng et al., "Goal-Congruent Default Network Activity Facilitates Cognitive Control," *Journal of Neuroscience* 34, no. 42 (2014): 14,108–14,114, http://www.jneurosci.org/content/34/42/14108.

6   David Hecht, "The Neural Basis of Optimism and Pessimism," *Experimental Neurology* 22, no. 3 (2013): 173–199, http://www .ncbi.nlm.nih.gov/pmc/articles/PMC3807005/.

7   James H. Fowler and Nicholas A. Christakis, "Dynamic Spread of Happiness in a Large Social Network: Longitudinal Analysis Over 20 Years in the Framingham Heart Study," *British Medical Journal* 337, no. a2338 (2008): 1–9, http://www.bmj.com/content/337 /bmj.a2338.

8   MindUP.org, the website of the Hawn Foundation, accessed October 29, 2016, https://www.mindup.org.

9   Karen Kleiman, "Try Some Smile Therapy," *Psychology Today*, July 31, 2012, https://www.psychologytoday.com/blog/isnt-what-i -expected/201207/try-some-smile-therapy.

10 Marianne Sonnby–Borgström, "Automatic Mimicry Reactions as Related to Differences in Emotional Empathy," *Scandinavian Journal of Psychology* 43, no. 5 (2002): 433–443, https://www.ncbi .nlm.nih.gov/pubmed/12500783.

11 David DiSalvo, "Study: Receiving a Compliment Has the Same Positive Effect as Receiving Cash," *Forbes*, November 9, 2012, http://www.forbes.com/sites/daviddisalvo/2012/11/09 /study-receiving-a-compliment-has-same-positive-effect-as -receiving-cash/.

12 Stephanie Watson, "Volunteering May Be Good for Body and Mind," *Harvard Health Blog*, June 26, 2013, http ://www.health.harvard.edu/blog/volunteering-may-be-good -for-body-and-mind-201306266428.

13 Eline Snel, *Sitting Still Like a Frog: Mindfulness Exercises for Kids (and Their Parents)* (Boston: Shambhala Publications, 2013).

REFERENCES AND RESOURCES

CHAPTER 1

Baumeister, Roy F., Ellen Bratslavsky, Catrin Finkenauer, and Kathleen D. Vohs. "Bad Is Sronger Than Good." *Review of General Psychology* 5, no. 4 (2001): 323-370. http://assets.csom.umn.edu/assets/71516.pdf.

Beckwith, Michael Bernard. *Life Visioning: A Transformative Process for Activating Your Unique Gifts and Highest Potential*. Boulder, CO: Sounds True, Inc., 2012.

Byrne, Rhonda. *The Secret*. Hillsboro, OR: Beyond Words, 2006.

Cerretani, Jessica. "The Contagion of Happiness." *Harvard Medicine*, Summer 2011. https://hms.harvard.edu/news/harvard-medicine/contagion-happiness.

Fredrickson, Barbara L., and Marcial F. Losada, "Positive Affect and the Complex Dynamics of Human Flourishing." *American Psychologist* 60, no. 7 (2005): 678-686. https://www.ncbi.nlm.nih.gov/pmc/articles/PMC3126111/.

Fritz, Robert. *The Path of Least Resistance: Learning to Become the Creative Force in Your Own Life*. New York: Fawcett Books, 1989.

Hicks, Esther and Jerry. *Ask and It Is Given: Learning to Manifest Your Desires*. Carlsbad, CA: Hay House, 2004.

————. *The Law of Attraction: The Basics of the Teachings of Abraham*. Carlsbad, CA: Hay House, 2006.

Hill, Napoleon. *Think and Grow Rich*. TarcherPerigee, 2013.

Lambert, Craig. "The Science of Happiness." *Harvard Magazine*, January /February 2007. http://harvardmagazine.com/2007/01/the-science -of-happiness.html.

Nardi, Dario. *Neuroscience of Personality: Brain Savvy Insights for All Types of People.* Los Angeles: Radiance House, 2011.

Ruge, Diane, Li-Min Liou, and Damon Hoad. "Improving the Potential of Neuroplasticity." *Journal of Neuroscience* 32, no. 17 (2012): 5,705-6. http://www.jneurosci.org/content/32/17/5705.

CHAPTER 2

Corsini, Raymond J., and Danny Wedding. *Current Psychotherapies.* 9th ed. Belmont, CA: Brooks/Cole, 2011.

Eisenberger, Naomi I., Matthew D. Lieberman, and Kipling D. Williams. "Does Rejection Hurt? An FMRI Study of Social Exclusion." *Science* 302, no. 5643 (2003): 290-2. http://www.ncbi.nlm.nih.gov /pubmed/14551436.

Garoli, Albert. *The Evolutionary Glitch: Rise Above the Root of Your Problems.* Ann Arbor: Loving Healing Press, 2010.

Jung, Carl. *Synchronicity: An Acausal Connecting Principle*. East Sussex: Routledge, 2008. First published 1955 in England.

————. *Two Essays on Analytical Psychology*. Princeton, NJ: Princeton University Press, 1972.

CHAPTER 3

Arnsten, Amy F. T. "Stress Signaling Pathways That Impair Prefrontal Cortex Structure and Function." *Nature Reviews Neuroscience* 10, no. 6 (2009): 410-22. http://www.ncbi.nlm.nih.gov/pmc/articles /PMC2907136/.

Church, Dawson. *The Genie in Your Genes: Epigenetic Medicine and the New Biology of Intention*. Santa Rosa, CA: Elite Books, 2007.

Comaford, Christine. "Got Inner Peace? 5 Ways to Get It NOW." *Forbes*, April 2012. http://www.forbes.com/sites/christinecomaford/2012 /04/04/got-inner-peace-5-ways-to-get-it-now/.

Fishman, Inna, Rowena Ng, and Ursula Bellugi. "Do Extroverts Process Social Stimuli Differently from Introverts?" *Journal of Cognitive Neuroscience* 2, no.2 (2011): 67-73. https://www.ncbi.nlm.nih.gov /pmc/articles/PMC3129862/.

Lipton, Bruce. *The Biology of Belief: Unleashing the Power of Consciousness, Matter & Miracles*. Hay House, 2008.

Mathews, Herbert L., and Linda Witek Janusek. "Epigenetics and Psychoneuroimmunology: Mechanisms and Models." *Brain, Behavior, and Immunity* 25, no. 1 (2011): 25-39. https://www.ncbi .nlm.nih.gov/pmc/articles/PMC2991515/.

The Myers and Briggs Foundation. "Extroversion or Introversion." Accessed October 29, 2016. http://www.myersbriggs.org/my-mbti -personality-type/mbti-basics/extraversion-or-introversion.htm.

Storr, Will. "A Better Kind of Happiness." Elements. *New Yorker*, July 6, 2016. http://www.newyorker.com/tech/elements/a-better-kind-of-happiness.

CHAPTER 4

Chavez, Thomas. *Body Electronics: Vital Steps for Physical Regeneration*. Berkeley: North Atlantic Books, 2005.

Eastman, P. D. *Are You My Mother?* New York: Random House, 1998.

Goleman, Daniel, Bruce H. Lipton, Candace Pert, Gary Small, Lynne McTaggart, Gregg Braden, Jeanne Achterberg et al. *Measuring the*

Immeasurable: The Scientific Case for Spirituality. Boulder, CO: Sounds True, 2008.

Isaacowitz, Derek M. "The Gaze of the Optimist." *Personality and Social Psychology Bulletin* 31, no. 3 (2005): 407-15. https://www.ncbi.nlm .nih.gov/pubmed/15657455.

Pinker, Steven. *The Better Angels of Our Nature: Why Violence Has Declined.* New York: Viking, 2011.

Roman, Andy. *Deep Feeling, Deep Healing: The Heart, Mind, and Soul of Getting Well.* Jupiter, FL: Spectrum Healing Press, 2011.

CHAPTER 5

Baker, Dan and Cameron Stauth. *What Happy People Know: How the New Science of Happiness Can Change Your Life for the Better.* New York: St. Martin's Griffin, 2003.

Carter, Sherrie Bourg. "The Benefits of Adding Gratitude to Your Attitude," *Psychology Today*, November, 2013. https://www.psychologytoday .com/blog/high-octane-women/201311/the-benefits-adding -gratitude-your-attitude.

Colbert, Don. *Deadly Emotions: Understand the Mind-Body-Spirit Connection That Can Heal or Destroy You.* Nashville: Thomas Nelson, 2003.

Hecht, David. "The Neural Basis of Optimism and Pessimism." *Experimental Neurology* 22, no. 3 (2013): 173-99. http://www.ncbi.nlm.nih.gov /pmc/articles/PMC3807005/.

Lewis, Jordan Gaines. "The Neuroscience of Optimism." *Psychology Today*, August 23, 2012. https://www.psychologytoday.com/blog/brain -babble/201208/the-neuroscience-optimism.

McCraty, Rollin, and Doc Childre. *The Appreciative Heart: The Psychophysiology of Positive Emotions and Optimal Functioning.* Boulder Creek, CA: Institute of HeartMath, 2002.

Schultz, Wolfram. "Reward Signaling by Dopamine Neurons." *Neuroscientist* 7, no. 4 (2001): 293–302. https://www.ncbi.nlm .nih.gov/pubmed/11488395.

Sugawara, Sho, Satoshi Tanaka, Shuntaro Okazaki, Katsumi Watanabe, and Norihiro Sadato. "Social Rewards Enhance Offline Improvements in Motor Skill." *PLOS ONE* 7, no. 11 (2012). http://journals.plos .org/plosone/article?id=10.1371/journal.pone.0048174.

CHAPTER 6

Carlson, Linda E., Tara L. Beattie, Janine Giese-Davis, Peter Faris, Rie Tamagawa, Laura J. Fick, Erin S. Degelman, and Michael Speca. "Mindfulness-Based Cancer Recovery and Supportive-Expressive Therapy Maintain Telomere Length Relative to Controls in Distressed Breast Cancer Survivors." *Cancer* 121, no. 3 (2015): 476–84. http://onlinelibrary.wiley.com/doi/10.1002 /cncr.29063/full.

Cerretani, Jessica. "*The* Contagion of Happiness." *Harvard Medicine*, Summer 2011. https://hms.harvard.edu/news/harvard-medicine /contagion-happiness.

Goldstein, Elisha. *Uncovering Happiness: Overcoming Depression with Mindfulness and Self-Compassion*. New York: Atria Books, 2015.

Gregoire, Carolyn. "The Habit of These Outrageously Successful People." *Third Metric* (blog). Huffington Post, July 5, 2013. http://www .huffingtonpost.com/2013/07/05/business-meditation-executives -meditate_n_3528731.html.

Kaliman, Perla, Maria Jesús Álvarez-López, Marta Cosín-Tomás, Melissa A. Rosencranz, Antonie Lutz, and Richard J. Davidson. "Rapid Changes in Histone Deacetylates and Inflammatory Gene Expression in Expert Meditators." *Psychoneuroendocrinology* 40

(February 2014): 96-107. https://www.ncbi.nlm.nih.gov/pmc /articles/PMC4039194/.

Kringelbach, Morten L., and Kent C. Berridge. "Towards a Functional Neuroanatomy of Pleasure and Happiness." *Trends in Cognitive Science* 13, no. 11 (2009): 479-87. https://www.ncbi.nlm.nih.gov /pmc/articles/PMC2767390/.

Matchock, Robert L. "Pet Ownership and Physical Health." *Current Opinion in Psychiatry,* 28, no. 5 (2015): 386-92. https://www.ncbi.nlm.nih .gov/pubmed/26164613.

Stephan, K. M., G. R. Fink, R. E. Passingham, D. Silbersweig, A. O. Ceballos-Baumann, C. D. Frith, and R. S. J. Frackowiak. "Functional Anatomy of the Mental Representation of Upper Extremity Movements in Healthy Subjects." *Journal of Neurophysiology* 73, no. 1(1995): 373-86. http://jn.physiology.org/content/jn/73/1/373.full.pdf.

CHAPTER 7

Aebersold, Paul C. *Radioisotopes: New Keys to Knowledge.* Washington, DC: The Smithsonian Institute, 1953.

Archer, Simon N., and Henrik Oster. "How Sleep and Wakefulness Influence Circadian Rhythmicity: Effects of Insufficient and Mistimed Sleep on the Animal and Human Transcriptome." *Journal of Sleep Research* 24, no. 5 (2015): 476-93. http://onlinelibrary.wiley.com /doi/10.1111/jsr.12307/pdf.

Aspinal, Peter, Panagiotis Mavros, Richard Conye, and Jenny Roe. "The Urban Brain: Analyzing Outdoor Physical Activity with Mobile EEG." *British Journal of Sports Medicine* 49, no. 4 (2015): 272-6. https://www.ncbi.nlm.nih.gov/pubmed/23467965.

Bergland, Christopher. "How Can Daydreaming Improve Goal-Oriented Results?" *Psychology Today,* November 26, 2014. https://www

.psychologytoday.com/blog/the-athletes-way/201411/how-can
-daydreaming-improve-goal-oriented-results.

Craft, Lynette L., and Frank M. Perna. "The Benefits of Exercise for the Clinically Depressed." *The Primary Care Companion to the Journal of Clinical Psychiatry* 6, no. 3 (2004): 104-11. http://www.ncbi.nlm .nih.gov/pmc/articles/PMC474733.

Dfarhud, Dariush, Maryam Malmir, and Mohammad Khanahmadi. "Happiness and Health: The Biological Factors—Systematic Review Article." *Iran Journal of Public Health* 43, no. 11 (2014): 1, 468-77. http://www.ncbi.nlm.nih.gov/pmc/articles/PMC4449495/.

Drew, Ramsey, and Jennifer Iserloh. *Fifty Shades of Kale: 50 Fresh and Satisfying Recipes That Are Bound to Please.* New York: Harper Collins, 2015.

Dunbar, R. I. M., Rebecca Baron, Anna Frangou, Eilund Pearce, Edwin J. C. van Leeuwen, Julie Stow, Giselle Patridge et al. "Social Laughter Is Correlated with an Elevated Pain Threshold." *Proceedings of the Royal Society B: Biological Sciences* 279, no. 1731 (2012): 1,161-67. http://rspb.royalsocietypublishing.org/content/279/1731/1161.

Laird, James D., and Charles Bresler. "The Process of Emotional Experience: A Self-Perception Theory." Vol. 13 of *Emotion: Review of Personality and Social Psychology,* edited by Margaret S. Clark. Newbury Park, CA: Sage, 1992. https://www.researchgate .net/publication/232517707_The_process_of_emotional _experience_A_self-perception_theory.

Leproult, Rachel, George Copinschi, Orefu Boxton, and Eve Van Cauter. "Sleep Loss Results in an Elevation of Cortisol Levels the Next Evening." *Sleep* 20, no. 10 (1999): 865-70. https://www.ncbi.nlm .nih.gov/pubmed/9415946.

Li, Qing. "Effect of Forest Bathing Trips on Human Immune Function."

Environmental Health and Preventative Medicine 15, no. 1 (2010): 9-17. https://www.ncbi.nlm.nih.gov/pmc/articles/PMC2793341/.

Mohajeri, M. H., J. Wittwer, K. Vargas, E. Hogan, A. Holmes, P. J. Rogers, R. Goralczyk, and E. .L. Gibson. "Chronic Treatment with a Tryptophan-Rich Protein Hydrolysate Improves Emotional Processing, Mental Energy Levels and Reaction Time in Middle-Aged Women." *British Journal of Nutrition* 113, no. 2 (2015): 350-65. https://www.ncbi.nlm.nih.gov/pubmed/25572038.

Nicoli, R. M., and J. M. Nicoli. "Biochemistry of Eros." *Contraception, Fertilite, Sexualite* 23, no. 2 (1995): 137-44. https://www.ncbi.nlm.nih.gov/pubmed/7894546.

Pert, Candace. *Molecules of Emotion: The Science Behind Mind-Body Medicine.* New York: Simon and Schuster, 1999.

Schwarz, Lothar, and Wilfried Kindermann. "Changes in Beta-Endorphin Levels in Response to Aerobic and Anaerobic Exercise." *Sports Medicine* 13, no. 1 (1992): 25-36. http://www.ncbi.nlm.nih.gov/pubmed/1553453.

Scutti, Susan. "7 Health Consequences of Going to Bed Past Midnight." *Medical Daily*, June 28, 2013. http://www.medicaldaily.com/7-health-consequences-going-bed-past-midnight-247247.

Sibold, Jeremy, and Jennifer Mears. Lecture to the 56th Annual Meeting of the American College of Sports Medicine, Seattle, WA, May, 2009.

Spalding, Kirsty L., Olaf Bergmann, Kanar Alkass, Samuel Bernard, Mehran Salehpour, Hagen B. Huttner, Emil Boström, et al. "Dynamics of Hippocampal Neurogenesis in Adult Humans." *Cell* 153, no. 6 (2013): 1,219-27. http://www.cell.com/abstract/S0092-8674(13)00533-3.

Weeks, David, and Jamie James. *Secrets of the Superyoung.* Berkeley Books, 1999.

Wenner, Melinda. "Smile! It Could Make You Happier." *Scientific American,*

September 1, 2009. http://www.scientificamerican.com/article
/smile-it-could-make-you-happier/.

Wikander, Tracy. "Want More Sexual Intimacy? This Plan Can Help."
mindbodygreen, November 30, 2014. http://www.mindbodygreen
.com/0–16331/want-more-sexual-intimacy-in-your-relationship
-this-plan-can-help.html.

CHAPTER 8

Bouchez, Colette. "Escape From Hormone Horrors—What You Can Do."
WebMD, November 19, 2008. http://www.webmd.com/women
/features/escape-hormone-horrors-what-you-can-do.

Korb, Alex. "Boosting Your Serotonin Activity." *Psychology Today*, November
17, 2011. https://www.psychologytoday.com/blog/prefrontal
-nudity/201111/boosting-your-serotonin-activity.

Lichterman, Gabrielle. "Female Hormone Cycle." Hormone Horoscope.
Accessed October 29, 2016. http://hormonehoroscope.com/the
-female-hormone-cycle/.

National Institutes of Health. "The Power of Love: Hugs and Cuddles
Have Long-Term Effects." *News in Health*, February 2007. https
://newsinhealth.nih.gov/2007/february/docs/01features_01.htm.

Otto, Michael W., Timothy S. Church, Lynette L. Craft, Tracy L. Greer,
Jasper A. J. Smits, Madhukar H. Trivedi. "Exercise for Mood and
Anxiety Disorders." *The Primary Care Companion to the Journal of
Clinical Psychiatry* 9, no. 4 (2007): 287-93. http://www.ncbi.nlm
.nih.gov/pmc/articles/PMC2018853.

Ranabir, Salam, and K. Reetu. "Stress and Hormones." *Indian Journal of
Endocrinology and Metabolism* 15, no. 1 (2011): 18-22. http://www
.ncbi.nlm.nih.gov/pmc/articles/PMC3079864/.

Van Cauter, Eve, Kristen Knutson, Rachel Leproult, and Karine Speigel.

"The Impact of Sleep Deprivation on Hormones and Metabolism." *Medscape Neurology* 7, no. 1 (2005). http://www.medscape.org /viewarticle/502825.

Young, Simon N. "How to Increase Serotonin in the Human Brain Without Drugs." *Journal of Psychiatry and Neuroscience* 32, no. 6 (2007): 394–99. https://www.ncbi.nlm.nih.gov/pmc/articles/PMC2077351/.

CHAPTER 9

Gibran, Khalil. *The Prophet.* New York: Alfred A. Knopf, 1923.

Morsella, Ezequiel. "What Is a Thought?" *Psychology Today,* February 9, 2012. https://www.psychologytoday.com/blog/consciousness-and-the -brain/201202/what-is-thought.

Watson, Stephanie. "Volunteering May Be Good for Body and Mind." *Harvard Health Blog,* June 26, 2013. http://www.health.harvard.edu/blog /volunteering-may-be-good-for-body-and-mind-201306266428.

Zeland, Vadim. *Reality Transurfing 1: The Space of Variations.* Translated by Gregory Blake. Ropley, UK: O Books, 2008.

CHAPTER 10

Krebs, James R., and Gayle A. Brazeau. "No Complaining…" *American Journal of Pharmaceutical Education* 75, no. 4 (2011): 67. http://www .ncbi.nlm.nih.gov/pmc/articles/PMC3138359/.

Selye, Hans. "Stress and Distress." *Comprehensive Therapy Journal* 1, no. 8 (1975): 9–13. https://www.ncbi.nlm.nih.gov/pubmed/1222562.

Whitbourne, Susan Krauss. "The Definitive Guide to Guilt." *Psychology Today,* August 11, 2012. https://www.psychologytoday.com/blog /fulfillment-any-age/201208/the-definitive-guide-guilt.

Wikander, Tracy. "How to Communicate More Mindfully: An 8-Step Plan." mindbodygreen, June 6, 2015. http://www.mindbodygreen

.com/0–20189/how-to-communicate-more-mindfully-an-8
-step-plan.html.

CHAPTER 11

Gordon, Amie M., Emily A. Impett, Aleksandr Kogan, Christopher Oveis, and Dachner Keltner. "To Have and To Hold: Gratitude Promotes Relationship Maintenance in Intimate Bonds." *Journal of Personality and Social Psychology* 103, no. 2 (2012): 257-74. https://www.ncbi .nlm.nih.gov/pubmed/22642482.

Mitchell, Ian J., Steven M. Gillespie, and Ahmad Abu-Akel. "Similar Effects of Intranasal Oxytocin Administration and Acute Alcohol Consumption on Socio-Cognitions, Emotions and Behavior: Implications for the Mechanisms of Action." *Neuroscience and Behavioral Reviews* 55 (May 2015): 98-106. https://www.ncbi.nlm .nih.gov/pubmed/25956250.

Tan, Chade-Meng. *Search Inside Yourself: The Unexpected Path to Achieving Success, Happiness (and World Peace).* New York: Harper One, 2012.

CHAPTER 12

Adams, Ryan E., Jonathan B. Santo, and William M. Bukowski. "The Presence of a Best Friend Buffers the Effects of Negative Experiences," *Developmental Psychology* 47, no. 6 (2011): 1786-91. https://www .ncbi.nlm.nih.gov/pubmed/21895364.

Cohen, Sheldon, William J. Doyle, Ronald Turner, and David P. Skoner. "Sociability and Susceptibility to the Common Cold." *Psychological Science* 14, no. 5 (2003): 389-95. https://www.ncbi.nlm.nih.gov /pubmed/12930466.

Fowler, James H., and Nicholas A. Christakis. "Dynamic Spread of Happiness in a Large Social Network: Longitudinal Analysis Over

20 Years in the Framingham Heart Study." *British Medical Journal* 337, no. a2338 (2008): 1-9. http://www.bmj.com/content/337 /bmj.a2338.

Harter, James, and Raksha Arora. "Social Time Crucial to Daily Emotional Wellbeing in U.S." Gallup.com, June 2008. http://www .gallup.com/poll/107692/social-time-crucial-daily-emotional -wellbeing.aspx.

Holt-Lunstad, Julianne, Timothy B. Smith, and J. Bradley Layton. "Social Relationships and Mortality Risk: A Meta-Analytic Review," *PLOS Medicine* 7, no. 7 (2010). http://journals.plos.org/plosmedicine /article?id=10.1371/journal.pmed.1000316.

Office of National Drug Control Policy. *Treatment Protocol Effectiveness Study (white paper).* Washington, DC: Office of National Drug Control Policy, 1996. https://www.ncjrs.gov/ondcppubs/publications /treat/trmtprot.html.

Schnall, Simone, Kent D. Harber, Jeanine K. Stefanucci, and Dennis R. Proffitt. "Social Support and the Perception of Geographical Slant." *Journal of Experimental Social Psychology* 44, no. 5 (2008): 1246-55. https://www.ncbi.nlm.nih.gov/pmc/articles/PMC3291107/.

Tuomela, Raimo. *The Importance of Us: A Philosophical Study of Basic Social Norms.* Redwood City, CA: Stanford University Press, 1995.

Young Women Social Entrepreneurs. http://www.ywse.org.

CHAPTER 13

Bargh, John A., Mark Chen, and Lara Burrows. "Automaticity of Social Behavior: Direct Effects of Trait Construct and Stereotype-Activation on Action." *Journal of Personal Social Psychology* 71, no. 2 (1996): 230-44. https://www.psychologytoday.com/files /attachments/5089/barghchenburrows1996.pdf.

Jerath, Ravinder, John W. Edry, Vernan A. Barnes, and Vadna Jerath. "Physiology of Long Pranayamic Breathing: Neural Respiratory Elements May Provide a Mechanism That Explains How Slow Deep Breathing Shifts the Autonomic Nervous System." *Medical Hypotheses* 67, no. 3 (2006): 566-71. https://www.ncbi.nlm.nih.gov/pubmed/16624497.

MindUP.org. Hawn Foundation. Accessed October 29, 2016. https://www.mindup.org.

Reynolds, Susan. "Happy Brain, Happy Life." *Psychology Today*, August 2, 2011. https://www.psychologytoday.com/blog/prime-your-gray-cells/201108/happy-brain-happy-life.

Rizzolatti, Giacomo, and Laila Craighero. "The Mirror-Neuron System." *Annual Review of Neuroscience* 27 (2004): 169-92. https://www.ncbi.nlm.nih.gov/pubmed/15217330.

CHAPTER 14

Bergland, Christopher. "How Can Daydreaming Improve Goal-Oriented Results?" *Psychology Today*, November 26, 2014. https://www.psychologytoday.com/blog/the-athletes-way/201411/how-can-daydreaming-improve-goal-oriented-results.

Orman, Suze. *The 9 Steps to Financial Freedom: Practical and Spiritual Steps So You Can Stop Worrying.* New York: Three Rivers Press, 2000.

Richardson, Alan. "Mental Practice: A Review and Discussion Part 1." *Research Quarterly* 38, no. 1 (1967): 95-107. http://www.tandfonline.com/doi/abs/10.1080/10671188.1967.10614808.

CHAPTER 15

Dispenza, Joe. *You Are the Placebo.* Carlsbad, CA: Hay House, 2014.

Lally, Phillippa, Cornelia H. M. van Jaarsveld, Henry W. W. Potts, and Jane Wardle. "How Are Habits Formed: Modelling Habit Formation in the Real World." *European Journal of Social Psychology* 40, no. 6 (2010): 998-1009. http://onlinelibrary.wiley.com/doi/10.1002/ejsp.674/abstract.

Selye, Hans. "Stress and Distress." *Comprehensive Therapy Journal* 1, no. 8 (1975): 9-13. https://www.ncbi.nlm.nih.gov/pubmed/1222562.

CHAPTER 16

Boothby, Erica J., Margaret S. Clark, and John A. Bargh. "Shared Experiences Are Amplified." *Psychological Science* 25, no. 12 (2014): 2209-16. http://pss.sagepub.com/content/25/12/2209.abstract.

Dunbar, R. I .M. "Gossip in Evolutionary Perspective." *Review of General Psychology* 8, no. 2 (2004): 100-110. http://allegatifac.unipv.it/ziorufus/Dunbar%20gossip.pdf.

Everett, Niko. "Meet Yourself: A User's Guide to Building Self-Esteem." TEDx video, 9:31. Posted February 11, 2013. http://tedxtalks.ted.com/video/Meet-Yourself-A-Users-Guide-to.

Frith, Chris. *Making Up The Mind: How the Brain Creates Our Mental World*. Malden, MA: Wiley-Blackwell, 2007.

Hamann, Stephan. "Cognitive and Neural Mechanisms of Emotional Memory." *Trends in Cognitive Science* 5, no. 9 (2001): 394-400. https://www.ncbi.nlm.nih.gov/pubmed/11520704.

Hatfield, Elaine, John T. Cacioppo, and Richard L. Rapson. "Emotional Contagion." *Current Directions in Psychological Science* 2 (June 1993): 96-100. http://cdp.sagepub.com/content/2/3/96.citation.

Levinson, Daniel B., Jonathan Smallwood, and Richard J. Davidson. "The Persistence of Thought: Evidence for a Role of Working Memory in the Maintenance of Task-Unrelated Thinking." *Psychological Science* 23, no. 4 (2012): 375-80. https://www.ncbi.nlm.nih.gov /pmc/articles/PMC3328662/.

McCraty, Rollin. "The Energetic Heart: Bioelectromagnetic Interactions Within and Between People." In *Clinical Applications of Bioeletromagnetic Medicine*, edited by P. J. Rosch and M. S. Markov, 6–16. New York: Marcel Dekker, 2004. https://www.heartmath.org/research /research-library/energetics/energetic-heart-bioelectromagnetic -communication-within-and-between-people/.

Morris, J.S., C. D. Frith, D. I. Perrett, D. Rowland, A. W. Young, A. J. Calder, and R. J. Dolan. "A Differential Neural Response in the Human Amygdala to Fearful and Happy Facial Expressions." *Nature* 383, no. 6603 (1996): 812-5. https://www.ncbi.nlm.nih.gov/pubmed/8893004.

Reynolds, Susan. "Happy Brain, Happy Life," *Psychology Today*, August 2, 2011. https://www.psychologytoday.com/blog/prime-your-gray -cells/201108/happy-brain-happy-life.

Spreng, R. Nathan, Elizabeth DuPre, Dhawal Selarka, Juliana Garcia, Stefan Gojkovic, Judith Mildner, Wen-Ming Luh, and Gary R. Turner. "Goal-Congruent Default Network Activity Facilitates Cognitive Control." *Journal of Neuroscience* 34, no. 42 (2014): 14,108-114. http://jneurosci.org/content/34/42/14108.

Stromberg, Joseph. "The Benefits of Daydreaming." Smithsonian.com, April, 2012. http://www.smithsonianmag.com/science-nature /the-benefits-of-daydreaming-170189213/.

CHAPTER 17

Frankl, Viktor. *Man's Search for Meaning.* Translated by Ilse Losch. 1959. Reprinted with foreword by Harold. S. Kushner and afterword by William J. Winsdale. Boston: Beacon Press, 2006.

Merali, Zeeya. "Quantum Physics: What Is Really Real?" *Nature* 521, no. 7552 (2015): 278-280. http://www.nature.com/news/quantum -physics-what-is-really-real-1.17585.

Tolle, Eckhart. *The Power of Now: A Guide to Spiritual Enlightenment.* Novato: CA: New World Library, 2004.

Weizmann Institute of Science. "Quantum Theory Demonstrated: Observation Affects Reality." *Science Daily*, February 27, 1998. https ://www.sciencedaily.com/releases/1998/02/980227055013.htm.

APPENDIX

DiSalvo, David. "Study: Receiving a Compliment Has the Same Positive Effect as Receiving Cash." *Forbes*, November 9, 2012. http://www .forbes.com/sites/daviddisalvo/2012/11/09/study-receiving-a -compliment-has-same-positive-effect-as-receiving-cash/.

Fowler, James H., and Nicholas A. Christakis. "Dynamic Spread of Happiness in a Large Social Network: Longitudinal Analysis Over 20 Years in the Framingham Heart Study." *British Medical Journal* 337, no. a2338 (2008): 1-9. http://www.bmj.com/content/337 /bmj.a2338.

Garoli, Albert. *The Evolutionary Glitch: Rise Above the Root of Your Problems.* Ann Arbor: Loving Healing Press, 2010.

Hecht, David. "The Neural Basis of Optimism and Pessimism." *Experimental Neurology* 22, no. 3 (2013): 173-99. http://www.ncbi.nlm.nih.gov /pmc/articles/PMC3807005/.

Kleiman, Karen. "Try Some Smile Therapy." *Psychology Today*, July 31, 2012. https://www.psychologytoday.com/blog/isnt-what-i-expected/201207 /try-some-smile-therapy.

LeVan, Angie. "Seeing Is Believing: The Power of Visualization." *Psychology Today*, December 3, 2009. https://www.psychologytoday.

com/blog/flourish/200912/seeing-is-believing-the-power
-visualization.

MindUP.org. Hawn Foundation. Accessed October 29, 2016. https://www
.mindup.org.

Schultz, Wolfram. "Reward Signaling by Dopamine Neurons." *Neuroscientist*
7, no. 4 (2001): 293-302. https://www.ncbi.nlm.nih.gov/pubmed
/11488395.

Snel, Eline. *Sitting Still Like a Frog: Mindfulness Exercises for Kids (and Their
Parents)*. Boston: Shambala Publications, 2013.

Sonnby–Borgström, Marianne. "Automatic Mimicry Reactions As Related
to Differences in Emotional Empathy." *Scandinavian Journal of
Psychology* 43, no. 5 (2002): 433-43. https://www.ncbi.nlm.nih
.gov/pubmed/12500783.

Spreng, R. Nathan, Elizabeth DuPre, Dhawal Selarka, Juliana Garcia, Stefan
Gojkovic, Judith Mildner, Wen-Ming Luh, and Gary R. Turner.
"Goal-Congruent Default Network Activity Facilitates Cognitive
Control." *Journal of Neuroscience* 34, no. 42 (2014): 14,108-114.
http://jneurosci.org/content/34/42/14108.

Stromberg, Joseph. "The Benefits of Daydreaming," *Smithsonian.com,* April
3, 2012. http://www.smithsonianmag.com/science-nature/the
-benefits-of-daydreaming-170189213/.

Watson, Stephanie. "Volunteering May Be Good for Body and Mind."
Harvard Health Blog, June 26, 2013. http://www.health.
harvard.edu/blog/volunteering-may-be-good-for-body-and
-mind-201306266428.

INDEX

ACKNOWLEDGMENTS

This book is my story, but the truth is, I didn't write *The Joy Plan*—it wrote me. It started as a blog post and then continued to pour out of me, almost faster than I could keep up with. It came to me at inconvenient times—in the middle of a Pilates class, in the bathtub, in the grocery store, in my sleep—and I wrote it on scraps of paper and on my iPhone—even on my hand—and in the wee hours of the night while my family was sleeping.

I had no choice. *The Joy Plan* was like a whirlwind love affair that swept me up and swallowed me whole. It showed me where I've been and lit the path to where I'm going. And in the process, everything that I've ever known to be true and real about myself and my life turned completely upside down, in the best possible way.

The people that love me could have told me I was crazy, not only for undergoing my Joy Plan experiment but for obsessively writing a book about it. But instead they supported me wholeheartedly and became an integral part of my story. With deep gratitude, I dedicate this book to the following people who are the behind-the-scenes team that made it possible:

To my parents, Andy, Carla, Lynne, and Paul: thank you for giving me such a colorful childhood. It gave me incredibly rich material to draw from, not only as I wrote this book but also as I became who I am. You are each powerful role models, and I am so fortunate to call you mine.

To Dan, you are my hero and my number one blessing. Thank you for being my biggest fan, thinking that my writing is sexy, and always encouraging me to follow my passions—even when I disappear for days on end, absorbed in my projects, or insist that we go off on wild adventures to far-off countries. I love cocreating life with you.

To Kira and Nava, thank you for giving me the opportunity to experience love that is bigger than I ever knew was possible—bigger than the universe. Being your mom is the greatest honor of my life.

To Alberto, you've given me more than you will ever know and more than I can express in words. "Thank you" does not do it justice but will have to suffice for now. Thank you.

To Susanna: I don't know if I've changed for the better, but because I know you, I have been changed for good. Thank you.

To Niko Everett, this all started because of you. You are my inspiration and the motivation that kept me going. Thank you.

To Michelle Lapinski, Sara Ellis Conant, Erin Reilly, Julie Kay Kelly, Tracy and David Wikander, Kristen Kanerva Richards, Melissa Weisner, Tess Delisa, Tammy Ford, Rachael Maxwell, Tara Kusumoto, Jen Heuett, Jen Musick, Gordon Cale, Dulcie Ford, Eli and Lynsey Pluzynski, Sean DeMarco, Lily Diamond, Daniella Remy, Elise Vogt, Guy Vincent, Fiona Hallowell, MeiMei Fox, Rachel Macy Stafford, Andrea Somberg (my fabulous agent), my editors at mindbodygreen, my blog readers, and everyone else who reached out to offer their support and encouragement as I birthed this book. Thank you for seeing the best in me and this project even when I doubted myself.

To my wonderful team at Sourcebooks, especially Anna Michels, editor extraordinaire. Thank you for believing in *The Joy Plan* and taking it on, not only as a work project but as a personal mission. You make publishing a totally joyful experience!

To the many researchers and authors whose material I've listed in the references and resources section, thank you for your groundbreaking work that made mine possible. I consider myself to be a curator of your ideas and discoveries, in hopes that your important work will reach and help even more people as much as it's helped me.

Lastly, to my wonderful mindfulness students: You are the future. I know you will take your mindfulness practices out into the world and make it a better place. You've shown me how quickly and easily simple techniques can change our perspectives and personalities for the better. Thank you for letting me be your teacher and, in turn, teaching me far more. The greatest compliment I ever received was from one of my students at Santa Cruz Children's School: "If it weren't for you, I wouldn't even know about my amygdala."

ABOUT THE AUTHOR

Photo © Julie Kay Kelly

Kaia Roman has been writing books since she was five years old. She believes in the healing power of words and stories. *The Joy Plan* is her first memoir/personal growth book. Over the past twenty years, Kaia has been a planner, publicist, ghost-writer, and editor for people, projects, and products working toward a better world. She's now a full-time writer and frequent blogger on mindbodygreen, the Huffington Post, and other wellness sites. She also has the honor of teaching mindfulness to elementary school children. When she's not in another country with her globe-trotting family, Kaia lives in Santa Cruz, California, with her husband and two magical daughters.

To sign up for Kaia's newsletter and read her blog, visit TheJoyPlan.com. You can also find her on Facebook, Twitter, and Instagram. She loves to hear from readers!